T0305198

CORPORATE DIVESTITURES

CORPORATE DIVESTITURES

A MERGERS AND ACQUISITIONS BEST PRACTICES GUIDE

WILLIAM J. GOLE
PAUL J. HILGER

WILEY

JOHN WILEY & SONS, INC.

For general information on our other products and services, or technical support, please contact our Customer Care Department within the United States at 800-762-2974, outside the United States at 317-572-3993 or fax 317-572-4002.

Wiley also publishes its books in a variety of electronic formats. Some content that appears in print may not be available in electronic books.

For more information about Wiley products, visit our Web site at www.wiley.com.

Library of Congress Cataloging-in-Publication Data

Gole, William J.
    Corporate divestitures : a mergers and acquisitions best practices guide / William J. Gole, Paul J. Hilger.
        p.   cm.
    Includes index.
    ISBN 978-0-470-18000-6 (cloth)
        1. Corporate divestiture.   2. Consolidation and merger of corporations.   I. Hilger, Paul J., 1959- II. Title.
    HD2746.6.G65   2008
    658.1'64–dc22
                                                                                    2007048495

To my brother, Henry, who ignited the flame of intellectual curiosity at an early age; and to my wife, Rosemary, who has supported me in all my endeavors, regardless of where they have taken us.

—WILLIAM J. GOLE

There isn't enough space to acknowledge all of the gifted professionals I've had the privilege of working with and who served as my role models over the years. But I would especially like to mention Bill Schlegel, whose peer as a leader and mentor I have yet to meet, and Joe Tomaselli, who transformed my understanding of effective communications. Finally, thanks to my wife, Isabel Czech, for her unending encouragement, and to my children, Lauren and Stephen, for their ability to make me laugh.

—PAUL J. HILGER

CONTENTS

PREFACE

WHY THE BOOK WAS WRITTEN

Over the course of our respective business careers, we have managed numerous corporate transactions, including both acquisitions and divestitures. Our experience has taught us that, while there are similarities, there are also important differences between these two types of transactions. Both acquisitions and divestitures share a similar transaction format and have a common purpose: to create shareholder value. Divestitures, however, have inherent downside risks for the selling corporation and present unique operational challenges to the divestiture team. Organizations also may have biases about divestitures that result in insufficient support for the team. Together, these challenges and impediments make corporate divestitures, in certain key respects, significantly more demanding than acquisitions.

In looking for guidance within the professional literature, however, we found that the available advice was significantly skewed toward the buy side; the literature related to divestitures would perhaps occupy a chapter within mergers and acquisitions books or warrant an occasional article in professional trade publications. Yet the number of divestiture transactions represents a surprisingly large percentage of all mergers and acquisitions, which leads us to suspect that we were not the only ones looking for guidance and not finding it.

Corporate Divestitures: A Mergers and Acquisitions Best Practices Guide (the *Guide*) is our effort to provide practical advice and guidance to those leading or participating in a divestiture transaction team. The *Guide* covers all major aspects of the divestiture process and promotes a structured, disciplined management approach. The principles and guidelines described in the *Guide* are the ones that worked best for us in practice, and it is our hope that readers will find them of similar benefit.

HOW THE *GUIDE* IS ORGANIZED

A key principle emphasized in the *Guide* is the importance of performing tasks in a specific logical sequence, to get to a successful outcome in the shortest possible time and to avoid certain pitfalls. Accordingly, the eight chapters of the *Guide*, and the sections within each chapter, are organized to follow a step-by-step approach through the phases of the transaction:

Chapter 1: Introduction differentiates corporate divestitures from acquisitions, introduces a transaction model and a staffing model for managing the divestiture, and discusses the importance of certain enabling principles that substantially enhance the likelihood of a successful outcome.

Chapter 2: Strategic Assessment describes the strategic issues and alternative approaches considered in the corporation's decision to divest a business unit, introduces the factors that influence the choice of a transaction structure, and presents the risks, exposures, and constraints inherent in a divestiture.

Chapter 3: Divestiture Planning describes the initial deliverables of the process—a recommendation for how the transaction should be structured, a corporate approval document, an organization plan, a retention plan, an execution plan, and a communication plan—and discusses the creation of the core divestiture team.

Chapter 4: Preparing for the Transaction discusses the engagement of external resources to advise and assist the divestiture team and describes the key steps in preparing for the divestiture: validating the transaction structure, developing marketing materials, identifying potential buyers, and preparing for due diligence.

Chapter 5: Disentanglement describes a critical preparatory step that must be undertaken before initiating the selling process: preparing for the operational separation of the divested business from its parent organization.

Chapter 6: Managing the Selling Process covers the initiation and management of the selling process: announcing the corporation's intention to sell, marketing the business, supporting buyers' due diligence, and managing bidding and negotiations.

Chapter 7: Structuring the Transaction focuses on the tax, legal, accounting, and regulatory details that the divestiture team must consider as it finalizes the transaction structure, negotiates legal agreements with the acquirer, and submits required governmental filings.

Chapter 8: **Closing** presents considerations for the team leading up to the close of the transaction and during the postclosing transition to new ownership, and then advocates a process for learning from the experience and ensuring knowledge transfer within the selling corporation. This chapter also includes a summary of the most important elements of successful divestiture transactions.

During our collaboration on the *Guide*, we spent considerable time thinking about how to share our experience in a way that is informative, useful, and readily accessible by those who are actually working on a live transaction. We appreciate how busy professionals are in today's business environment and have a sense of how much busier they become when working on a divestiture transaction. So we wrote the *Guide* with an eye toward optimizing its usability. All chapters, as mentioned, present a step-by-step transaction flow for the applicable phase of the transaction, so that readers can turn to the relevant phase of the divestiture and easily navigate through its process steps. The discussion within each section is compartmentalized into bulleted segments, so readers can rapidly scan the segment headings for points of interest. Alternatively, a recap with cross-references is presented at the end of each chapter, so readers can jump there, scan our bottom-line thoughts for that phase of the transaction, and then turn back to the more detailed discussion if desired. In addition, a detailed index is included at the end of the *Guide* for readers who need to locate the treatment of a specific topic. We also present numerous exhibits throughout the *Guide*, which readers may find helpful as templates, checklists, or reminders for the corresponding aspects of their transaction.

ACKNOWLEDGMENTS

We'd like to thank the friends and colleagues who generously invested their time to provide insightful comments on the manuscript. Darren Pocsik, Christopher Caridi, Paul Walsh, Tony Donofrio, Frank Licata, and Donna Santarpia provided experience, wisdom, honesty, and clarity of thought that greatly improved our efforts. Our editors at John Wiley & Sons, Inc., Sheck Cho and Stacey Rympa, provided the perfect mix of encouragement and friendly guidance to keep us on track.

INTRODUCTION

1.1 OVERVIEW

Merger and acquisition (M&A) transactions provide organizations with important mechanisms for adjusting to challenges and opportunities in an ever-changing business environment. Divestment activities in general, and corporate divestitures in particular, play a significant role in that adjustment process. They enable organizations to periodically realign their product/service portfolios with the market, to monetize undervalued assets, and to generate cash for higher value uses.

This introductory chapter establishes a foundation for the thorough discussion of the planning, preparation, and execution of corporate divestiture transactions that follows in the remainder of this book. This initial foundational discussion begins with a definition of divestitures, the reasons they occur, why they are important, and the factors that distinguish them from other M&A transactions, and ends with an explanation of how this book can assist those tasked with executing or assisting with these transactions and a summary of key points covered in the chapter. The intervening sections of this chapter describe the three major components of a practical, experience-based approach to managing divestiture transactions. These sections present:

- An overview of a *transaction model* that provides guidance on the planning, preparation, and execution of divestiture transactions
- An overview of a *staffing model* that provides guidance on resourcing and managing a transaction
- A discussion of *enabling principles,* underlying elements of the process that are critical to its efficient and effective execution

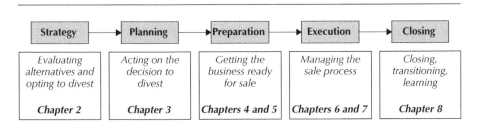

Strategy	Planning	Preparation	Execution	Closing
Evaluating alternatives and opting to divest	Acting on the decision to divest	Getting the business ready for sale	Managing the sale process	Closing, transitioning, learning
Chapter 2	Chapter 3	Chapters 4 and 5	Chapters 6 and 7	Chapter 8

Exhibit 1.1   Transaction Flow

The succeeding chapters elaborate on these themes. Organizationally, they follow the divestiture transaction flow, as illustrated in Exhibit 1.1.

Although there is ample discussion of underlying M&A principles and concepts, the treatment herein can best be characterized as practical and directive. Accordingly, the discussion is focused on process management and the application of experience-based best practices. The pragmatic, transactional approach presented is intended to equip those involved in divestiture transactions with tools that, if employed, will substantially enhance the potential for a successful transaction.

1.2 CHARACTERISTICS OF CORPORATE DIVESTITURES

(a) INTRODUCTION   Corporate divestitures, to be distinguished from the sale or liquidation of an entire enterprise, involve the sale of the stock or assets of portions or segments of a business (a business unit). These business units may range in size and nature from relatively small, niche properties, such as individual products or product lines, to more substantial properties, such as divisions or subsidiaries.

Divestiture decisions are generally made as the result of an organization's disciplined strategic planning or portfolio assessment process, which is briefly discussed in section 1.3(c)(i) and described in detail in Chapter 2, which focuses on investment and divestment options targeted to meet market needs and preferences, to optimally restructure the entity for profitable growth, and, ultimately, to enhance enterprise and shareholder value.

The divestment aspect of this process employs an addition-by-subtraction approach. Its focus is on the strategic objectives of the business and, in that context, considers such issues as the strategic fit of the various components of the business's product/service portfolio, the historical and prospective financial performance of its individual business segments, and the impact of individual components of the portfolio on the financial markets' perception of the consolidated entity's value. To the extent that individual segments of the business do not support the strategic objectives of the organization, they become candidates for divestment initiatives. Although there are a number of other divestment options available to the organization, such as carve-outs, spin-offs, or joint ventures, arguably the most commonly chosen alternative is the divestiture or outright sale of the business unit.

(b) WHY DO ORGANIZATIONS CHOOSE TO DIVEST BUSINESS UNITS? As noted, the generic reason for divesting is the strategic incompatibility of the business being divested. More specifically, divestiture rationales fall into one or more of these four categories:

1. **Sale of a well-performing but nonstrategic unit.** Clearly, superior financial performance does not equate to strategic fit. However, superior performance can inhibit the decision to divest, because it can mask the lack of strategic fit and it can induce management to equivocate and opt for short-term financial gain. Therefore, the decision to sell a well-performing business unit requires a high degree of discipline on the part of management, and usually is presented in the context of an investment strategy for the proceeds from the sale.

2. **Sale of an underperforming unit that is diluting consolidated growth and profitability.** This rationale is generally based on management's recognition that the targeted unit is no longer well aligned with its market and is not a good candidate for further investment. In such situations, noninvestment or underinvestment is very likely to lead to a downward spiral of deteriorating performance, further lack of investment, and continued poor performance. Unless the property can be realigned with its market, further investment is destined to lead to unmet expectations and the misutilization of both managerial and financial resources. Under these circumstances, management will generally opt to dispose of the unit.

3. **Sale of a profitable unit to raise cash.** Occasionally organizations sell properties that are both profitable and strategically compatible in order to generate cash. Usually this is done to enable the organization to pay down debt and to restructure its financial position. In relatively rare cases, it may be done to generate operating cash, a rationale that suggests structural business problems.

4. **Sale of a unit perceived by the market to cause undervaluation of the seller's entire enterprise.** The organization's strategy and business structure do not exist in a vacuum and are subject to critical analysis by relevant constituencies, such as the organization's shareholders or the investment community in general. Management must consider that financial markets make their own judgments as to strategic fit and value and that those judgments can negatively impact shareholder and enterprise value. In situations where the investment community perceives that an existing business unit is undermining the value of the larger enterprise, management may feel it is necessary or desirable to take corrective action in the form of a divestiture.

As all of these rationales indicate, corporate divestitures should not be seen as isolated financial transactions that are executed to eliminate an unwanted business unit or simply to generate cash. Divestitures are reflective of an underlying strategy to reposition or restructure an organization with the objective of enhancing the organization's value.

(c) **WHY ARE DIVESTITURES IMPORTANT?** As noted, corporate divestitures are an important component of an organization's strategic planning process and any resulting portfolio adjustment decisions. Therefore, it is not surprising that they are relatively common in occurrence, affecting large numbers of organizations annually, as well as many of the managers within those organizations. In addition, they are notable for the substantial transfers of value that result.

More specifically, corporate divestitures have consistently accounted for over one-third of all announced M&A activity from 2002 to 2006, with the number of transactions averaging well over 3,000 during that period (see Exhibit 1.2).

YEAR	TOTAL M&A TRANSACTIONS*	NUMBER OF DIVESTITURES*	DIVESTITURES AS % OF TOTAL	AVG. PURCHASE PRICE (IN MILLIONS)†
2002	7,303	2,691	37%	$165.0
2003	7,983	3,188	40%	$130.7
2004	9,783	3,560	36%	$175.5
2005	10,332	3,570	35%	$171.5
2006	10,660	3,375	32%	$228.9

Source: *Mergerstat Review* 2007
*These include all announced transactions. As a result, the numbers are likely to be substantially *understated* since many transactions go unreported.
†Average purchase price is based on transactions where the purchase price was disclosed (1,495 in 2005).
EXHIBIT 1.2   DIVESTITURES AS A PERCENT OF TOTAL M&A TRANSACTIONS, 2002 TO 2006

The absolute number of divestiture transactions—approximately 16,000 over the five-year period cited—indicates broad involvement by a large number of firms and the management personnel within those firms. As illustrated in the listing of *Divestiture Activity by SIC: 2002 to 2006* in Appendix 1A, these transactions cut across all industries. Although there are notable concentrations in industries such as communications, financial services, and computer products and services, virtually all industries engage in a substantial level of divestiture activity. And many of the most active divesters are large organizations with familiar names. As Appendix 1B demonstrates, they include such companies as GE, Carlyle, Hilton, JPMorgan Chase, Citigroup, Blackstone Group, Honeywell, Clear Channel Communications, Kohlberg, Viacom, Ford, Prudential, Alcoa, Bank of America, Exxon Mobil, and H. J. Heinz.

It is also important to note that these same data indicate that, in addition to transactions being large in volume, the average transaction is also significant in size. From 2002 to 2006, the transaction value of the average divestiture where the purchase price was disclosed was approximately $175 million, an amount that is material to most sellers. In addition, the total value of transactions in which a purchase price was disclosed—only about half the total transactions announced—exceeded $342 billion during that period.

In short, corporate divestitures are pervasive in occurrence and material in effect, both individually and in aggregate. They are a major component of M&A activity and a significant class of economic transaction. Additionally, within the thousands of divesting organizations each year, tens of thousands of managers are tasked with the responsibility of managing these high-value transactions.

(d) HOW DO DIVESTITURES DIFFER FROM ACQUISITIONS?   Those who have participated only on the buy side of a transaction or transactions (i.e., acquisitions) may tend to view divestitures as the mirror image of those transactions. In fact, there are some very significant differences between the two, and these differences impact important aspects of the divestiture process. The most notable differences are:

- **Psychology of the transaction.** Attitudes of executives and managers within organizations that are divesting a property are generally quite different from attitudes of those same individuals toward acquisitions. Acquisitions almost invariably generate enthusiasm and excitement, which usually results in broad-based support for, and a desire to be involved in, the transaction. Despite their importance, divestitures have a tendency to be viewed as dead-end transactions that have little payoff for participants. This attitude can lead to organizational indifference and a lack of enthusiastic support across the organization, and may result in an under-resourcing of the transaction. This tendency and its attendant risks are discussed in detail in section 2.4(c). Suffice it to say here that while all M&A transactions are inherently risky, this psychological barrier to enthusiastic participation in divestitures adds an additional layer of risk that is generally not encountered with acquisitions.

- **Need for intense planning and rapid implementation of the organizational separation of the entity being sold**. The divestiture counterpart to postacquisition integration is organizational separation or "disentanglement," a process that is thoroughly discussed in Chapter 5. Unquestionably, successful acquisitions require a great degree of focus on integration planning and implementation. However, divestiture disentanglement presents different, and in some ways more difficult, challenges. Whereas the implementation of the integration plan is something that occurs posttransaction, divestitures require both planning *and implementation* of the separation process *before the transaction is consummated*. This is an important distinction because the disentanglement process can be very complex. The property being divested frequently has been owned by the seller for an extended period of time and its infrastructure is likely to have been integrated into that of the seller. Therefore, separation of the entities requires rigorous analysis and intensive participation on the part of a broad cross-section of both entities' operational personnel. Arguably, the disentanglement process, in contrast to the integration process, is more complex, less forgiving, and definitely planned and performed under substantially tighter deadlines.

- **Need for the preparation and staging of the transaction.** The nature of the activities associated with divestitures is substantially different from those involved with acquisitions. Whereas members of an acquisition team focus on review, analysis, and validation, those on a divestiture team predominantly focus on preparing and positioning the business for sale. For example, the acquisition team *attends* the management presentation, whereas the seller *develops and presents* it. Similarly, the buyer *conducts* due diligence, while the seller *manages* the process. In short, the preparatory activities sellers engage in are substantially different from the evaluative efforts of acquirers and, therefore, require substantially different approaches and skills.

- **Existence of substantial communication and management challenges.** Corporate divestitures present significant communications and management challenges. The announcement of the prospective sale of the business unit generally occurs months before the identity of the buyer is known. In those ensuing months, the selling organization must communicate a message of stability to the employees and customers of the business being divested, in an environment of uncertainty. For employees, this is a particularly challenging time because the announcement will generate a host of unanswerable questions about such things as the timing of the transaction, its impact on their jobs, the effect of the change in ownership on their benefits, and the potential for relocation of the business. As a result, the business unit will be vulnerable to employee demotivation, loss of productivity, loss of personnel, and erosion of its assets.

To minimize the impact of these vulnerabilities, the organization must develop a well-thought-out and well-executed communication plan (see section 3.8 for a discussion of the content and section 6.3(a) for a discussion of the implementation of such a plan) that addresses both employee and customer concerns and whose message is sustained over this period of uncertainty. That plan and the message it communicates must be complemented by aggressive management efforts to minimize business erosion and employee defection. A major element of those efforts will generally take the form of a retention plan designed to retain and motivate key employees, also discussed in section 3.4. These activities have no clear counterpart in the acquisition process.

- **Lack of a robust knowledge base.** M&A literature focuses inordinately on acquisition activity, to the virtual exclusion of substantive discussion of divestitures. We believe that this lack of attention to virtually all aspects of corporate divestitures in the professional literature is replicated in practice, resulting in a very thin layer of shared or institutionalized knowledge on the topic in most organizations. A major factor influencing that phenomenon is the organizational indifference that is frequently associated with divestiture transactions. In addition, it is in the nature of the transaction to lose a significant number of participants and their acquired expertise. The executive management team of the unit being sold, which may represent as much as half the number of active participants in the process, is routinely transferred with the business upon the closing of transactions. This combination of indifference or inattention and the erosion of the organization's knowledge base conspire to undermine the development of a body of knowledge that can be accessed by participants in future divestiture transactions. (Note that section 8.5 discusses approaches to institutionalizing lessons learned from divestiture transactions.)

- **Need to maintain leverage throughout the transaction.** Parties to all M&A deals try to optimize their negotiating leverage throughout a transaction. In an acquisition of an entire enterprise, the acquirer's, as well as the seller's, leverage might be characterized as binary (i.e., throughout the negotiations, the parties maintain leverage by retaining the right to walk away from the transaction if key terms and conditions are unacceptable and cannot be negotiated further). Divestiture transactions have different negotiating dynamics. In the case of a divestiture, negotiating leverage tilts toward buyers when the initial announcement is made and will shift even more dramatically to a buyer if the seller makes an exclusive commitment to that buyer prematurely. This situation arises because the seller has publicly committed to the sale, and a decision to terminate negotiations would present extremely unattractive options, such as reopening negotiations with a previously eliminated bidder or pulling the property from the market. As a result, the seller will want to try to retain as many alternative buyers as possible, for as long as possible, to keep favorable pressure on price and conditions of sale. Doing this generally argues strongly for the use of a public auction process with the involvement of multiple potential buyers, right up to the finalization of the sale (see section 4.6(b) for a discussion of auction sales). If the size of the transaction warrants it, the seller may also find it desirable to keep other options, such as a carve-out, a spin-off, or a leveraged buyout (LBO), on a parallel track, if the potential opportunities justify doing so.

1.3 TRANSACTION MODEL

(a) **INTRODUCTION**   The most progressive organizations active in the M&A arena develop and adapt best practices through trial and error and the thoughtful retrospective analysis of past transactions. These organizations recognize that merger and acquisition activity is more than a series of unique transactions. Although they appreciate that no two transactions are exactly alike, they have come to realize that there are certain disciplines that can be standardized, documented, and improved on, just like any other repeatable business process. Employing a logical, structured approach that incorporates lessons learned from prior transactions and that is built on a platform of thoughtful planning, detailed preparation, and disciplined execution has enabled such organizations to become accomplished managers of M&A transactions.

Development of best practices in M&A is extremely important because the stakes involved are almost invariably high and missteps are likely to entail substantial actual, as well as opportunity, costs. Corporate divestitures or disposals are subject not only to these risks; risks may be exacerbated by what has been characterized as the organizational indifference, or the "orphan treatment," that can frequently befall them. Even those organizations that have institutionalized best practices in the management of acquisitions historically have been slow to apply the same rigor to divestiture transactions. The potential for orphan treatment is discussed in detail in section 2.4(c), but suffice it to note here that, in contrast to acquisitions, which have a certain cachet that causes executives and managers to want to be associated with them and which attract an abundance of resources, involvement in divestiture transactions has substantially less appeal to corporate executives and managers. As a result, in addition to the lack of a standardized framework for conducting the transactions, they can be at risk to be underresourced.

These largely psychological barriers tend to mask the value creation opportunities that divestiture transactions represent as well as the development opportunities they afford their manager/participants (as discussed in section 8.6(b)). Therefore, the execution of divestiture transactions requires an intense focus on the efficient and effective use of resources and should be based on a highly structured and disciplined process. The discussion that follows presents a best practice approach intended to emphasize the underlying logic and the desirable characteristics of a well-executed disposal transaction.

(b) BEST PRACTICE APPROACH   M&A transactions may differ from each other in numerous ways, but they all invariably should follow a logical sequence of steps designed to get the managers of the process to the optimal solution in the shortest possible time. Our experience has shown that getting out of sequence or eliminating a step in this logical sequence is likely to result, at a minimum, in prolonging the process and may end up suboptimizing value or even causing a failed transaction. Therefore, we believe that a fundamental characteristic of best practices relative to M&A transactions in general, and divestitures in particular, is a disciplined process orientation. Exhibit 1.3 provides an overview of a best practice divestiture process model.

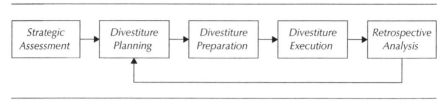

EXHIBIT 1.3   BEST PRACTICE DIVESTITURE PROCESS MODEL

The model depicted outlines a process that starts with the strategic assessment of the organization's portfolio (generally as part of a periodic strategic planning exercise) and, when appropriate, leads to a decision to dispose of a business unit or units. That decision is followed by the planning, preparation, and execution of the actual transaction. Once the transaction has been finalized, the seller should evaluate its performance and ensure that any lessons learned are duly noted, documented, and incorporated into its institutional memory.

(c) ELEMENTS OF THE DIVESTITURE PROCESS   The major elements of the five phases of the divestiture process depicted in Exhibit 1.3 are summarized and illustrated in the sections that follow. Each summary refers to the chapter in which that particular phase of the process is described in greater detail.

(i) Strategic Assessment.   The assessment phase of the process has these components and follows the sequence indicated.

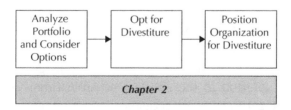

This phase places the proposed transaction within the context of the strategic planning process. Accordingly, it evaluates the organization's business portfolio in relation to its strategic objectives and the dynamics of the market(s) it serves. A key aspect of this evaluation is the thorough consideration of all reasonable strategic alternatives to divestiture, with the objective of ensuring that the course of action selected is the one with the greatest potential for optimizing shareholder value. The assessment process is discussed in detail in Chapter 2.

(ii) Transaction Planning. The planning phase of the process is depicted in the next illustration.

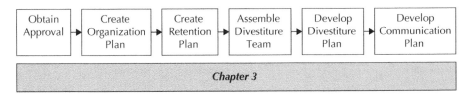

This is the phase of the process during which the business case is made for the divestiture. It is also when the seller puts into process those measures that are designed to ensure the proper staging and management of the transaction. Doing so includes the development of organization and retention plans, the assignment of a divestiture team leader, the creation of the divestiture team, and the development of the divestiture and communication plans. Chapter 3 describes this phase of the process in detail.

(iii) Transaction Preparation. The sequencing of the preparation phase of the process is depicted in the next illustration.

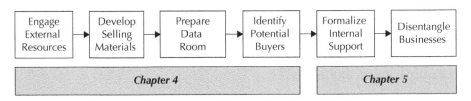

This phase of the process is focused on getting the business unit being divested ready for sale. It has two distinct components: (1) preparation for the selling process; and (2) preparation for the separation of the business being sold from its parent. The former, discussed in detail in Chapter 4, relates to the first four steps depicted in the illustration and entails the engagement of external resources and the creation of selling materials (i.e., an offering document or prospectus and a management presentation) and the staging of steps that will be used in the course of the selling process. The latter component, described in Chapter 5, relates primarily to the final two steps depicted and includes formally assigning the internal resources necessary to support the transaction and the initiation of the process of disentangling the business being sold from the seller's organization.

(iv) Transaction Execution.   The next chart illustrates the flow of the execution phase of the process.

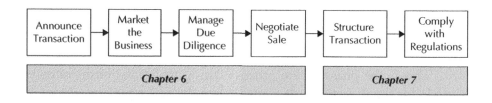

This phase of the process spans the announcement of the intent to sell through preclosing agreement on contract terms and compliance with any prescribed legal and regulatory requirements. Accordingly, it covers the management of the selling process: announcing the prospective sale, soliciting offers from potential buyers, and managing the due diligence process, all topics covered topic in Chapter 6, and the negotiation of final legal documents and ensuring compliance with regulatory requirements, covered in Chapter 7.

(v) Transaction Close, Business Transition, and Retrospective Analysis. In this phase, as illustrated next and discussed in Chapter 8, the transaction is finalized, ownership is transferred, and process improvement measures are memorialized.

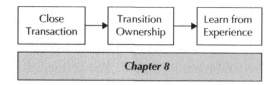

Once the transaction is closed and the business is transitioned to new ownership, the seller should perform a retrospective analysis of the transaction and record all relevant information that can be accessed by those in the organization who are tasked with responsibility for divestitures in the future. This would entail the identification of lessons learned, both positive and negative, and the documentation of those findings to ensure that these lessons are incorporated into the seller's institutional memory.

1.4 STAFFING MODEL

(a) DIVESTITURE TEAM STRUCTURE Divestitures generally require the participation of a substantial cross-section of functions, and managers within those functions, in the organizations involved in the sale. They also require the involvement of a number of external experts. The internal participants typically can be broken down into two categories: the core team that has day-to-day responsibility for managing the transaction and a group of line managers and subject area specialists whose participation and expertise will be drawn on periodically. External expertise should be engaged based on the needs of the transaction and the availability of specific resources and expertise within the selling organization. The various participants are briefly profiled in the next section and described in greater detail in Chapter 3. In addition, the changing nature of team member involvement, as the transaction progresses, is outlined in this section. This section ends with the description of an alternative staffing approach that may be appropriate for small companies that engage in divestiture activity infrequently and are likely to encounter significant staffing challenges when they do.

(i) Core Team. The core team generally consists of executives from the business development (i.e., the function responsible for strategic planning and merger and acquisition activity), human resource, legal, and finance and accounting functions, as well as the executive staff of the business unit being divested. As noted, this team will shepherd the organization through the transaction.

(ii) External Resources. Divestiture transactions require the support of various external experts. As indicated, the extent to which such expertise is required is situation-specific. However, it will generally include a business broker or investment banker to assist in the sale process and an independent accounting firm to assist in the preparation of standalone financial statements. Depending on the size and

sophistication of the seller, it may also include the engagement of external legal, tax, or human resource expertise. These participants generally will be intensely involved during the preparation stage of the transaction and, in the case of the broker/banker, the actual selling process.

(iii) Internal Resources. The need for involvement of internal managers is also heavily dependent on the size and nature of the transaction and the degree of interdependency between the business being sold and the parent organization. Generally, the most significant variable in determining the extent of involvement of internal staff is the level of interdependency that has been established between the two businesses. Frequently, the interdependence is significant and requires the involvement of a broad range of line managers within functions such as information technology, facilities management, real estate management, and operations. In addition, as the transaction proceeds toward the negotiation stage, the involvement of members of the seller's executive management team typically will be required to deal with contractual issues.

(b) POTENTIAL UNDERSTAFFING As noted, the volume and mix of internal and external resources needed is dependent on a number of variables. The burden of determining the nature and extent of support falls on those tasked with managing the transaction. In smaller organizations with limited internal expertise or in larger organizations that are unwilling to dedicate the necessary internal resources, this team leader must evaluate needs quickly and thoroughly to ensure that the initiative is appropriately supported. To the extent that internal resources are not available, or are not made available, the team leader must be empowered to engage outside experts and consultants to fill gaps on the team. A model for doing so is described and illustrated in section 1.4(d). It is incumbent on the team leader to ensure that those who are ultimately responsible for the transaction understand that underresourcing the effort will put the transaction at substantial risk.

(c) EXPANSION, CONTRACTION, AND MODIFICATION OF THE DIVESTITURE TEAM The discussion that follows identifies various key points or stages in the transaction that require the expansion, contraction, or refinement of the divestiture team. These stages do not neatly coincide with the five phases of the transaction described in section 1.3(c) and may occur "midphase," such as when the core team is formalized midway through the planning process. The points at which the team undergoes significant adjustment are listed next, illustrated in Exhibit 1.4, and discussed in detail in the sections that follow.

- **Nonformalized collaboration.** A period of analysis during which a divestiture is considered and ultimately recommended
- **Formalization of a core team.** The point at which those tasked with the transaction are identified and they initiate the planning process
- **Transaction preparation.** The stage in the process when external resources are engaged and added to the divestiture team
- **Organizational preparation.** The stage in the process when additional internal resources are assigned to the divestiture team
- **Formalization of the negotiating team.** The point when the negotiation team is formed and the role of supporting staff is defined
- **Posttransaction activities.** The stage in the process following the close when the business is transitioned to the new owners and when lessons learned are incorporated into the selling organization's institutional memory

(i) Nonformalized Collaboration.   Nonformalized collaboration is the early assessment and planning stage of the process that precedes the formal creation of the core team. It spans the assessment, approval, organization, and retention planning steps of the process, described in section 1.3. Participants at this stage usually include executives from business development, finance and accounting, and human resource functions, and may also require input from certain specialists, such as tax advisors to determine the tax implications of the option considered. In this stage, the desirability of divesting the property is evaluated, options are entertained, and the decision to divest is made. The initial steps in this stage of the process require substantial strategic and financial analysis, since all options and their implications should be considered.

Planning				Preparation					Execution				
Approve Process	Organization and Retention Plans	Assemble Team	Create Plans	Engage External Resource	Develop Sales Materials	Identify Buyers	Engage Internal Resources	Separate Business	Announce Transaction	Accept Bids	Manage Due Diligence	Negotiate Terms	Close

CORE TEAM

Business Development/Team Leader

Finance and Accounting

Human Resources

Legal

Business Unit Executives

EXTERNAL RESOURCES

Broker/Banker

Accounting Firm

Other External Resources

INTERNAL RESOURCES

Tax

Information Technology

Executive Management

Line Managers and Subject Area Experts

EXHIBIT 1.4 DIVESTITURE TEAM: DURATION OF PARTICIPATION BY FUNCTION

(ii) Formalization of the Core Team. The next stage of the process is initiated by the formalization of the core team. The choice of the individual who will lead the initiative should be established and/or confirmed. More often than not the team leader will be drawn from the business development function, although there may be situations in which that individual will be the lead financial manager in the project or a line executive who is closely associated with the unit being sold. In any event, core team members generally will be drawn from business development, finance and accounting, human resource, and legal functions. The lead attorney in the process often plays a key role throughout and very often functions as a co-equal partner of the team leader. The team will also include members of the senior executive management of the business unit being divested. Those in this group will vary but typically include the chief executive and a number of that individual's direct reports. The relationships within the core team are illustrated in Exhibit 1.5.

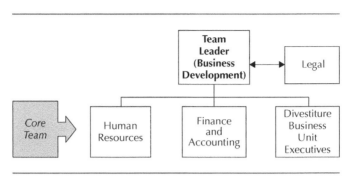

EXHIBIT 1.5   CORE DIVESTITURE TEAM

In addition to the creation of the team, this is the stage that includes development of the divestiture plan and timeline, the creation of the communication plan, and the initial identification of the internal and external resources necessary to implement the plan.

(iii) Transaction Preparation.   The transaction preparation stage of the process is initiated by the identification and engagement of external resources to assist in the preparation of the sale and extends through the actual staging and preparation of the transaction. Activities include the identification of potential buyers, the preparation of stand-alone financial statements, the development of selling materials, and population of the data room. The external parties generally include a business broker and/or investment banker and an accounting firm, and may include other subject area specialists, depending on the nature of the transaction. The expanded team is illustrated in Exhibit 1.6.

(iv) Organizational Preparation.   The organizational preparation stage of the process is when the involvement of the internal managers who will assist in the transaction is formalized. Typically these managers include representatives from information technology, facilities management, real estate, and operations functions, and specialists in areas such as taxation, intellectual property, and business insurance. The focus of that involvement generally will be the disentanglement process. Executive management of the parent company will also be apprised of the role they will be expected to play in the process; usually they serve as advisors to decisions made regarding the separation of the businesses

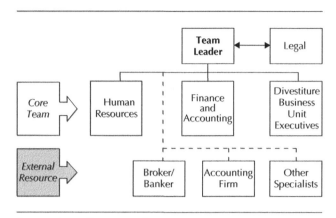

EXHIBIT 1.6 EXPANDED TEAM: ADDITION OF EXTERNAL RESOURCES

and the negotiation of noncompetition aspects of the contract. The addition of these individuals to the team is illustrated in Exhibit 1.7.

(v) Formalization of the Negotiating Team. When the process reaches the stage where the finer details of the contract and supporting documents are to be negotiated, the structure and responsibility of those

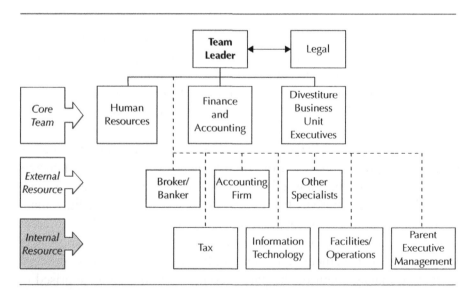

EXHIBIT 1.7 FULL TEAM: ADDITION OF INTERNAL RESOURCES

on the team should be refined. The selling organization should clearly empower a single individual, usually the team leader, as chief negotiator to represent its position in negotiations. That individual would work closely with, and rely heavily on, the lead attorney to manage negotiations and revise and finalize documents with the buyer as well as ensure compliance with applicable regulations and law. Together, these two individuals would comprise the negotiating team and would directly interface with the business and legal negotiators representing the buyer.

The negotiating lead should have broad authority to speak on behalf of the organization and ready access to senior management when decisions that exceed that authority are encountered. Additionally, the negotiating team should have access to various line managers and subject area experts to review and sign off legal documents and provide input and make recommendations on a wide range of issues that will be beyond the capacity of the lead negotiator to address.

In most instances, some of the participants in the process to this point will have completed their assignments and rotated off the divestiture team. This would include outside accountants, whose work will have been completed, and the business unit executive team, whose personal objectives and fiduciary responsibilities would place them in a conflicted position (an issue discussed more fully in section 7.3(b)). This would generally also include the seller's broker or its banker.

The relationship between the negotiators and the advisory team is illustrated in Exhibit 1.8.

(vi) Posttransaction Activities.   The posttransaction stage of the process is initiated by the close of the transaction. It includes the transfer of assets to the new owners and generally also includes the provision of transition services by the seller to the buyer. At that point, the divestiture team would effectively be disbanded, and services will have been contracted on an arm's-length basis.

The nature and extent of transition services will depend on two variables: the degree to which the transferred business is a stand-alone entity; and the extent to which the buyer has an infrastructure that can support something less than a stand-alone business. For example, a financial buyer (e.g., private equity firm) is unlikely to be able to provide back office support to a business that had relied on the seller for such services.

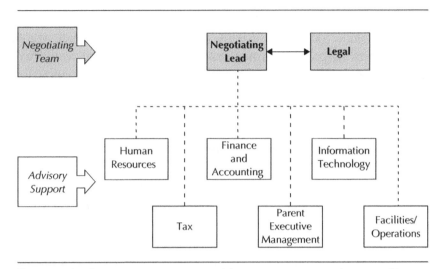

EXHIBIT 1.8   RELATIONSHIP BETWEEN THE NEGOTIATORS AND THE ADVISORY TEAM

The nature and extent of transition services also will dictate which functions within the seller's organization will be required to remain involved with the business unit after the transaction. As a general rule, the seller will want to limit both the extent of services and their duration.

Ideally, the final responsibility of the team leader will be to review the transaction with an eye toward identifying lessons learned and worth institutionalizing. This is a step that is easily ignored, to the detriment of the organization. Without a feedback process in place, organizations frequently face the prospect of reinventing the wheel with each successive transaction. In more sophisticated organizations, the building of this knowledge base may take the form of entries to a corporate intranet. In other environments, it may take the form of memos, reports, and exhibits housed in a binder that is accessible to those tasked with divestitures in the future. Regardless of the form documentation takes, the objective should be the same: to provide a feedback mechanism for process improvement and knowledge transfer.

(d) SMALL-COMPANY APPROACH   We believe that the model just described is the optimal staffing approach to the divestiture process. However, for smaller companies with limited available personnel and for small transactions generally, the level of internal resources recommended may be unrealistic. A more practical approach for such situations may be to rely on external resources to a much greater extent, under the direction of a project leader. This approach would require the engagement of an M&A advisor, in addition to an M&A attorney, a financial advisor (broker or banker), and, possibly, an accounting firm. It may also require the engagement of other specialists in areas such as information technology and human resources/compensation. This approach would not obviate the need for input and some degree of involvement on the part of line management within the selling company, but it would relieve functional managers of the need to get deeply involved in the divestiture process. They would essentially function as internal consultants. In this approach, the project leader plays a critical role, both directing the activities of the various external advisors and, importantly, making the major decisions related to the deal. While external consultants can do more of the work, they cannot supplant the seller's ownership of the transaction.

The extensive use of external resources would enable the seller to address a void in M&A expertise and to reduce the level of internal distraction. However, this approach comes at some cost. In addition to the financial cost of external consultants, which may be quite significant, it also entails a reduction in the level of accountability on the part of internal management, since it is extremely unlikely that minimally involved managers will be imbued with a sense of ownership in the transaction. While not the preferred approach to the process, it does enable the small company to find a balance between the competing considerations of resource availability, transaction staffing, management accountability, and management distraction. The approach is depicted in Exhibit 1.9.

1.5 ENABLING PRINCIPLES

(a) INTRODUCTION   As reflected in the text, corporate divestitures are protracted, complex, and demanding transactions. In addition, frequently they are conducted in a resource-starved environment. The combination of a demanding transaction and the tendency of organizations to hedge on committing the appropriate level of support heightens the need for those tasked with the disposal to adopt an approach that is

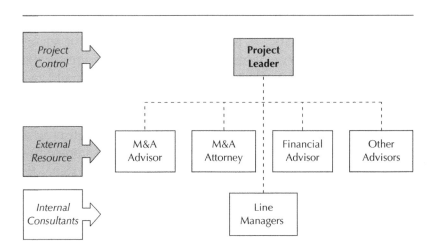

Exhibit 1.9 Divestiture Team: Small-Company Approach

highly structured and makes optimal use of the resources that are made available. That approach requires a strong focus on high-quality analysis, thorough planning, detailed preparation, and disciplined execution as well as adherence to principles that *enable* the effective execution of the transaction.

It has been our experience that a well-structured process, such as that presented in the preceding section, even when fully resourced, is a necessary but not sufficient ingredient of an effective and efficient transaction. In addition, we believe that the organization conducting the transaction must adopt enabling principles that add rigor to that process. These enabling principles, their rationale, and their impact are discussed next.

(b) EMPOWERED LEADERSHIP Early in the divestiture process, an individual will be assigned to a leadership role and be tasked with managing the transaction. This individual will have responsibility for directing a core team of senior executives and for coordinating internal and external support on an as-needed basis. It is critical to the success of the transaction that this team or project leader is empowered by senior executive management, typically the chief executive officer (CEO) of the selling entity. Empowerment in this context has several aspects. At the appropriate time or times, the CEO must clearly communicate to all relevant parties that the team leader has both the responsibility *and the* *authority* to execute the transaction. While such authority cannot be a blank check, it must be defined broadly enough so that the team leader need not continually seek approval to engage resources or make commitments on behalf of the organization. Therefore, the span of authority must be broad, mutually understood by CEO and team leader, and effectively communicated to all relevant parties. Empowerment also implies timely and structured access to the CEO. A predetermined mechanism for communication must be established to assure seamless management of the transaction when issues arise that exceed the decision-making authority of the team leader. Empowerment also implies the commitment of the resources necessary to manage the transaction. The point has been made repeatedly that there is a significant risk of the under-commitment of resources to disposal transactions. That risk must be mitigated by the CEO's willingness to provide, and the team leader's insistence on, access to sufficient resources. Thus empowered, the team leader will be positioned to aggressively execute the transaction.

(c) TEAM COHESIVENESS AND OWNERSHIP IN THE TRANSACTION
As noted, the project leader will head a small team of managers—typically, senior executives in the human resources, finance and accounting, and legal functions, as well as the most senior executives of the business being disposed—who will have responsibility for the ongoing management of the transaction. These individuals must approach their roles with a team mentality and a keen sense of ownership of the transaction, reinforced by the knowledge that they are engaging in an important value-creation enterprise. This translates into a commitment to the success of the transaction at the expense of individual personal gain. While this may sound idealistic, in practice it is simply a form of enlightened self-interest, a realization that "credit" will result only from a successful transaction. Key elements of team cohesiveness in the context of the transaction are information sharing, a holistic approach to the project, and a cross-functional managerial approach.

Divestitures are complex transactions, comprised of multiple steps, involving a large number of individuals over an extended period. This creates an environment of constant change. Sharing relevant information completely and quickly is critical to keep the transaction on track. Those running the transaction must also resist the temptation to take a narrow, functional view of their responsibilities. Given the functional bounds within which they are used to operating, this will require a different mind-set. It means shedding their silo mentality and adopting a comprehensive or holistic approach to the transaction. In this regard, they must take ownership in the entire transaction, not a piece or an aspect of it. An outgrowth of this approach is the need to engage in aggressive cross-functional resource management (i.e., the management of those involved across the organization as well as the contract professionals and consultants who are providing advice and expertise).

(d) CLEARLY DEFINED ROLES, TASKS, AND DELIVERABLES Divestiture transactions entail numerous and diverse activities, frequently involving subgroups of the larger team, and generally occurring over the better part of a year. Effective management of a process of this magnitude requires a high degree of discipline. That discipline can be exercised only by clearly defining (and redefining, when necessary) and unambiguously communicating what has to be done, by whom, and when and by regularly holding those responsible accountable for delivering.

(e) FREQUENT AND REGULAR COMMUNICATION The need for communication in the context of a divestiture transaction is multifaceted. Communication is critical to the management process. In that regard, it is a lubricant. Although process management communication may take many forms, such as e-mail, formal and informal meetings, conference calls, and telephone conversations, arguably the key communication component should be regular status meetings run by the team leader or subgroup project leaders, as frequently as weekly. This is also where communication intersects with the definition of roles, tasks, and deliverables. These meetings should be structured around formal project management documents that identify assignments, the individuals responsible, deliverables, and their deadlines.

Equally important is the communication associated with protecting the asset being divested. In this regard, communication is a deterrent. The announcement of the prospective sale can be expected to have a disruptive impact on the business unit being sold. Left unattended, disruption can lead to employee defection and business erosion. Effective communication can minimize employee distraction and its impact on the business. Therefore, it is critically important for parent company management to maintain frequent and regular two-way communication with this employee base. After the initial announcement is made, mechanisms, such as regular meetings and a dedicated Web site, should be established to provide these employees with news and developments relative to the sale as well as to enable them to get timely answers to their inquiries.

(f) **AMPLE USE OF DOCUMENTATION**   The need for formal documentation permeates the entire divestiture process. The process requires deliberation on key issues, the development of a wide array of plans, the management of various projects, and the accumulation and transfer of knowledge. These are all activities that should be reduced to written form whenever possible.

While PowerPoint presentations have become the preferred presentation media in today's business environment, their use should not preclude the development of underlying text documents. Such documents foster quality analysis, informed decision making, and structured thought, and enable clear communication and knowledge transfer. Clear and comprehensive documentation is particularly relevant to the deliberative process. Key decisions, such as the decision to divest, are made based on the analysis of complex issues and the consideration of various alternatives. Written documentation not only provides the opportunity for a clear and complete record, it *drives quality analysis,* the basis for good decision making.

With regard to planning and project management, perhaps the two most prevalent aspects of the divestiture process, documentation *promotes clarity and structure.* Documentation works in conjunction with the definition of responsibilities and communication, principles discussed earlier, as enabling tools for the management of these transactions. Insofar as the knowledge transfer process is concerned, documentation of lessons learned from each succeeding transaction is fundamental to building and maintaining a contemporary knowledge base for managers of future transactions.

1.6 HOW THIS *GUIDE* CAN HELP

(a) **WHY A GUIDE ON DIVESTITURES?**   As noted, corporate divestitures are generally very challenging yet commonplace transactions. It is therefore surprising that there is little in the way of dedicated discussion of them in the professional literature. To the extent one can find discussions of divestitures, they appear as sections or, at best, chapters of books on mergers and acquisitions and strategic planning. That lack of published guidance on the topic appears to be replicated in practice. Many, if not most, corporations engaged in M&A activity treat divestitures as poor cousins to acquisitions and tend to deal with them as isolated events rather than repetitive transactions that lend themselves to standardization and process improvement. This volume has been written to fill this void in the professional literature and, by extension, in practice.

(b) WHY WILL IT HELP?   The focus of the *Guide* is on process management. Consistent with that focus, it has a distinct transactional orientation and a directive tone. It promotes a structured, practical approach and contains detailed guidance on how to manage all major aspects of the divestiture process. We believe that a work with this orientation will have the greatest benefit to the largest audience, because it spans the entire divestiture process and has application to a broad cross-section of managers who may be called on to play a role in such a transaction.

(c) WHO WOULD BENEFIT?   Anyone involved with a divestiture transaction who does not have extensive experience in that capacity will benefit from this *Guide*. However, the nature and extent of the utility of the *Guide* is dependent on a number of factors. From an organizational perspective, its relative usefulness is illustrated in Exhibit 1.10.

Large, sophisticated corporations with active portfolios, such as GE, Microsoft, Cisco Systems, and JPMorgan Chase, have established systems and procedures governing M&A transactions. Even in these organizations, though, the systems and procedures associated with divestitures may be less robust than those associated with acquisitions due to the poor-cousin treatment frequently endured by divestitures. In such instances, the *Guide* can be used to supplement practices that may have been established but not fully developed.

Other Fortune 500 companies with less active portfolios generally do not encounter disposals as often and are less likely to have established divestiture procedures. However, they usually have an M&A experience base to draw on that will provide a foundation for

	TYPE OF DIVESTER		
	SOPHISTICATED	**EXPERIENCED**	**OCCASIONAL**
Type of Organization	Fortune 50	Rest of the Fortune 500	Small to moderate-size companies
Experience Profile	Have large, actively managed portfolios. Have established M&A processes but may not have robust divestiture process or adequate knowledge transfer mechanism for disposals.	Have acquisition experience but are unlikely to have established disposal process and are very unlikely to have adequate knowledge transfer mechanism for disposals.	Have limited M&A experience and are unlikely to have established M&A processes in general and even less likely to have an established process for disposals.
Utility of the *Guide*	A best practice template for the disposal process. Supplements established practices.	Systematized guidance for the disposal process. Increases efficiency and effectiveness and provides insights for avoiding major pitfalls.	Provides detailed guidance to those who are likely to be exposed to disposals infrequently.

EXHIBIT 1.10 USEFULNESS OF THE *GUIDE*

adequately managing many disposals. These organizations will benefit in the short run from the systematized guidance provided in the *Guide*. And, in the long run, this volume provides the basis for a process improvement approach that would enable users to develop and adapt best practices going forward.

The needs of smaller companies are less frequent but more intense. For them, divestitures are generally an uncommon occurrence. Typically they are viewed as isolated transactions that do not warrant the dedication of resources necessary to systematize their management. That said, when they are encountered, the need for assistance can be acute. For these organizations, the *Guide* can provide extremely valuable guidance and support.

From a functional perspective, the contents of the *Guide* would be of value to a wide variety of managers, professionals and consultants. However, the primary audience is the front-line manager—the business development, financial management, legal, and human resources executives responsible for the day-to-day management of the disposal process. Undoubtedly, other participants in the process, such as line managers and outside consultants and advisors, would find substantial value in the *Guide* since its comprehensive view of the process provides important context, as well as specific, practical guidance.

KEY POINTS

1. Corporate divestitures are not isolated financial transactions that are executed to eliminate an unwanted business unit or simply to generate excess cash. Divestitures reflect an underlying strategy to reposition or restructure an organization with the objective of enhancing the organization's value. (Section 1.2(b))

2. Corporate divestitures are an important class of business transaction by virtue of their pervasiveness and their size. They represent more than one-third of all M&A transactions, average approximately $175 million in transferred value, and annually involve thousands of organizations and tens of thousands of managers within those organizations. (Section 1.2(c))

3. Corporate divestitures have unique characteristics that distinguish them from other M&A transactions. Most important:
   - They are often subject to organizational indifference due to the perceived dead-end nature of the transaction. (Section 1.2(d))

- They require intense planning and rapid implementation of *preclosing* structural disentanglement. (Section 1.2(d))
- They present substantial communication and management challenges because of the potential instability that may result from the announcement of the *prospective* sale. (Section 1.2(d))
- The announcement of the prospective transaction creates negotiating challenges not encountered in other sale and acquisition transactions. (Section 1.2(d))

4. Effective divestiture transactions require a high degree of structure. Employing a logical, structured approach that incorporates lessons learned from prior transactions and that is built on a platform of thoughtful planning, detailed preparation, and disciplined execution will enable organizations to become accomplished managers of these transactions. (Section 1.3(b))

5. To the extent that internal resources are not available—or are not made available—for the transaction, the divestiture team leader must be empowered to engage outside experts and consultants to fill gaps on the team. It is incumbent upon the team leader to ensure that those who are ultimately responsible for the transaction understand that underresourcing the effort will put the transaction at substantial risk. (Section 1.4(a))

6. Structure and resources are critical elements of a successful transaction but, in the absence of enabling principles, they are just the roadmap without a means of transportation. Concepts such as empowered leadership, accountability, and effective communication and documentation must be operationalized to ensure optimal results. (Section 1.5(a)–(f))

DIVESTITURE ACTIVITY BY STANDARD INDUSTRIAL CLASSIFICIATION: 2002 TO 2006

TOP 10 INDUSTRIES	
SELLER INDUSTRY	5-YEAR TOTAL OF DIVESTITURES
Broadcasting	1,794
Computer Software Supplies and Services	1,584
Miscellaneous Services	1,395
Leisure and Entertainment	935
Wholesale -and Distribution	640
Retail	576
Banking & Finance	542
Electric, Gas, Water, and Sanitary Services	505
Communications	499
Drugs, Medical Supplies, and Equipment	489

Source: *Mergerstat Review,* 2007

AGGRESSIVE DIVESTERS: 2005 AND 2006

SELLER 2006	NO. OF TRANSACTIONS	SELLER 2005	NO. OF TRANSACTIONS
UTEK Corp	26	General Electric	17
General Electric	17	Carlyle Group	11
Clear Channel Comm.	11	El Paso Corp.	11
El Paso Corp.	10	Hilton Hotels	10
Federated Dept Stores	10	JPMorgan Chase	10
Bank of America	9	UTEK Corp	10
The McClatchey Co.	9	The Blackstone Group	9
CitiGroup	8	CitiGroup	9
ConAgra Foods	8	Honeywell International	8
Hilton Hotels	8	Clear Channel Comm.	7
CBS	7	Kohlberg Kravis	7
Exxon	6	Viacom	7

Source: *Mergerstat Review,* 2006 and 2007

STRATEGIC ASSESSMENT

2.1 OVERVIEW

(a) PLANNING PROCESS   Any meaningful discussion of acquisition and divestment activity should be grounded in an understanding of the role that strategic planning plays in the corporate decision-making process. Most companies, and particularly multidivisional corporations that regularly engage in such activity, routinely update or reinforce their business development strategy annually, generally in the guise of a formal planning document. Even smaller companies that may not employ a formal, structured strategic planning process will still be guided by long-term objectives and a stated or implied business strategy supporting those objectives, which are broadly understood within the organization. In either case, well-run organizations will not view investment and divestment initiatives opportunistically or in a vacuum, but rather as vehicles to realize broad, long-range strategic goals that ultimately will enhance shareholder value.

The approach to the strategic planning process employed may vary among organizations but typically will include a validation or refinement of established strategic objectives and an evaluation of trends in the general environment and the enterprise's specific market(s). This would be followed by an evaluation of the organization's business portfolio, the consideration of various investment and divestment alternatives, and a decision to pursue those initiatives that best support the enterprise's strategic objectives.

(b) MANAGING THE PROCESS   The development of a fluid planning process generally evolves over time as an organization matures. Initially organizations may engage planning consultants to assist them and, as they evolve and grow, create staff functions (a business development or strategic planning group) with responsibility for driving the planning process and coordinating investment and divestment activities, such as, acquisitions, corporate divestitures, and the development of strategic alliances.

The executive management of most large organizations will generally provide their operating units with broad guidelines and assign the planning team (operating management of divisions and business units, along with strategic planning and finance staff members) with responsibility for developing the plan and identifying initiatives to enable its execution. In this way, corporate headquarters provides general direction and parameters for investment, while those closest to the business and the markets served are able to develop a market-focused plan that will then be reviewed, possibly modified, and approved by corporate management.

2.2 STRATEGIC ASSESSMENT PROCESS STEPS

(a) ASSESSMENT OF THE BUSINESS PORTFOLIO A key aspect of the strategic planning process for a multidivisional corporation is the assessment of its business portfolio. This entails the determination of what additions and modifications should be made to the portfolio to optimize shareholder and enterprise value. That assessment has both an investment and a divestment component. Investment initiatives typically include those associated with product development, market expansion, and infrastructure improvement. Once the organization has determined what investment initiatives it wishes to pursue, it must then determine how they will be pursued, that is, whether they will be organically developed, acquired, or jointly developed with a strategic ally. Similarly, the planning process may identify potential divestment initiatives, those that suggest that the organization should realign its portfolio, monetize undervalued assets, or simply generate cash for higher-value uses. The organization would then consider alternatives, such as reinvestment in, liquidation of, or divestment of the relevant assets, before selecting the optimal course.

(b) CHAPTER FOCUS The focus of the discussion in this chapter is on the *divestment analysis and decision-making and their role in value creation.* We characterize this as the strategic assessment phase of the divestiture transaction process. Strategic assessment is illustrated in Exhibit 2.1 and consists of:

- Analysis of an organization's business portfolio intended to determine if there is a need for portfolio realignment
- Targeting of those properties that are candidates for divestiture
- Positioning of the organization to execute the divestiture transaction or transactions

This chapter outlines the process and discusses key preliminary considerations that the organization should take into account to minimize the risks and optimize the opportunities associated with the prospective transaction.

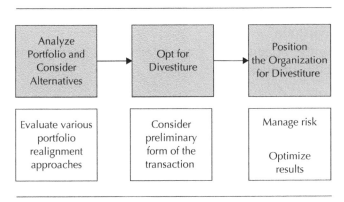

EXHIBIT 2.1 STRATEGIC ASSESSMENT PROCESS FOR DIVESTMENT

2.3 ANALYZE PORTFOLIO AND CONSIDER ALTERNATIVES

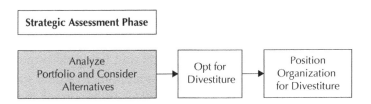

(a) STRATEGIC FIT As a first step in the strategic assessment process, the planning team should analyze the business's portfolio in the context of the company's overarching strategic objectives. Meaningful analysis, with an eye toward identifying potential divestments, requires the planning team (and the corporation) to ask probing questions about the consistency of the portfolio's makeup, given the strategic focus and direction of the overall enterprise. These questions would include:

- Are the individual markets or market segments in which the business operates fundamentally attractive in the long term?
- Are poorly performing properties well aligned with the organization's strategic objectives and with their markets?
- Regardless of the relative success of a business unit from a financial perspective, do the properties in the portfolio support the strategic objectives of the organization?

- How do financial markets perceive the individual elements of the portfolio?
- Does the organization's need for cash supersede other nonfinancial considerations?

The answers to these questions will generally identify any elements of the business portfolio that may require some form of corrective action. Divestment is but one of a number of options an organization may consider when addressing the issue of portfolio realignment. In fact, other, less dramatic options should usually be evaluated before divestiture is even entertained. This is because divestment activities in their various forms (divestiture options are discussed in section 2.4(c)) consume time and resources, can be extremely distracting to management, and may entail a substantial degree of risk. Divestment activities can tie up dozens of managers for as much as a year or more, and there is always the risk that their outcomes will not meet organizational expectations. In fact, a failed transaction is very likely to negatively impact shareholder value, distract and then frustrate operational management, and demotivate employees of the business unit being divested.

Also, because the enhancement of shareholder value is the driving force behind whatever option is exercised, it is important that the net benefit of divestment is measured against its alternatives to determine which course of action is likely to yield the optimal result, before any recommendations or decisions are made. The evaluation process associated with various portfolio realignment scenarios is discussed next.

(i) Disposition of Properties in Unattractive Markets.   Regardless of the performance of the entity's individual business units, those in markets offering limited growth opportunity should be closely scrutinized. Therefore, a fundamental step in the strategic planning process is the evaluation of the markets served by the organization's businesses. That evaluation should focus on the long-term attractiveness of those markets. This would include such things as size, growth potential, and the competitive dynamics in the market environment. In those instances where a market or markets are stagnating or contracting, planners should try to determine whether these conditions are likely to persist. If so, the organization should seriously consider exiting those sectors. Alternatively, even though a business is underperforming, the organization may be pointed in a completely different direction if the market holds promise for future growth. This direction would include some form of corrective action, such as a more aggressive investment posture, perhaps even acquisition.

(ii) Disposition of a Poorly Performing Property. A poorly performing property should not be deemed strategically incompatible simply by virtue of its substandard results. Other factors, such as poor management, underinvestment, short-term market disruption, or simply temporary loss of strategic focus, may be at the core of the business unit's performance. In such cases, it is clearly more desirable to address the underlying problem than to divest the property. However, poor performance is an important indicator of the need for some type of corrective action, so the planning team should routinely evaluate poor performers to determine its underlying cause. A preliminary determination can then be made whether continued investment is prudent or whether disposal should be considered.

Even in cases where the property is strategically marginal, it may be desirable to consider teaming with an arm's-length partner, in either a joint venture or in the form of a less formal strategic alliance, to buttress the performance of the unit rather than to divest. Also, if the unit has evolved into a nonstrategic asset and its poor performance is not addressable through corrective action, it may be more desirable to liquidate the assets than to endure the disruption and incur the costs associated with divestment. This option may be particularly preferable to divestment when the property is small and liquidation can be accomplished gradually by milking its profits over time.

(iii) Disposition of a Well-Performing but Nonstrategic Property. It is important that the planning team assess the strategic fit of all elements of the business portfolio and not fall into the trap of considering only poor performers as candidates for divestiture. That said, there are a number of challenging issues associated with deciding whether a well-performing property falls outside the scope of an organization's strategy and should be divested.

First of all, there is no guarantee that there will be unanimity of opinion among those making that determination. There is a significant degree of subjectivity in making such a judgment. Second, if there is recognition that the property is a poor strategic fit, there still may not be the discipline to take the appropriate action. Operational managers are frequently reluctant to consider the disposal of a nonstrategic but otherwise healthy business unit, since this may imply failure of management and entails the loss of control over assets as well as the authority and responsibility that accompany them. (Some of the factors that may cause organizational resistance are discussed in section 2.5(c).) Those in the strategic planning function can play an important role in this area. Planning managers can frequently balance this reluctance with a more objective view of the strategic fit of business units in question. Finally, it may not be obvious to nonmanagement stakeholders, such as shareholders and investors, that the property is a poor strategic fit.

If the organization believes that divestment is the best option, it is important, if not imperative, that any decision to divest is accompanied by a clearly articulated plan to reinvest the proceeds in activities that will yield better returns in the long term. Such a plan should act as a catalyst to galvanize internal opinions and to stimulate action as well as a vehicle for conveying an understandable and convincing rationale for stockholders and investors. If the organization cannot articulate such a plan, it may want to reconsider the decision to divest.

(iv) Disposition of a Property that Is Undervalued by the Financial Markets.   The financial market's view of a corporation's business portfolio may be at odds with management's perceptions. The markets may consider elements of the portfolio to lack strategic cohesiveness. As a result, investors and analysts may attribute little or no value to these assets, with the effect of suboptimizing enterprise value. If the market places minimal value on certain properties in a corporation's portfolio, management is faced with a difficult challenge if it wishes to change these perceptions. The markets generally favor focused (pure-play) strategies over diversified (conglomerate) strategies and frequently will undervalue the latter. Efforts to convince stakeholders and market commentators, in and of themselves, are of dubious value. The only option available to the corporation under these circumstances is to focus on results in the form of either:

- Demonstrable and quantifiable synergies between the property or properties in question and other elements of the portfolio or
- The consistent superior profitability of the suspect business

Absent the conviction that such results will be forthcoming, the organization is well advised to strongly consider divestiture.

(v) Disposition of a Property to Generate Cash. A property can be divested to generate cash for two distinctly different reasons. One is to generate operating cash when under duress and when all other options have been exhausted. If this is the case, the decision to be considered is not whether to divest, but which property or properties to put on the market. The difficulty associated with that choice is generally that the most valuable and attractive properties to potential buyers are those that are the most important strategically to the organization, and whose sale will further weaken an already weak core business. Under these circumstances, the potential of the transaction to enhance value is quite limited.

A second scenario is one in which the organization perceives that divestment of certain assets will result in a better use of funds. Organizations that are highly leveraged and wish to reduce their debt burden frequently exercise this option. If this is likely to be viewed favorably by the market, it can be an effective value creation strategy.

Although not exhaustive, these scenarios highlight the most common situations planners encounter during the strategic assessment process. Once they have conducted an analysis that considers all forms of corrective action to realign the business's portfolio, they can incorporate their final recommendations into the strategic planning document. The discussion that follows assumes that the decision to divest has been made. At that point, the organization must begin to consider how the prospective transaction will be structured.

2.4 OPT FOR DIVESTITURE

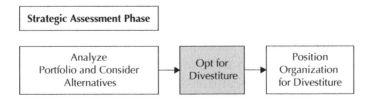

(a) DIVESTITURE EVALUATION PROCESS: OVERVIEW   If the evaluation of alternatives, as discussed in the preceding section, yields a conclusion that the optimal choice is to divest of certain elements

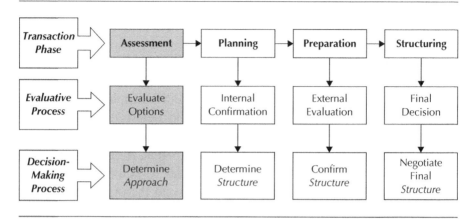

EXHIBIT 2.2   TRANSACTION APPROACH AND STRUCTURE EVALUATION CONTINUUM

of the business portfolio, a process of refining the specifics of that course of action would begin. That refining process will intensify during the planning phase of the transaction (discussed in Chapter 3), when possible transaction structures are thoroughly analyzed and an initial preference will be agreed on internally. During the preparation phase (discussed in Chapter 4), input from the seller's financial advisor would be sought, to validate the structure that had been internally arrived at; and during the structuring phase (discussed in Chapter 7), the final form of the transaction would be determined in negotiations with the buyer. This process is illustrated in Exhibit 2.2.

As illustrated, the initial step in the evaluation process occurs in the assessment phase and results in a decision on the *approach* to the disposition of the properties being considered for divestiture (i.e., whether they should, in fact, be divested or whether an alternative approach would yield greater value in the long term). This decision would be effectively affirmed by the approval of the strategic plan by corporate management. Assuming that divestiture is the path chosen, the next benchmark in the transaction structuring process will be drafting of an approval document that would contain a recommendation regarding the *structure* of the transaction, that is, the form that the divestiture would take (e.g., an outright sale or some other type of divestment transaction).

Although the rigorous analysis and decision making associated with the structure of the transaction will occur during the planning phase, the planning team would generally devote some preliminary, high-level thought to the realistic options available in anticipation of drafting the approval document. The range of divestiture options available are discussed next and presented in greater detail in section 3.1(b).

(b) DIVESTITURE OPTIONS   The divestiture options available include the outright sale of the property or properties to be divested, the creation of a separate entity in which the corporation may or may not retain an ownership interest, and the exchange or swapping of assets, and possibly other consideration, with another corporation.

- **Outright sale.** This is the most common type of divestiture, and it can take a number of forms, including the sale of the business unit's assets (and, generally, selected liabilities) or the sale of its stock, which, in turn, may be executed in a variety of ways. These options all have different tax, legal, and accounting implications that have to be considered before the final decision on transaction structure can be made.
- **Creation of a separate entity.** In certain cases, the organization may choose to create a separate entity to either sell the shares in an initial public offering (IPO) or retain majority ownership and distribute the shares to its stockholders in the form of a dividend. The former is referred to as an equity carve-out and the latter, a spin-off. Both are feasible only if the business being divested is of substantial size, but they entail substantial legal, regulatory, and advisory costs as well as the dedication of significant managerial resources for an extended period.
- **Swap of assets with another corporation.** This type of arrangement involves the exchange of assets by two organizations, both of which consider the other's properties to be more in line with their strategic objectives. These types of situations are relatively rare but, when they occur, provide both entities the opportunities to enhance the value of their respective portfolios.

(c) FACTORS INFLUENCING THE STRUCTURE OF THE DIVESTITURE TRANSACTION As previously indicated, at this point in the process the planning team will not dedicate an inordinate amount of its time and effort to a detailed analysis to determine the most attractive transaction structure. However, it should consider the range of possible structures and narrow its focus on the realistic alternatives available, based on the facts and circumstances surrounding the prospective transaction. Generally the most relevant factors to be considered by the team relate to the size of the transaction, the conditions of the financial markets, the extent to which the business is self-sufficient, the breadth of the market for the business, and the preferences and priorities of the seller.

- **Size of the entity.** As a general rule, the larger the business being considered for divestiture, the broader the range of divestiture options open to the seller. Obviously, the sale of a $5 billion subsidiary can be expected to have a substantially different impact on shareholder value than the sale of a $50 million product line and, therefore, would warrant a hard look at the full range of options available. Conversely, transactions involving smaller business units rarely will justify the level of management attention (and distraction from the core business) or the legal, regulatory, and advisory cost associated with such transactions. Accordingly, transaction size may broaden or narrow the range of possibilities and will generally influence the choice of transaction structure.

- **Condition of financial markets.** The conditions of the financial markets also have the potential to expand or contract the range of divestiture options and to impact value. Buoyant public markets and low interest rates are likely to enhance marketability and stimulate competition among potential buyers, making it sufficiently attractive to the seller to consider a wide variety of divestiture options. In contrast, depressed markets and tight credit tend to narrow a seller's options. These conditions may eliminate certain transaction structures, such as those involving public offerings, as well as exclude certain types of potential bidders, such as financial buyers.

- **Self-sufficiency of the business.** The ability to present the business as a stand-alone entity can have a significant impact on its marketability. (See section 5.4(a) for a discussion of the desired end state of the business.) Self-sufficiency is a prerequisite for some transaction structures (e.g., IPOs) and for attracting some categories of buyers (e.g., financial buyers without businesses that can supply missing elements of infrastructure). Conversely, the lack of self-sufficiency will generally limit the market to strategic buyers and, more specifically, to those strategic buyers that have a robust enough infrastructure to support the business being sold. As a result, the degree of self-sufficiency can affect the range of transaction types open to consideration.
- **Breadth of the market for the property.** Some properties will have a broad range of potential buyers while others will have a very narrow range, independent of the factors just noted. Where the business stands along this spectrum will influence the structure the seller chooses. If the market is large, the options open to the seller can be numerous. If the market is extremely narrow, the seller may in fact have no option but to deal with a small number of, or even a single, buyer. This will have a direct impact on the seller's leverage, in general, and on its ability to dictate structure, in particular.
- **Preferences and priorities of the selling corporation.** The prospective divestiture will not occur in a vacuum. The corporation will almost invariably have other initiatives, such as acquisitions, other divestitures, or financing activities, which will be competing for attention and resources. The relative importance of the divestiture will have an impact on the level of investment and management attention that the organization is willing to dedicate to the transaction. This, in turn, will impact the range of options that the corporation will entertain relative to the divestiture transaction.

Occasionally the facts and circumstances surrounding the transaction may be such that they lead the team to a quick and obvious recommendation with minimal input from tax and legal advisors. However, especially if the transaction is large, it may be desirable to consult with a financial advisor (i.e., business broker or investment banker) for a third-party view of the market potential and the range of realistic alternatives. (This type of consultation should not be confused with the formal engagement of a financial advisor to manage the transaction, a function that is described in Chapters 4 and 6.) In any event, more often than not, the optimal choice of structure is not readily apparent and the process requires extensive evaluation and input from specialists with tax, legal, accounting, and transaction expertise as well as line managers with in-depth knowledge of operational issues.

As noted, the assessment of transaction structure made at this point is preliminary and is intended to narrow the range of possibilities rather than to identify the optimal structure. Potential complexities that generally influence the final form of the transaction are considered in the development of the approval document, which is discussed in section 3.3.

2.5 POSITION THE ORGANIZATION FOR THE DIVESTITURE

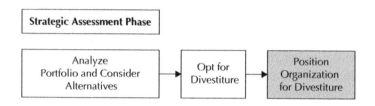

(a) PROCESS MANAGEMENT   As the process proceeds from its assessment to its approval and planning phase, the planning team will expand to include others who will either provide advice or become engaged as active members of the divestiture team (see section 1.4 for a description of the divestiture staffing model). Typically, planning and finance executives have substantial merger and acquisition (M&A) experience and understand what a divestiture transaction entails. However, operational managers very often have considerably less M&A experience and may not have been exposed to the sell side of such transactions at all. Therefore, it falls to the planning and finance professionals to sensitize those being brought into the process to some of the important issues and considerations they can expect to encounter. Because of the risks associated with the transaction (material impairment of value or a failure to close the deal), this responsibility goes beyond basic project management. It requires the ability to mobilize, educate, and motivate the team and the organization as well as a grasp of the intricacies of the transaction to minimize potential risks and optimize results. Some of the specific challenges that these professionals face are detailed in the sections that follow.

(b) FOCUS ON VALUE CREATION It is important to the success of the transaction that the participants understand that it is not simply an effort to get rid of an unwanted property. Those leading the project should emphasize that divestitures are common strategic initiatives (more than one-third of all M&A activity takes the form of a corporate divestiture) that are used by corporations to sharpen their strategic focus and in doing so create shareholder value. As managers are assigned to the divestiture team, those in leadership positions should make it clear that the team will be engaging in an important value-creation undertaking and that the difference between a well-executed and poorly executed transaction can be substantial in dollar terms. With transactions averaging approximately $175 million in recent years, the stakes can be dramatized by noting that suboptimizing a sale can easily cost tens of millions of dollars in lost proceeds. A necessary ingredient in optimizing the transaction is the commitment, enthusiasm, and effectiveness of the team—qualities that are substantially enhanced by casting the initiative in a positive light.

(c) RISKS, EXPOSURES, AND CONSTRAINTS In this early stage of the transaction, it is important that those who are brought into the process understand some of the risks, exposures, and constraints they will be working under. These items—confidentiality, organizational resistance, infrastructure interdependency, and regulatory constraints—all address issues that, if mishandled, can have a substantial impact on the risk profile of the transaction, that is, the increased potential for either a suboptimal transaction (one in which materially less than full value is realized for the properties being sold) or a broken transaction (one in which a sale is not consummated).

- **Confidentiality.** If news of the divestiture inadvertently becomes known by the management and employees of the properties being sold, the seeds of uncertainty will have been sown and the potential for loss and/or disaffection of key employees will be heightened. For these reasons, *it is imperative that the discussions of the potential sale are kept confidential during the planning and preparation stages of the process.* During this period, the circle of those who know about the proposed divestiture should be kept as small as possible and be expanded only on a need-to-know basis. As individuals are brought into the process, they should be advised that all information related to the transaction under consideration must be kept in the strictest confidence. They should also be apprised of the reasons why confidentiality is critically important and the negative consequences of a premature release of information.

Team members should understand that a breach of confidentiality will create an environment of uncertainty and speculation, and will leave management with only unattractive options. For example, denial of an event that will soon be announced would only undermine management's credibility at a time when that credibility is critical to managing and motivating employees of the business to be divested through the sale process. Similarly, ignoring the questions and speculation of employees can be harmful to morale and productivity and, in fact, invites wild speculation that may go well beyond rumors about the intended transaction. Also, acknowledging the planned divestiture effectively takes the timing of the announcement out of the hands of the organization and can short-circuit the important planning and preparation processes that are critical to the effective execution of the transaction. As a result, heavy emphasis should be put on the need for confidentiality until the transaction is formally announced.

- **Organizational resistance.** Team members should understand that some level of organizational resistance to divestiture transactions is not unusual. It can take any or all of these forms: outright opposition, delay, underresourcing, and management inattention.

The importance of divestitures as a value-creation activity notwithstanding, managers frequently resist selling off parts of their portfolio. Inappropriately, but realistically, the decision to sell may be seen as an admission of failure on their part. Additional resistance may come from some quarters because the prospective sale represents the diminution of the involved managers' authority and responsibility. Even after the decision to divest has been made, the residue of these attitudes may result in a tendency to delay implementation. Operating management may argue that the timing is poor due to a depressed market for the properties to be sold, it may be unwilling to commit limited resources to the management of the disposal process, or it may simply find it easier to procrastinate than to act.

The underresourcing of the divestiture effort, once the decision to sell has been made, is also a common pitfall associated with divestiture transactions, and generally stems less from a conscious effort to withhold support than from the psychological dynamics surrounding the divestiture process. There will be those in the organization who view the transaction as a low priority and, when called on to provide assistance, will be reluctant to do so. The resistance or inattentiveness of senior management, when it occurs, generally is more subtle or less conscious. They are prone to adopt an out-of-sight, out-of-mind mentality once the decision to divest has been made. This is the function of a need and desire to focus on issues associated with running and building the business that will be retained, but it can result in a blind spot regarding the support and resourcing of the transaction. That tendency can be further exacerbated if the business being divested is placed into discontinued operations (see section 7.4(b)) for financial reporting purposes.

These problems are by no means insurmountable. Strong leadership from those charged with responsibility for the transaction can counter them. However, an important step in doing so is to anticipate these attitudes and behaviors and alert team members to their potential in advance.

- **Infrastructure interdependency.** When the unit being divested is a stand-alone business with its own infrastructure, financial representation of the entity's historical performance and condition are relatively straightforward. Comprehensive historical financial statements for the business will exist, and a self-sufficient enterprise, with the entire necessary infrastructure, can be presented for sale.

However, this is rarely the case. It is more common that the business unit being divested has been owned by the seller for an extended period, in some cases for decades, and that the operational support of the property is very likely to have become intertwined with those of the parent. As a result, from both a financial reporting and operational perspective, the unit may be difficult to present as a true stand-alone operation. Addressing this issue typically requires a considerable amount of thought, planning, and management effort.

These factors are thoroughly discussed in Chapter 5. Suffice it to say here that team members should have a full understanding of the impact of infrastructure interdependency on the management and timing of the transaction. In many, if not most, corporate divestitures, disentangling the business being divested from that of the seller and the creation of representative financial statements are two of the most important and challenging aspects of the transaction. Under the best of circumstances, they can substantially delay the progress of the deal. When poorly handled, they can have a material negative impact on the value at which the business is sold.

- **Regulatory constraints.** Regulatory compliance, specifically compliance with the Hart-Scott-Rodino Antitrust Improvements Act of 1976 (HSR), can be a significant rate-limiting step and an area of potential exposure for the transaction. As detailed more completely in Chapter 7, HSR established a premerger program requiring those engaged in "large" M&As to notify the Federal Trade Commission (FTC) and the Department of Justice (DOJ) of the impending transaction. The parties to such a transaction must submit a Notification and Report Form with information about their businesses and wait a specified period before consummating the transaction. The objective of the act is to inhibit transactions that result in monopolistic entities.

Despite the act's reference to "large" M&As, the threshold established by HSR is quite low and, as a result, affects a significant number of transactions. Although thresholds may be adjusted upward periodically, they generally apply to transactions in which one of the parties has $100 million or more in annual net sales or total assets and the other has $10 million or more, and the size of the transaction is in excess of $59.8 million (in 2007). As a result, a very large percentage of divestitures are subject to FTC and DOJ scrutiny.

Although most corporate divestiture transactions meet the reporting criteria for HSR, most do not result in anticompetitive combinations. Clearly, those that do either will have to ameliorate that situation through disposal of certain properties or terminate the prospective transaction. Those that do not will have the consummation of the transaction delayed. The filing generally is not made to the FTC and the DOJ until a purchase agreement has been signed, and, once signed, the waiting period is 30 days, unless a request for early termination is granted. There is no guarantee that early termination will be granted; in fact, if one of these bodies requests additional information, the review period can be extended. Therefore, the planning for the transaction should accommodate a delay in closing the deal after the contract has been executed.

Perhaps more important, members of the team should be aware of the potential for undue complications if the information submitted with the Notification and Report Form (or any additional information requested) in any way suggests that the resulting combination would have an anticompetitive effect on a market. Accordingly, team members should be advised that judicious use of language about the business and its markets is critical. The seller should avoid sales hyperbole, and all internal communications and selling materials (such as the offering document and the management presentation) should steer clear of characterizations that would appear to diminish competition as a result of the transaction. The failure to do so will only invite the unnecessary scrutiny of these governmental bodies. At a minimum, that will further delay the transaction. In the extreme, it could eliminate some of the most attractive potential buyers or even cause the termination of the transaction.

2.6 NEXT STEPS

At the end of the assessment phase of the process, the organization should be positioned to move forward with detailed planning of the transaction (discussed in Chapter 3). If the assessment phase has been managed properly, the stage will have been set for the development of a formal recommendation, the staffing of the divestiture team, and the development of all the necessary plan documents that will initiate the process.

KEY POINTS

1. Any meaningful discussion of acquisition and divestment activity should be grounded in an understanding of the role of strategic planning in the corporate decision-making process. Divestitures are an output of the planning process and must be seen in the context of portfolio realignment and value creation. (Section 2.1(a))

2. Divestment is one of a number of options an organization may consider when addressing the issue of portfolio realignment. In fact, other, less dramatic options usually should be evaluated before divestiture is even entertained, because divestment activities in their various forms consume substantial amounts of time and resources, can be extremely distracting to management, and may entail a substantial degree of risk. (Section 2.4(b))

3. Possible structures should be analyzed based on the facts and circumstances surrounding the prospective transaction. The most relevant factors to be considered by the team relate to:
   - Size of the transaction
   - Conditions of the financial markets
   - Extent to which the business is self-sufficient
   - Breadth of the market for the business
   - Preferences and priorities of the seller (Section 2.4(c))

4. It falls to the leaders of the planning team to sensitize those being brought into the divestiture process to the key issues

and challenges they can expect to encounter. Because of the risks associated with the transaction (material impairment of value or a failure to close the deal), this responsibility goes beyond basic project management; it requires the ability to mobilize, educate, and motivate the team and the organization as well as a grasp of the intricacies of the transaction to minimize potential risks and to optimize results. (Section 2.5(a))

5. It is important to the success of the transaction that the participants understand that it is not simply an effort to get rid of an unwanted property. Those leading the project should emphasize that divestitures are common strategic initiatives (more than one-third of all M&A activity takes the form of a corporate divestiture) that are used by corporations to sharpen their strategic focus and in doing so create shareholder value. (Section 2.5(b))

6. It is imperative that the discussions of the potential sale be kept confidential during the planning and preparation stages of the process. Team members should understand that a breach of confidentiality will create an environment of uncertainty and speculation and will leave management with only unattractive options. (Section 2.5(c))

CHAPTER 3

DIVESTITURE PLANNING

3.1 OVERVIEW

(a) INTRODUCTION   Once the decision has been made that a business unit is no longer compatible with the strategic direction of its parent company, formal, detailed divestiture planning can begin in earnest. As we note throughout this *Guide,* the importance of thoughtful planning (as well as careful preparation and disciplined execution, which are discussed in the chapters that follow) cannot be overemphasized. Although detailed planning and preparation and disciplined execution will not guarantee success, their absence dramatically increases the probability of a protracted process and/or an unfavorable outcome (i.e., a failed transaction or a sale at a price that does not reflect the true value of the property being sold).

(b) RECOMMENDING THE STRUCTURE OF THE DIVESTITURE   As illustrated later in Exhibit 3.3, the planning phase of the process is initiated by the development of an approval document. However, before the approval document can be drafted, the originators of the document, with input from corporate management and financial, tax, legal, and accounting advisors, will have to decide which structure will optimize the organization's objectives. This is a critical juncture in the evaluation and negotiation process that ultimately leads to the final form the transaction will take. Each transaction is unique, and the option chosen is specific to the facts and circumstances surrounding it. The next sections discuss the options available, the selection process employed over the course of the transaction, and the interplay of the various factors that impact that selection.

(i) Options.   The divestment options available to an organization include: the outright sale of the property or properties to be divested, in the form of an asset sale or various types of stock sales; the creation of a separate entity in which the corporation may or may not retain an ownership interest; and the exchange or swapping of assets, and possibly other consideration, with another corporation. Exhibit 3.1 provides an overview of the major types of transactions and some of their more salient characteristics. A more detailed description of these options and technical analysis of their tax and accounting ramifications is presented in section 7.4.

Transaction Type	Characteristics
Sale of assets	Usually results in a higher sales price than other outright sales (i.e., a stock sale) because of the tax benefits to the buyer but may result in the retention of unwanted assets and/or liabilities by the seller and may be complicated by the transferability or assignability of assets or contracts.
Sale of stock	Usually results in a lower sales price than an asset sale because of the tax treatment required by the buyer, but the buyer assumes ownership of entire legal entity, along with all assets and liabilities.
Section 338(h)(10) sale of stock	Section 338(h)(10) of the IRS Code allows stock sales that comply with its provisions to be treated as asset sales for tax purposes. This may or may not result in beneficial tax treatment for the seller.
Section 368 sale of stock	Section 368 of the IRS Code allows the seller a tax-free sale transaction but requires that the proceeds it receives are in the form of the buyer's stock.
Equity carve-out	Involves the nontaxable sale of a portion of the equity of the subsidiary business to the public, generating cash proceeds. Execution of the transaction requires substantial advisory costs and protracted management attention.

Exhibit 3.1   Transaction Structure Characteristics (Continued)

Transaction Type	Characteristics
Spin-off	Involves the creation of a corporate entity distinct from the seller and distribution of the resulting stock to the selling corporation's shareholders. Properly structured, it results in a tax-free transaction, but it too requires significant advisory costs and management time and attention.
Asset swap	Involves the exchange of assets between the seller and another entity. It is analogous to conducting an assets sale and an asset acquisition simultaneously. It would result in the recognition of a gain or a loss and would be taxed accordingly.

Exhibit 3.1 Transaction Structure Characteristics

(ii) Selection Process Overview. As we indicated in Chapter 2, once the assessment process yields a conclusion that the optimal choice is to divest certain elements of the business portfolio, a process of refining the specifics of that course of action then begins. That refining process will intensify during this planning phase of the transaction, when the team thoroughly analyzes possible transaction structures and makes a specific recommendation. During the preparation phase (discussed in Chapter 4), input from the seller's financial advisor is also sought, to validate the structure that had been internally arrived at; and during the structuring phase (discussed in Chapter 7), the final form of the transaction is determined in negotiations with the buyer. This process is illustrated in Exhibit 3.2.

(iii) Factors Affecting Selection of the Optimal Structure. The planning team will have to recommend a transaction structure in the context of competing priorities and objectives that may be in conflict. The priorities of the organization will be influenced by other strategic activities that may be taking place, such as acquisitions, other divestitures, or financing activities. Those making the recommendation will also have to consider strategic, tax, accounting, legal, and operational factors.

The starting point in attempting to rationalize potentially conflicting objectives is understanding the strategic rationale for the divestiture and its impact on the associated financial considerations. This can be accomplished by determining whether the objective is to exit

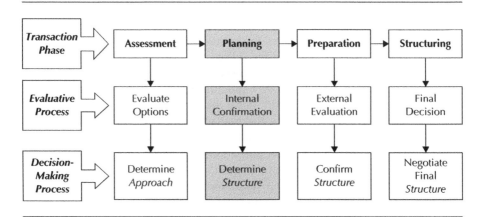

EXHIBIT 3.2   TRANSACTION APPROACH AND STRUCTURE EVALUATION

unattractive markets or to raise cash. If the objective is to generate cash, certain options, such as a spin-off, an asset swap, and tax-free IRS Section 368 stock sale, will be eliminated, since none of these will generate cash proceeds. In this case, the decision is somewhat simplified but still requires an analysis of multiple options and their ramifications.

If the objective is market exit to maximize shareholder value, the entire range of options may be open to consideration. The team will then have to determine whether a tax-free structure is likely to yield greater value, at an acceptable level of risk, than a taxable transaction. If a taxable structure appears to be more attractive and/or less risky, the team must decide whether the net benefits of an asset sale outweigh those of a stock sale. The team may also have to take into account the accounting treatment associated with the prospective transaction, specifically discontinued operations reporting.

Operational considerations also come into play and, regardless of the underlying objective of the transaction, they can make the decision-making process even more complex. They include such things as:

- Cost and distraction associated with executing certain types of transactions, specifically equity carve-outs and spin-offs
- Difficulty associated with getting the business being divested into a stand-alone condition (discussed in further detail in Chapter 5)

- Time and level of management commitment that would be tolerable to the organization
- Stability or fragility of the business being sold

As should be apparent from this discussion, the factors affecting the decision are many and complex. Deciding which structure is best for the selling corporation requires that these disparate factors somehow be *weighed against each other*. Before the planning team can make a reasoned, albeit still subjective, decision, the selling corporation should provide guidance by defining corporate goals in a *measurable* way and by *prioritizing* them.

It is not much help to the team if the objectives for the divestiture expressed by the corporation are too general, such as "get as high a price as we can, but as rapidly as possible, while minimizing the distraction of our management." While three factors have been expressed—price, speed, and management distraction—they cannot be made actionable because they cannot be measured. The lack of sufficient specificity begs clarifying questions, such as:

- What is the minimum valuation the corporation would accept?
- What specific time frame equals "rapid"?
- The distraction of how many people for what period of time would be acceptable?
- Which factor is more important than the others?

If the objectives are defined in a measurable way and priorities are clearly expressed, the team has a much more solid basis on which to craft a recommendation. It can then make its recommendation in terms of the corporation's priorities and the specifics of the prospective transaction. The recommendation might then take this form:

> If we opt for an IPO (i.e., equity carve-out), we would likely get up to $X more for the business than from an outright sale, but this would require X months more than a sale to close the transaction. Within this time frame, we would require X more man-years of effort and $X higher expenses to provide for the increased regulatory, disentanglement, and advisory aspects of the IPO. In comparison, we anticipate that a sale of stock,

based on our tax analysis, would generate net proceeds of $X to $X+ lower than an IPO but anticipate closing X months more quickly than an IPO and requiring X man-years less effort and $X lower transaction costs. Based on these estimates and considerations, and in light of the corporation's objectives and priorities for this divestiture, we preliminarily recommend the following course of action. [Insert plan.]

Once financial advisors are retained, we will ask them to review our assumptions, after which we will confirm or revise the recommended divestiture transaction structure.

As illustrated by this example, the decision is ultimately one that the corporation must make based on the facts and circumstances and informed by its own priorities and preferences, but it can be facilitated by articulating those priorities and preferences as unambiguously as possible. Ideally, they should be established and communicated to the team as soon as possible after the divestiture is approved, so that the actions and focus of the team and its advisors can be directed at crafting a recommendation that can be presented to the ultimate decision makers as part of the formal approval process (described next).

3.2 PLANNING PHASE PROCESS STEPS

(a) INTRODUCTION   In the remainder of this chapter we outline a comprehensive approach to the divestiture planning process, supported by illustrative documents, which will assist managers who have been tasked with the disposal of a business unit. The elements of this approach are illustrated in Exhibit 3.3. They include:

- Development of an *approval document* that articulates the rationale for the divestiture as well as key facts and considerations relating to the proposed transaction.
- Development of an *organization plan* that identifies the elements (i.e., products, functions, facilities) necessary for the business being divested to operate on a stand-alone basis and that determines those employees who will be part of the transaction and those who will not.

- Identification of *key* personnel who will remain with the divested property and development of a *retention/bonus plan* designed to retain those individuals.
- Creation of a *core divestiture team* (i.e., those individuals who will manage the transaction on a day-to-day basis).
- Development of an *execution plan* for the divestiture, to include a clear assignment of responsibilities and a description of the dynamics and steps involved in the sales process.
- Development of a *communication plan* to ensure clear and consistent messaging to all of the constituencies affected by, or with an interest in, the transaction.

(b) IMPORTANCE OF PROCESS Individual divestiture transactions may differ in many respects, but their planning (as well as preparation and execution) have their own internal logic that should be followed, if a given transaction is to have the chance of an optimal outcome. It is important to recognize that the elements of the planning approach just described should be seen in the context of a *process*; that is, the logic and sequencing of the approach is as important as the individual and collective elements of the plan. Getting out of sequence, even if all of the elements of the plan are present, usually will result in significant inefficiencies and, possibly, an impaired transaction. For example, the untimely creation and implementation of a retention plan can result in key employee defections and impairment of the business. Similarly, a delay in the assembly of the divestiture team can result in a rudderless

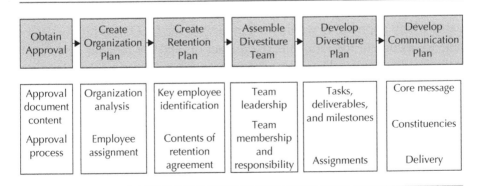

EXHIBIT 3.3 DIVESTITURE PLANNING STEPS AND CONSIDERATION

process. These early stage steps are consistent with the adage "Well begun is half done."

Exhibit 3.3 illustrates the logical flow of the planning process.

3.3 APPROVAL

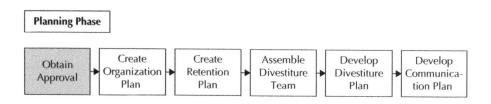

(a) INTRODUCTION As we discussed in Chapter 2, broad agreement by senior management on the desirability of divesting a property—generally as a result of a strategic planning exercise or a strategic assessment of the company's portfolio—would trigger the disposal process. Once such a consensus had been reached, the decision would require formal approval by those within the corporate organization with decision-making authority. The nature of the approval process is generally dependent on the size of the property being disposed of and the size and structure of the company doing the disposing. Small divestitures may be within the purview of the company's chief executive officer (CEO), but more material disposals by larger organizations typically require the approval of corporate headquarters (if the CEO reports into another layer of corporate management, such as officers of a holding company) and/or the approval of the company's board of directors. However, even in cases where approval is within the purview of the CEO, it is highly desirable to document the rationale, the impact of, and the process associated with the divestiture. Therefore, the first tangible output of the planning process should be a brief paper, in some organizations referred to as a board paper, that contains all of the descriptive and analytical information needed for those with approval authority to make an informed decision.

The originator(s) of the document may also differ based on the nature of the organization involved. In larger organizations, the originator typically would be the business development function, which has responsibility for the company's strategic planning process. If the parent/seller entity is a smaller company, the originator may be a senior line manager with responsibility for the property being considered for disposal. Regardless of who drafts the paper, at this point in the process it is advisable that the circle of those involved in considering the divestiture is kept small, as discussed in section 2.4(c).

(b) VALUE OF DOCUMENTATION   We believe that the creation of a clear and comprehensive written document of record is representative of best practices in that it provides an invaluable foundation for the proposed transaction. A requirement to document the deliberative process tends to drive the quality of analysis and ensures that there is a clear and fulsome discussion of the issues and alternatives involved as well as the conclusions reached. As the next graphic illustrates, documentation drives the quality of analysis, which in turn assures informed decision making—a process that ultimately results in validation of the underlying strategy and enhanced transaction value.

In addition, full documentation of the issues surrounding the transaction provides much of the basis for follow-on documents, such as the communication plan and the offering document, and downstream decision making, such as the approach to and structure of the transaction that will be adopted (discussed in Chapters 4 and 7). It also limits the potential for misunderstanding, disagreement, or the second guessing that can occur with the passage of time or changes in personnel, especially if the transaction gets derailed.

(c) APPROVAL DOCUMENT CONTENT   The objective of the approval document is to present a well-considered case for the disposal of the relevant business unit in the context of the core company's business strategy (and the underlying intent to increase shareholder value) as well as to outline the process to be employed in executing the transaction. Frequently, larger organizations that are active in the merger and acquisition (M&A) arena will have guidelines for the disposal process as well as what should be included in a document requesting approval. And, clearly, the specific information included in an approval document will be dependent on the facts and circumstances relevant to that transaction. However, in the absence of corporate guidance, the items discussed next should be considered when seeking approval and outlining the key aspects of a proposed transaction. In addition, an outline of an approval document is illustrated in Exhibit 3.4.

- **Executive summary.** The executive summary should contain a formal request for approval to proceed with the divestiture and a discussion of the strategic rationale for recommending to do so. (Note that in Chapters 1 and 2 we characterize the generic rationales for divesting business units in the context of an organization's strategic plan.) If the property had been acquired within the prior several years, the specific issue of why it was no longer a strategic fit should also be addressed. In addition, this section of the approval document generally includes a brief overview of the business unit recommended for disposal, a discussion of the financial impact of the transaction on the seller, and, possibly, an indication of how the proceeds from the transaction will be used. In short, this section should provide sufficient information for the reader to understand what is being recommended for disposal and why.
- **Business and market served.** This section should include a brief discussion of the history of business unit (i.e., its origins and evolution) and a description of the unit, including characteristics such as size, location(s), employee base, and corporate structure and organizational leadership. The business description should also include a description of the unit's products and/or services and should be accompanied by a discussion of the market in which the business unit operates. This discussion typically focuses on the sizing and dynamics of the market and the position of the business unit being recommended for disposal in that market (e.g., whether it is a major participant, niche player, or minor participant and whether it has a positive, neutral, or negative reputation). This discussion should avoid hyperbolic references to the market position of the business unit (e.g., terms such as "market dominance" and "market leader").

This approach fosters fact-based analysis that can be drawn on later in the process. It also ensures that the narrative does not unnecessarily invite Department of Justice or Federal Trade Commission scrutiny—or their equivalents in the European Union and other regions, if the deal has an international character—in the context of noncompetitive business combinations. We discuss this topic in section 7.7, where all the requirements and implications of regulatory compliance are considered.

- **Financial performance trends.** The financial section of the document generally should outline the recent historical financial performance of the business (at least the last three complete years) and any trends or anomalies associated with that performance. It should also indicate expectations for current year results as well as projections for the next two to three years and the forces affecting those anticipated results. This presentation should provide insight into overall trends in the business and the basis for determining the impact of the proposed disposal on the earnings (dilution or accretion) and growth (revenue and income) of the core business. This section should also address the issue of treating the business unit as a discontinued operation, if appropriate. We discuss discontinued operations treatment in some detail in section 7.4(b).

- **Financial impact of the transaction and sale considerations.** This section should include a discussion of potential buyers and the state of the market as reflected by such things as recent transactions, the vibrancy of the capital markets, and the impact of competitive forces in the market in which the unit operates. It should also include a discussion of the anticipated or preferred form of the sale (stock or assets), valuation estimates and how they were arrived at, and estimates of one-time transaction costs (such as broker, legal, and accounting firm fees and retention bonuses), the pretax and after-tax gain or loss the sale can be expected to generate, along with any associated tax implications. It is important to note that the ultimate form of the transaction is the result of ongoing internal deliberations that originate in the strategic assessment process, as we discussed in Chapter 2, and that culminate during the structuring phase of the process, as we discuss in Chapter 7.

- **Alternatives approaches to divestiture to be considered.** The document should contain a discussion of all reasonable alternatives to the divestiture option being recommended and how the option being recommended will optimize shareholder value. The options that should be evaluated will depend on factors specific to the individual transaction under consideration; alternatives, such as hold and invest, creation of spin-off or carve-out entities, or partnering with another entity in a joint venture, are options that we have discussed in sections 2.3(a) and 3.1(b) and that may be included in the evaluation and analysis presented in this section of the document.
- **Operational impact on the core business.** A major element in many, if not most, divestitures is the need to disentangle the business being divested from the core or parent entity. This section of the approval document should provide a preliminary view of the divestiture's impact on the infrastructure of the core business and any implications it may have on its organization, personnel, and customer base. It should also provide a high-level assessment of the ease or difficulty of positioning the business being sold as a stand-alone entity and any implications this may have on the salability of the unit. In most cases, disentanglement will have significant implications for the property being divested, due to its likely reliance on the core business for back-office support (e.g., human resources, finance and accounting, information technology). Although, as noted, key assets and capabilities that are critical to the viability or value of the disposal should be cataloged at this stage in the process, it is generally not feasible to address all of the issues associated with the business unit's infrastructure in detail. That effort should be the subject of a thorough, focused initiative in the disposal preparation process. Accordingly, we treat disentanglement as a major component of the transaction preparation phase and discuss it in great detail in Chapter 5.
- **Management of the disposition process.** Whereas the preceding components of the document focus on the rationale and justification for approval, *this section of the document should outline the issues associated with the planning,*

preparation, and execution of the transaction. The first element to be addressed in the implementation aspect of the transaction is that of project leadership. Effective implementation is highly dependent on leadership, and effective leadership is highly dependent on empowerment. Accordingly, the individual chosen to champion the transaction must have the explicit and ongoing support of those approving its execution. In establishing that support, the extent of the transaction champion's authority should be broad and, at the appropriate point in time (generally when the prospective transaction is announced), well understood by all relevant parties within the organization. In addition, there should be a clearly understood mechanism for the project leader to obtain approval from the appropriate decision maker when decisions that exceed his or her authority are required. Choice of the project leader will vary, depending on the size and relative importance of the transaction and on the size and structure of the core business, but commonly the individual designated will be the originator of the approval document and certainly will be a senior manager within the selling company. That individual will ultimately lead a core group of internal managers, whose composition and roles are discussed in section 3.6, and whose participation generally would be confirmed subsequent to the decision to proceed with the transaction. This section of the document should also identify the additional resources necessary to implement the transaction, such as a business broker or investment banker to help manage the transaction, an accounting firm to perform an audit or other agreed-on procedures to validate the business unit's financial statements, and any other consultants/specialists required to assist in the divestiture process. In identifying resources, it may also be appropriate to include a discussion of any apparent risks associated with the transaction, their potential impact, and any measures and resources recommended to mitigate those risks. This section should conclude with a view of project duration, anticipated proceeds, and estimated expenses, and provide a detailed timetable outlining the steps in the process. See Appendix 3A for an illustration of such a timetable.

Executive Summary

- Request for approval to proceed
- Brief overview of the business
- Strategic rationale underlying the decision to divest

Business and Market Served

- Brief history of the business
- Description of the business and its products
- Overview of the market and the market position of the business

Financial Performance Trends

- Discussion of the historical performance, current-year estimate, and near-term (e.g., 2 to 3 year) projected performance
- Impact of disposition on current-year results (dilutive or accretive)
- Impact of disposition on near-term projected performance (effect on revenue and income growth)
- Discontinued operations treatment (if applicable)

Financial Impact of the Transaction and Sale Considerations

- Potential buyers
- Valuation estimates
- Costs associated with the transaction
- Form of sale (stock or assets)
- Projected pretax and after-tax gain or loss
- Tax implications

Alternatives Approaches to Divestiture to Be Considered

- Hold and invest
- Spin-off
- Leveraged buyout
- Joint Venture

Operational Impact on the Core Business

- Management implications
- Overhead implications
- Customer implications

Management of Disposition Process

- Leadership and empowerment
- Resources required and measures necessary to prepare the business for sale
- Risks and risk mitigation
- Timetable

EXHIBIT 3.4 APPROVAL DOCUMENT OUTLINE

(d) FINAL APPROVAL   Approval will require additional dialogue and clarification between those recommending the disposal and those with decision-making authority. Therefore, any relevant material changes to the recommended course of action (e.g., the structure of the transaction, or limitations placed on sales price or terms of the sale) should be documented as well. It is at this point that general agreement on the approach (i.e., fix, fold, or sell) and structure of the transaction (e.g., outright sale, carve-out, or leveraged buyout [LBO]) is established. The organization's position on these issues will be revisited when a financial advisor is engaged and the business unit is taken to market (discussed in Chapter 4) and reconfirmed when the transaction goes through the final structuring phase (discussed in Chapter 7). However, consensus on the optimal deal structure, factoring in the strategic, financial, and operational objectives of the organization, should be reached. Once such consensus and overall approval to move forward have been reached, detailed planning of the divestiture process, beginning with the development of an organization plan, would be triggered.

(e) ANTICIPATING A COMMUNICATION LEAK   Once the transaction has been approved, the organization should consider the possibility that news of the transaction may prematurely become public or that rumors of an impending sale become so rampant as to have the same effect. Such a situation presents unattractive options, reinforcing the importance of strict confidentiality, as we discussed in Chapter 2. However, a communication leak is always a possibility, and the organization should proactively consider its options in advance in case it does occur.

While, theoretically, there are four courses of action—to deny, to ignore, to counter, or to accelerate the announcement—practically, there are only three, since denial is rarely if ever a good choice. Denial of a decision whose announcement is imminent can only undermine the credibility of management and the effectiveness of its future communications with major constituencies, most important the employees of the business being divested. Alienation of this employee population will only increase the potential for diminished productivity and impairment of the value of the business.

Therefore, if a leak occurs, the selling organization should consider whether to:

- Ignore it.
- Counter it with statements that neither confirm nor deny it (e.g., "While we are not presently engaged in an active effort to sell any our properties, evaluation of our portfolio is a continuous process.").
- Accelerate the development of the communication plan (described in section 3.8) and the announcement of the plan to sell (discussed in section 6.3).

The option chosen will depend on the specific circumstances surrounding a given transaction, particularly the size and importance of the business to be sold and the amount of time between the leak and the planned announcement. At this early stage of the divestiture process, the important point is that the selling organization has anticipated the possibility of a leak, has considered its options in advance, and therefore is positioned to react if it occurs.

3.4 ORGANIZATION PLAN

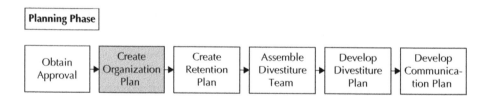

(a) **INTRODUCTION**   It is not uncommon that business units that are candidates for divestiture have been part of the parent company's portfolio for an extended time, frequently for decades. As a result, an environment of functional interdependency and shared operational infrastructure is likely to have evolved over that time. Predictably, the greater the level of interdependency, the more complex the disentanglement process will be when the business unit is sold. The countervailing issues associated with that process are the desire to present the disposal as a stand-alone entity to the greatest extent possible—so that its sales potential can be optimized by making it attractive to financial as well as strategic buyers—versus the reality that its operation is likely to have been substantially interwoven into the fabric of the parent/seller. The first step in the effort to rationalize the structures that will result from the divestiture is the development of an organization plan. As previously noted, we describe a more rigorous and detailed plan of disentanglement to be initiated later in the divestiture process in Chapter 5. The organization plan developed during this phase of the process generally follows the logic outlined in the next illustration.

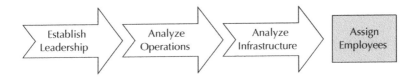

(b) BUSINESS UNIT LEADERSHIP The determination of who will lead the business unit being divested should be the first step in the development of the organization plan. Those chosen typically include the business unit's chief executive and that individual's senior management team. This decision usually should be made by a small group consisting of the parent company CEO, the project leader, and senior executives in the human resource and finance functions. The determination of who will staff the leadership team of the company being divested is important for a number of reasons, most immediately in assisting in the development of the organization plan. The team members' knowledge of the business, its dynamics, its personnel, and its market can be critical to analyzing operations, infrastructure, and staffing and identifying all products and/or services, functions, facilities, and personnel that should logically comprise the business being divested. In addition, they will necessarily be major participants in the divestiture process going forward. They will be integral to the selling process and, among other things, will play a prominent role in describing what the business is and in crafting and articulating a vision of what it can become. Finally, they will play a critical role in ensuring that the operation remains focused on performance during the sales process. Therefore, early identification of these individuals and vigorous efforts to retain them are important initial steps in the divestiture process. Although formalization of their retention arrangements generally will have to await the creation and approval of the retention plan (as we discuss in the next section), at this point in the process the executives identified should be informed of the company's intention to provide them with generous stay incentives.

(c) OPERATIONAL ANALYSIS   Once business unit leaders have been confirmed, an analysis of operations should be conducted. This is generally a fairly straightforward process consisting of the identification of customer-facing operations and functions. This analysis should specifically identify these aspects of the unit's operation:

- All of the elements of the product and/or service portfolio of the business
- Functions that are integral to the creation and delivery of those products/services
- Facilities, physical plant and equipment, intellectual property assets, and operational capabilities necessary for product creation or product/service delivery
- All functions that support revenue generation of the unit

(d) INFRASTRUCTURE ANALYSIS   The determination of infrastructure functions necessary to establish the business as a freestanding unit is generally more complex than the operational analysis just described. Whereas the customer-facing operations are fairly obvious, infrastructure operations and functions are frequently interwoven into the fabric of the parent company. This is typically true of functions such as human resources, finance and accounting, and information technology. Although a granular evaluation of many aspects of these shared services will not begin to be addressed until a disentanglement project team is formulated, the basic functions necessary for the unit to be a stand-alone business should be identified. Doing this would entail identifying all staff and back-office functions that currently support the business unit and determining what can be transitioned with the sale. This determination will enable the next step in the process, employee assignment, as well as the identification of gaps in support that will have to be filled.

(e) EMPLOYEE ASSIGNMENT   The employee assignment process follows logically from the identification of the functions necessary for the business unit to be freestanding. Once the determination of necessary operational and infrastructure functional support is made, it must be translated into headcount and then into the specific identification of those individuals who will staff those functions as well as those affected individuals who will be retained by the parent company. As noted, in the case of customer-facing functions, the determination should be readily apparent. In the case of shared services/infrastructure, the determination would less obvious in some cases and may have to be based on the best judgment of those crafting the plan. Those judgments should generally be informed by the input of the business unit's executive team.

In the course of the analysis of infrastructure, two other issues often arise: those of "stranded" employees and "fractional" employees. In some cases, there may be a group of employees that would be stranded (i.e., overall headcount in shared functions may be reduced as a result of the divestiture and a group of employees may be subject to termination when the transaction is finalized). Conversely, in some cases there may not be sufficient personnel within the support functions to be split between parent and business unit. This case generally results in the understaffing of the entity being divested, and the back-filling of those positions postacquisition would have to be considered in the development of any pro forma and prospective financial statements provided to potential buyers.

Ultimately, the determination of which employees will be part of the transaction is situation-specific. In the sale of a freestanding division or subsidiary, the level of shared services and integration is likely to be minimal. At the other extreme, if the prospective sale involves a highly integrated business unit, such as a product line, the complexity of disentanglement may be quite substantial. As noted, a key factor in making decisions about personnel is that of salability. Generally, the more freestanding the unit being sold, the larger the potential market of buyers and the higher the value placed on the property. This does not mean that extraordinary efforts should necessarily be made to make the unit a stand-alone entity, but the seller should realize that the market will be limited to those with an appropriate infrastructure if it is not. For example, a substantial market of financial buyers that do not possess the necessary infrastructure to support an incomplete business may be ruled out, as would the option of a LBO or initial public offering (IPO).

Once a clear determination on personnel is reached and approved by senior management, a plan can then be developed to retain key personnel.

3.5 RETENTION PLAN

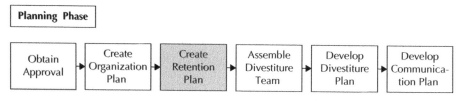

(a) **INTRODUCTION**   Besides considering the overall staffing needs of the company to be divested, there invariably are key employees, in addition to its executive management team, who are critical to the ongoing operation of the business being divested. The loss or demotivation of these individuals would have a serious negative impact on the near-term performance of the business, which in turn would impact the ability of the parent to sell the business at a price that reflects its true market value.

(b) **IDENTIFICATION OF KEY EMPLOYEES**   It is important that all key individuals are identified as early as possible in the process and that a plan is formulated to reward them for staying with the property being sold, for at least as long as it takes to execute a transaction. There may be a tendency for those who are in decision-making positions, yet removed from the day-to-day operation of the business, to assume that it is sufficient to provide executive managers of the unit being sold with stay incentives. This attitude can be shortsighted and may result in the defection of those who directly or indirectly generate substantial streams of revenue. Such employees generally include sales personnel but may also include operational personnel (such as key programmers in a software business or those with strong business relationships in a service business) whose loss might have an immediate impact on the financial performance of the business.

A prudent approach to determining the value of employees to the short-term health of the business is for senior human resource and finance personnel to perform a thorough review of the organization by functional area, using as a criterion the importance of each function to *delivering* revenue over the next one to two years. The use of the concept of revenue *delivery,* rather than revenue *generation,* broadens the scope of the review and ensures that all those functions that may be critical to the near-term success of the business are captured. Once those critical functional areas have been identified, the analysis can drill down to the individual level to determine those for whom retention incentives would be appropriate.

(c) **DEVELOPMENT OF THE RETENTION PLAN**   The retention plan should identify all those who are being recommended for stay incentives and the nature of the incentives to be awarded. In developing the plan, several factors should be considered:

- **Size of the transaction and the anticipated proceeds associated with it.** These factors will influence the decision regarding the amount to be dedicated to the plan and its breadth of coverage.
- **Risk associated with the loss of key personnel.** Retention payouts should be viewed in the context of insurance. While there are no hard-and-fast rules governing retention payouts, it is useful to assess the impact of certain classes of personnel turnover on near-term revenue goals and, ultimately, on valuation. In some environments, such as manufacturing, exposures may be slight. In others, such as service businesses that are highly reliant on personal relationships, that exposure may be substantial. Those exposures should be determined and quantified when formulating the retention plan.
- **Number of employees to be included in the plan.** The number of employees included will affect the shape of the plan. If it is desirable to include a large number of employees in the plan, consideration should be given to having several levels or categories of retention bonuses, based on the relative importance of each person to the near-term health and salability of the business.
- **Conditions to be met to earn the incentive.** In many cases it is not desirable to tie the incentives solely to retention (i.e., the

requirement of simply remaining with the business). Plan developers must keep sight of the fact that its goal is to ensure that the value of the business is optimized. The incentives, therefore, should reward behavior that supports that objective. In the case of senior management, this may translate into incentives to reward them for the success of the sale (i.e., that the sale is consummated and/or that a predetermined sales price is attained). For sales personnel, this may mean additional incentives to reach near-term sales goals. And for those in operational functions, this may simply translate into remaining productive employees in good standing until the business is sold.

- **How incentives are characterized.** As noted, there are no hard-and-fast rules governing retention agreements, but a common approach to quantifying incentives is to express them in terms of a percentage of annual salary. Doing this enables some degree of standardization and equity as well as ease of comparability. The approach is also consistent with other incentive arrangements most likely experienced by those involved.

- **Avoidance of agreements that might inhibit the sale.** Retention plans must strike a balance between motivating the key personnel and avoiding any arrangements that might sour a deal during due diligence. Accordingly, agreements should not include terms that saddle potential buyers with costly obligations or limit their flexibility in making personnel decisions.

The cost of employee retention generally is estimated in the approval document; a more precise estimate is made during the development of a formal retention plan. Senior managers in human resource and finance functions typically have responsibility for the development of the plan, which ultimately would be approved by the parent CEO, and may require approval at a higher level if the plan results in a cost materially greater than the original estimate. For an illustration of a retention plan, see Appendix 3B.

(d) EXECUTION OF THE RETENTION PLAN The approval of the retention plan should trigger the creation of letters of agreement between the seller/parent and the key employees. These letters should clearly document the terms and conditions under which the employee would receive his or her incentive. As noted, the incentives and, therefore, terms and conditions of individual agreements may differ by type of employee. Exhibit 3.5 contains an outline of key elements that should be considered in the drafting of a retention agreement.

Acknowledgment of the Intent to Sell

This introductory paragraph indicates that the controlling entity intends to sell the business unit that employs the addressee.

Acknowledgment of the Importance of the Addressee to the Business Being Divested

This text indicates the desire of the controlling entity to incent the addressee to remain with the business unit until a sale is transacted or for a specified period thereafter (a transition period).

Definition of the Mechanisms that Would Trigger the Awarding of the Retention Bonus

This text characterizes the event or occurrence that would make the addressee eligible for payment of the award. It may entail employment of the addressee until the closing of the prospective sale or some period thereafter or the attainment of other specified objectives.

Definitions of the Conditions to Be Met to Earn Awards

Awards more often than not fall into three categories: (1) retention bonuses, (2) performance bonuses, and (3) success bonuses. Retention bonuses are awarded for remaining an employee in good standing beyond a specified date, usually the close of the divestiture transaction. Performance bonuses generally are awarded for attainment of a specific goal, such as targeted sales or revenue and/or earnings, and are conditioned on employment through the close of the transaction or another specified date. Success bonuses are awarded for the closing of the transaction (frequently at a specified valuation) and are conditioned on employment through the close of the transaction or another specified date.

Quantification of Potential Awards

Awards are usually expressed in terms of percent of annual salary and can vary significantly but can range from 15% to 20% for retention bonuses

---

EXHIBIT 3.5 RETENTION LETTER OUTLINE (CONTINUED)

for lower level managers to 100% or more for performance and success bonuses for key managers.

Impact of Early Termination on Awardees

Early termination provisions will generally honor bonus awards, if such termination is originated by the controlling entity or its successor for reasons other than cause. If the employee elects to voluntarily terminate employment or is terminated for cause, the employee would forfeit his or her award.

Impact of a Failed Transaction

In the event that a divestiture transaction is not consummated, most bonuses would not be paid, although stepped-down payments to the most senior or critical employees may be made.

End Date

All letters should have an end date beyond which awards would not be paid, unless the controlling entity chose to extend it.

EXHIBIT 3.5 RETENTION LETTER OUTLINE

3.6 ASSEMBLING THE DIVESTITURE TEAM

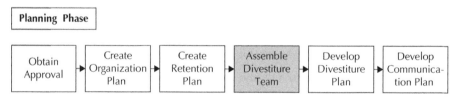

(a) INTRODUCTION   A critical element of the planning process is the creation of the team that will help formalize the divestiture plan, drive the divestiture process, and ensure that it stays on track. Almost invariably, the challenge facing the team tasked with a divestiture is, simply stated, *to get the deal done under optimal terms with minimal disruption to the parent organization.* Doing this requires an intense focus on efficiency and generally dictates that the core team must be lean, must rely heavily on external resources, and must be able to selectively access internal resources on an as-needed basis.

(b) TEAM STRUCTURE   Leading up to this point in the process, at a minimum, finance, human resources, and business development managers, with possible input from legal, have been involved in the request for approval and in the development of the organization and retention plans, and a team leader generally has been designated as a result of the approval process (the preferred and recommended approach). If a team leader has not been designated when the divestiture was approved, such an appointment should be made at this point.

The team leader, whenever assigned, should be designated by the parent company CEO. The choice of lead manager would vary, depending the size and structure of the parent organization, but, in larger organizations, responsibility generally should be assigned to the business development function, whose purview includes M&A activity. In smaller organizations without a business development group, the assignment may fall to a senior member within the finance function or, less likely, a line manager associated with the business unit being divested.

In any case, the core members of the divestiture team consist of a small group of senior managers as well as the executive management of the property being divested. It is important that they are empowered by senior management to drive the transaction to closure and that they have the authority to draw on corporate resources, as needed. As the process gains momentum, the team should be complemented by outside consultant/professionals with specific skills and knowledge as well as other line managers and subject matter experts within the seller's corporate structure, who would be accessed when their expertise is needed. Each of these components of the team is discussed in detail in the sections that immediately follow.

(c) CORE TEAM MEMBERS   Core members of the team generally consist of senior managers from the business development, finance and accounting, human resource, and legal functions of the seller's organization. The team should also include the executive management of the property being divested, usually the CEO (or the functional equivalent), the chief financial officer (CFO), and the senior tier of management. Although information technology managers generally play an advisory role in the process, they may be included on the core team in those situations where significant revenue of the business unit is tied to technology assets and/or capabilities. The roles of core team members in the process are described next.

- **Business development.** Many larger companies are staffed with a planning group typically headed by an executive titled senior vice president (SVP) of strategic planning or SVP of planning and business development. This group would be the logical choice to provide the executive who would take the lead role in the divestiture process. Undoubtedly, this individual would have played a central role in articulating the strategic rationale for the divestiture and could be expected to work very closely with the lead financial manager (i.e., the relevant senior financial executive in managing the divestiture process, whether that is the CFO, controller, or a designee).

- **Finance and accounting.** Finance and accounting personnel play a major role in any divestiture transaction. As noted, the lead financial manager may in fact be the default choice for overall divestiture team leader in some instances. In any event, the lead financial manager will have had substantial involvement in the development of the approval document, the organization plan, and the retention plan, and, going forward, should play an active role in the development of an offering document (or prospectus) and management presentations, the creation of the data room, and the orchestration of the due diligence process. That individual should also manage or comanage the relationships with outside accountants, tax specialists, and brokers and play an important part in negotiating final legal documents during the execution phase of the process.

- **Legal.** Many large organizations, especially those that are active in the M&A arena, have attorneys on staff that have in-depth M&A transaction experience. In those situations where that is not the case, it is critical that the seller engage seasoned M&A counsel. Arguably, he or she will be the most important member of the disposal team. A knowledgeable and capable M&A attorney will help the team avoid critical mistakes and provide invaluable positive input while protecting the interests of the seller throughout the transaction process. Counsel should participate in the disposition process from beginning to end and should be consulted early and often by the other members of the core team. Although the attorney need not attend every meeting or be involved in every discussion involving the other members, he or she must be kept abreast of developments and should provide input on all major decisions affecting the transaction. By training and experience, the attorney will be able to provide the technical knowledge and expertise to deal with important legal issues. By being deeply involved throughout the process, counsel will have established the context for making critical legal/business judgments and for ultimately comanaging final contract negotiations.

- **Human resources.** Because of the sensitive nature of the personnel issues involved, human resource staff should play a prominent role in the process, particularly in communicating with the employees of the business being put up for sale. Senior members of the human resources staff will have been major participants in developing the organization plan and creating and managing the execution of the retention plan and, now, for coordinating the communication plan with corporate communications or media relations staff. This early involvement will also position them to monitor and report on the morale and the productivity of the employees of the business being sold. Additionally, as the process progresses, they will also be required to provide critical input into the disentanglement initiative and in final contract negotiations.

- **Business unit executives.** As previously noted, executive managers of the property being divested can be expected to be key participants in the divestiture process. They will wear several hats. They will be expected to continue to manage the business day to day. They will also play a prominent part in developing, assembling, and presenting the information required for due diligence. Under the direction of the core members of the team (and usually a broker or banker engaged to assist in the sale), they will be the ones primarily tasked with the creation of a prospectus, conducting management presentations and participating in follow-up interviews, and populating a data room. More important, they will also play a critical role in the sale process insofar as they are an integral part of what is being sold. To the potential buyers, they effectively will be the face of the business.

(d) CONSULTANT/PROFESSIONALS   In addition to the core internal team, the parent/seller frequently will engage a range of consultant/professionals with specialized expertise. These would generally include a business broker or investment banker, external legal support, and external accounting and tax resources, all discussed next.

- **Business broker.** The term "business broker" generally refers to intermediaries who are active in the M&A arena in representing sellers or potential sellers. Their clients are frequently privately held companies or public companies wishing to divest of small to midsize business units. (Investment bankers, discussed next, generally fulfill this intermediary role in larger transactions involving the sale of large business units of publicly traded companies.) Brokers usually focus on discrete industries; if their business is more broad-based, they are organized along industry lines, with individuals or small groups focusing on specific segments of the broader market. Their industry focus enables them to be fully conversant in all aspects of the industry/market they cover. The best brokers understand the makeup and dynamics of their respective markets and generally are intimately familiar with its participants and their strategic interests.

  As noted, brokers generally represent sellers, but they themselves try to remain networked with potential buyers, both strategic and financial, throughout the industry so that they are able to service their clients effectively. Brokers clearly have their own agendas, but their motivation is in large part consistent with those of a seller. Because they are compensated on a commission/transaction basis, all things being equal, they have a vested interest in selling a business at the highest possible price. They are generally compensated on percentage basis, frequently a variation of the so-called Lehman Formula, a standard industry formula that is illustrated in Exhibit 3.6.

  When a divestiture is contemplated, it is highly advisable to engage a broker (or banker) to assist in the transaction. As noted, dual objectives are being served in a divestiture transaction: to optimize the sales price and to minimize management

COMMISSION	PURCHASE PRICE
5%	First $1 million
4%	Second $1 million
3%	Third $1 million
2%	Fourth $1 million
1%	All amounts over $4 million

EXHIBIT 3.6 LEHMAN FORMULA

distraction and business disruption. An effective broker, with strong market knowledge, good industry contacts, and expertise in the management of auction sales, can relieve the seller's management team of much of the administrative and sales burden generated by the transaction as well as assist in the effort to realize an optimal price for the business.

- **Investment bankers.** Investment bankers serve a role similar to that of brokers, but differ in a number of ways. Whereas brokers bring market expertise to a transaction, bankers generally bring financial expertise and capabilities. As noted, bankers generally play an intermediary role in larger transactions. Investment banking operations, more often than not, are part of a larger financial institution, usually a bank or brokerage house. These institutions generally have other financial relationships with clients they represent and may be involved periodically with public and private placements of their securities. Bankers can be valuable resources, especially for large divestitures, where they may also play a role when a transaction requires debt or equity financing or when a "fairness opinion" (discussed in section 4.3(c)) may be desirable in justifying the sale price and other aspects of the transaction to shareholders. Staple financing is another banker service that has gained prominence in recent years. It is a financing arrangement provided to the buyer by the lending function within the investment bank representing the seller, and is intended to facilitate the financing of the transaction. Similarly, facilitating equity financing, when the seller chooses to spin off the business unit or to initiate a public offering of the unit, is another important service bankers are able to offer. When an outright sale of a business unit is contemplated—particularly in the case of a large transaction—there are rare occasions where both a banker *and* broker (as "second seat") may be engaged. This arrangement provides the seller with both the broker's sales expertise and the banker's financial clout. Generally, though, bankers are not as active as business brokers in the midmarket (transactions of less than $250 million), where a large percentage of divestiture transactions take place. We discuss the relative merits of brokers and bankers and their impact on the selection process in section 4.3(b).

- **Outside legal.** As noted, sellers that do not possess in-house M&A legal expertise will avail themselves of the support of external counsel, which would play a role comparable to that of in-house counsel, as described earlier. However, in those cases where the lead M&A attorney (whether internal or external) needs additional support, he or she may draw on legal experts who specialize in areas such as employment, intellectual property, real estate, tax, or insurance law. Additional resources may also be accessed if the transaction is complex and beyond the scope of the expertise of the lead attorney(s), such as transactions that involve business operations outside the United States.

- **External accounting/tax expertise.** The need for outside accountants and/or taxation specialists in the divestiture process depends on two factors: the degree of complexity associated with the transaction and the availability of internal resources. This may be the case when there are international or multijurisdictional issues that are beyond the scope of the selling organization's internal capabilities or when internal resources are simply not available to support the transaction.

(e) OTHER INTERNAL EXPERTISE   In addition to those on the core team and supporting consultant/professionals, certain internal experts will be called on to provide support on an as-needed basis. These experts generally reside within the larger corporate structure of the seller and may include:

- **Corporate tax department.** Early in the process, discussions should include the input of a tax specialist. If this expertise was not resident within the parent's corporate structure, it would have to be accessed on a consulting basis. This individual should be enlisted as early as the approval stage if there were serious tax considerations attached to the transactions, and should remain in the contact with the core team, generally through the lead financial manager team member, throughout the divestiture process.

- **Information technology (IT) expertise.** Information technology has become thoroughly embedded in today's business environment, and issues associated with all manners of connectivity, hardware, and software can be expected to come into play when two businesses are being disentangled. Arguably, IT issues will be the most pervasive and complicated facing those managing the transaction. When the disentanglement process (discussed in Chapter 5 in detail) is initiated, best practice suggests that a dedicated project team be assigned the responsibility of identifying interdependencies and making recommendations for their resolution. Often IT issues loom so large in the disengagement process that it is advisable to create a separate project team to deal with them. Whether a separate team or not, it is generally wise to have the IT representatives vet all operational (i.e., non-IT) disentanglement decisions to ensure that they do not have an unforeseen impact on the technology infrastructure of either entity.

- **Executive management.** It will be necessary to obtain input periodically from the executive management staff of the parent company. That input will generally relate to personnel, customer, and competitive issues. It will be particularly important when crafting the description of the business being sold and the provisions of noncompetition covenants for the purchase and sale agreement, to ensure that the parent's ability to compete in the marketplace postacquisition is not impaired in any way.

- **Other resources.** Typical functions that may need to be accessed include those responsible for facilities management, real estate management, and business insurance. The need for other internal resources is situation-specific. For example, in a manufacturing environment, production expertise would be needed.

In highly regulated businesses, such as banking, brokerage, and pharmaceutical manufacturing, access to resources related to compliance would be required.

3.7 DEVELOPMENT OF THE DIVESTITURE PLAN

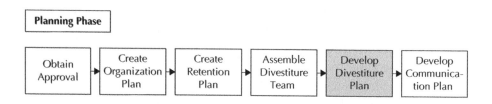

(a) **INTRODUCTION**   Once the team is formalized and members are confirmed, they would develop a detailed divestiture plan under direction of the team leader. This plan should be extremely specific and should:

- Outline the steps associated with the divestiture transaction.
- Identify all material tasks, deliverables, and milestone accomplishments associated with the transaction.
- Assign responsibility and establish deadlines for those tasks, deliverables, and milestones, including transitional tasks or services after the close of the transaction.
- Identify key decision points, such as the selection of outside resources (brokers and accounting firms), the announcement of the intent to sell, and the selection of bidders, and any criteria associated with their execution.

The shape of the plan will be influenced by the specifics of the transaction. For example, the need for accounting assistance may be dependent on whether there are existing stand-alone financial statements for the entity being sold. Similarly, the need for a Hart-Scott-Rodino (HSR) filing will depend on whether the specifics of the transaction meet the criteria established by the act. Also, although we strongly recommend the engagement of a broker or banker for most divestiture transactions, the decision to do so is clearly at the discretion of the seller. There are transactions for which a banker or broker may not be necessary, such as those that involve a small property or a preemptive bid.

(b) PHASES OF THE TRANSACTION PROCESS The divestiture plan can be broken down into three major phases: (1) the planning phase, (2) the preparation phase, and (3) the execution phase. Within each phase, there are a number of discrete, sequential steps. The planning phase is described in detail throughout this chapter. Although we discuss preparation and execution exhaustively in Chapters 4 through 7, the next sections provide overviews of these key phases of the transaction and their relationship to the planning process.

(c) PREPARATION PHASE The preparation phase consists of those steps necessary to position the business for the sale and has two components: preparation for the selling process and preparation for the separation of the business being sold from the seller. The former, which we describe in Chapter 4, includes:

- Engagement of a broker or banker to assist in the sales process
- Engagement of an accounting firm to prepare stand-alone financial statements for the entity being sold
- Creation of an offering document or prospectus that describes the business, its products, the market it serves, and its fundamental attractiveness to potential buyers
- Development of presentations to be made by the business unit executive team to potential buyers
- Identification of the pool of potential buyers
- Preparation of the data room, where all documents to be provided for due diligence purposes to potential buyers are located

In Chapter 5, we detail the other aspect of the preparation phase, the initiation and implementation of the disentanglement process.

(d) EXECUTION PHASE The execution phase of the divestiture plan, the topic we cover in Chapters 6 and 7, consists of those steps that are necessary to initiate and manage the selling process. The steps generally include:

- Announcement of the intent to sell (essentially, the initial phase of the communication plan)
- Solicitation of bids from potential, qualified buyers

- Management of the due diligence process
- Determination of the winning bidder
- Negotiation and structuring of the transaction
- Finalization of the sales contract and creation of supporting documents
- Compliance with HSR requirements, if appropriate

Although planning, preparation, and execution are essentially sequential steps in the process, a number of the preparation and execution steps must be initiated or staged in advance of their implementation. For example, the effort of identifying the pool of possible external resources that will be engaged, such as brokers and accounting firms, must be initiated in advance of their selection and the actual initiation of the preparation process. Similarly, the managers who will participate in the disentanglement effort must be mobilized in advance of implementation. There are similar staging efforts associated with the execution phase, the most important of which is the continued consideration of the structure of the transaction whose deliberations start in the planning phase and extend through the preparation and execution phases.

Exhibit 3.7 illustrates the duration and intensity of activities within the various phases of the transaction. Light gray indicates the

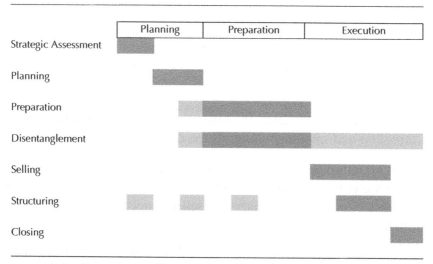

Exhibit 3.7 Phases of the Divestiture Process

staging and deliberations that precede or trail implementation, and dark gray indicates the duration of the activity when efforts are most intense. A more granular illustration of the process appears in Appendix 3A.

(e) ASSIGNMENT OF RESPONSIBILITIES   As we discussed in section 1.5(d), a key enabling principle for the successful execution of a divestiture transaction is clearly defined roles, tasks, and deliverables. Accordingly, divestiture planning should include a clear assignment of responsibilities associated with each step in the divestiture process. We recommend that the team develop tools to capture this information and to manage the divestiture process on a week-by-week basis, at a minimum. Examples of documents that can be used for these purposes appear in Appendix 3C and Appendix 3E. These examples are not meant to be comprehensive; rather, they are intended to be representative of the types of documents that should be utilized in managing the transaction. Appendix 3C, "Weekly Action Item Control," enables the team to clearly identify the tasks to be completed, to assign responsibility for those tasks, and to establish deadlines for their execution. Appendix 3E, "Issue and Resolution Control," provides the team with a tool to identify cross-functional issues raised in the course of the process and assign responsibility for their resolution.

3.8 DEVELOPMENT OF A COMMUNICATION PLAN

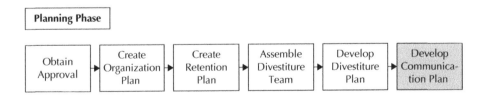

(a) INTRODUCTION   Implementation of the communication plan, which is initiated by the actual announcement of the prospective transaction, does not occur until the execution phase of the process. However, development of the communication plan should begin as soon as possible after the decision to sell has been made and the team has been assembled, since its development entails a substantial amount of coordination among the team members and because the organization will want to retain as much flexibility as possible with regard to the timing of its execution.

The underlying objective of the divestiture transaction is to optimize shareholder value, and the communication plan should be consistent with that objective. The plan should be designed to deliver a clear, consistent, and positive message about the parent company's intent to sell the business unit—as well as its rationale for doing so—to all relevant constituencies. These constituencies are graphically illustrated in Exhibit 3.8.

The communication plan typically consists of two major elements: an external communications element directed at constituencies that can be characterized as *External Stakeholders, Involved Third Parties*, and *Interested Third Parties*; and an internal communications element directed at *Internal Stakeholders*. Development of the plan typically is coordinated by the parent company's human resource function, with the input and approval of members of the core team and the parent company CEO. For material transactions, the media or investor relations department within the larger corporate structure of the parent generally will take the lead on third-party messaging and communication. (See Appendix 3D.)

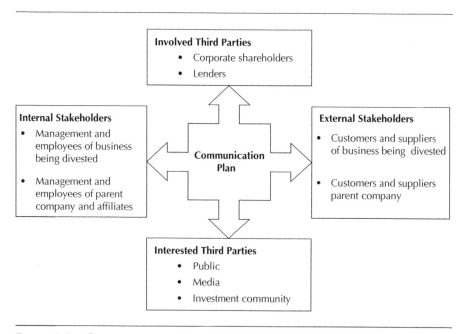

EXHIBIT 3.8 CONSTITUENCIES TO BE ADDRESSED IN COMMUNICATION PLAN

Announcement of Intent to Divest

The announcement of the intent to sell should include the identification of all major properties to be included in the transaction.

Presentation of Strategic Rationale

The rationale for the sale should include reference to the strategy the parent company is pursuing and that the divestiture will focus the organization more sharply on that strategy to the long-term benefit of the organization (and, by inference, its shareholders).

Inherent Value of the Business Being Sold

The announcement should emphasize the inherent value of the property being divested and that the decision to sell has been made solely because the property is no longer compatible with the strategic direction being pursued by the seller.

Identification of the Party Assisting in the Transaction

The announcement should identify the broker or banker assisting in the transaction.

Anticipated Timing of the Transaction

The announcement should provide a general indication of the anticipated timing of the transaction.

EXHIBIT **3.9** CORE ELEMENTS OF DIVESTITURE MESSAGE

(b) CORE MESSAGE Although messaging should be customized to address the issues relevant to each discrete audience, there are core elements of the message that the selling organization will want to convey to all constituencies. These core elements include:

- Announcement of intent to sell
- Strategic rationale for the divestiture
- Inherent value of the property being sold
- Identification of any broker or banker assisting in the sale
- Indication of the anticipated timing of a transaction

These elements are outlined in Exhibit 3.9, which is followed by a discussion of messaging issues specific to each of the various constituencies.

(c) EXTERNAL COMMUNICATIONS   There is usually a direct relationship between the size and impact of the transaction and the desirability of informing the investment community and shareholders of the selling entity. In cases where an announcement is appropriate, the corporation's media or investor relations department generally should take the lead in the positioning of the divestiture, and would do so in a manner designed to emphasize the beneficial aspects of the transaction and the positive impact it will have on shareholder value. If the decision to divest is based, as it should be, on a sound rationale arrived at as part of a strategic assessment exercise, crafting a positive message should be quite straightforward.

Material transactions generally will be announced via a press release, which often are picked up by the business and trade media. If the corporation maintains contact with analysts in the investment community, after the formal announcement investor relations personnel often notify the analysts of the impending transaction, its rationale, and the ultimate benefit to the corporation. The intensity of the campaign to publicize the transaction should be in direct relation to the size and importance of the transaction. Small transactions will not generally register on radar of the business press. Larger transactions may get intense proactive treatment by investor relations (e.g., webcasts or personal contact with analysts) to ensure that the rationale and benefits are well understood by stakeholders and interested parties, such as investors, lenders, and shareholders.

The corporation will also want to emphasize its strategic rationale and that a lack of strategic fit, and not any inherent weaknesses of the property being sold, is the driving force behind the decision to divest. It is important to make this distinction, since the corporation wants to optimize the price it will get for the property and would not want to leave any impression in the marketplace that might impair the property's value. The organization may also want to indicate what it will do with the proceeds from the transaction, to reinforce the value creation theme and the strategic underpinnings of the decision to sell.

Other key constituencies of the seller are the customer bases of both the parent company and the business unit being divested. The basic message to these stakeholders, in all cases, should be that maintenance of superior service and customer satisfaction remain the primary objectives of the organizations. Several factors may affect the delivery of that message. Customer bases of the two entities may overlap, and this would have an impact on both the message and the manner in which it is delivered. Also, often some customers are more important than others. It may be desirable to segment the customer base and to use different vehicles (personal contact, phone contact, written contact) or combinations of vehicles to communicate with the various segments, based on their size and importance to the business. For customers in general and key customers in particular, mechanisms such as management briefings by the sales force and continuous feedback loops from sales personnel to senior management can be effective tools for identifying customer concerns and maintaining customer satisfaction. This is especially true in businesses with big-ticket products with long sales cycles.

Other external constituencies may include major suppliers and contractors. Supplier/vendor relationships are usually a lesser concern than those of customers, unless assignability of contracts will have a major impact on the transaction. Regardless, it is generally desirable to contact major vendors proactively in the interest of maintaining positive relationships with them. Proactive contact ensures that these groups will receive the information about the prospective transaction firsthand, accurately and within the proper context.

(d) INTERNAL COMMUNICATIONS   The internal component of the plan should address the messaging to two distinct audiences: the employees of the unit being divested and the employees of the parent company. The objectives of these internal communications are to minimize the disruption of the business being sold and to assure employees of the parent company that management remains committed to their business and that no other major changes are currently anticipated.

The management of the message to the employees of the parent company is relatively straightforward. If the divestiture involves a large business unit or one that is significantly integrated into the parent's operation, communication of its planned sale generally should consist of a live announcement by the parent company's CEO to its employee population, followed by a written announcement immediately thereafter. If the company being divested is not material to the operation of the parent, written communication is generally appropriate. A major objective of this aspect of the announcement is to assure this employee population that the transaction represents the full extent of the organization's realignment effort and that there is not another proverbial shoe to drop. A clear, crisp, and credible announcement can be key to assuaging any employee concerns.

Effective management of communication with the employees of the company being sold is usually more complex. It has both immediate and ongoing components. It is generally advisable for the CEO or a senior executive of the parent company to meet with the relevant employees to announce the decision to sell the business unit and to be prepared to respond to questions that these employees may pose. (What does this mean to me? Is my job in jeopardy? What will happen to my benefits? etc.) It is also good practice to develop and distribute a package of information that addresses obvious potential concerns of this audience and to have human resource representatives available to answer questions during the period immediately following the announcement, as well as to provide mechanisms to receive and respond to employee questions subsequent to this initial stage of the process. This can be accomplished by establishing a dedicated e-mail address for inquiries (and making sure that such inquiries are responded to in a timely fashion) and by providing employees with updates, both in writing and via meetings with business unit senior management.

(e) CAVEAT It is also important to be aware of the limitations and realities associated with the decision to divest and the announcement to do so. It is very likely that the announcement, at the business being divested, will result in a period of distraction, accompanied by an initial decline in productivity. The goal of the team should be to minimize the duration of such a period and the extent of any loss of productivity. Additionally, it is not possible to eliminate all employee concerns, particularly because it is not possible to answer many of the questions—Who will be the new owner? Will the new owner eliminate my position? Will the company be relocated?—that employees will have. As a result, the team should realize that the aftercare of those employees will be an ongoing need and that concerns can only be mitigated, not eliminated.

KEY POINTS

1. Planning is the bedrock of the divestiture process. It does not guarantee a success but, without it, the probability of a protracted or even broken transaction is dramatically increased. (Section 3.2(b))

2. Failure to begin addressing organizational separation early in the divestiture process can have a catastrophic effect on the transaction. Disentangling the infrastructure of the seller from the unit being sold is frequently the single most difficult step in the process and requires detailed analysis, thorough planning, and crisp execution. (Section 3.4(a))

3. The seller cannot afford to be penny-wise and pound foolish when it comes to key personnel. Retention plans should be viewed as insurance policies, and the premiums paid should be aligned with the attendant risks. (Section 3.5(c))

4. M&A transaction are people-intensive activities, and corporate divestitures are no exception. These transactions cannot be brought to a successful conclusion unless they are fully resourced and managed by empowered leaders. (Section 3.6(a))

5. A plan without clear assignments, specific deliverables, and definitive deadlines is undermined from the outset. Defining (and redefining, when necessary) and unambiguously communicating what has to be done, by whom, and when *and* by regularly holding the responsible parties accountable for their deliverables are critical components of a successful transaction. (Section 3.7(a))

6. The communication plan is more than a document describing how the transaction will be announced. It is an important vehicle for safeguarding the assets being sold, communicating the selling organization's strategic intent, and optimizing shareholder value. (Section 3.8(a))

ILLUSTRATIVE
DIVESTITURE TIMELINE

Month	1	2	3	4	5	6	7
Planning							
Develop approval document	↑						
Develop organization plan	↑						
Develop retention plan	↑						
Assemble divestiture team	↑						
Develop divestiture plan		↑					
Develop communication plan		↑					
Preparation							
Select financial advisor	↑	↑	↑	↑			
Select accounting firm		↑	↑	↑			
Create Offering document			↑	↑	↑	↑	
Identify potential buyers			↑	↑	↑		
Develop management presentations				↑	↑	↑	

Month	1	2	3	4	5	6	7
Prepare data room				↑			
Assemble disentanglement team		↑	↑				
Execute disentanglement plan			↑	↑	↑	↑	
Execution							
Announce intent to sell				↑			
Solicit bids				↑			
Manage due diligence					↑	↑	
Accept winning bid						↑	
Structure terms						↑	↑
Comply with regulatory requirements						↑	↑
Close							↑

RETENTION PLANNING DOCUMENT

This document illustrates a step-by-step analysis of the risk associated with the loss of key employees. Although there are no cookbook approaches to such an analysis, a structured approach like the one outlined should help guide those who are tasked with developing a retention plan.

1. **Establish expected enterprise value.**

   Using a valuation model and/or recent market transactions as a basis, determine estimated value of the enterprise.

   Example: The enterprise is projected to generate $150 million in revenue and $30 million in EBITDA in the current year. Over the last 18 months, comparable businesses have sold for amounts ranging from 1.8 to 2.1 times revenue. Because of the enterprise's market position and profitability, it can be expected to sell toward the top of this range, at approximately $300 million.

2. **Identify exposures.**

   Using their impact on revenue delivery as a criterion, determine any material exposures associated with the loss or demotivation of key employees.

   Example: These categories of staff have been identified as "key" for the reasons indicated:

   o *Executive management is key to the ongoing stability of the business and to the divestiture sales process. Loss of members of this group would impair enterprise value in the eyes of potential buyers.*

○ *The sales force plays a vital role in the attainment of this year's revenue targets.*

○ *Product development personnel are critical to the introduction of three new products that are scheduled for introduction in the fourth quarter.*

3. Quantify exposures.

The potential impact of the exposures identified should be quantified.

Example: Turnover or demotivation of key personnel is estimated to have these impacts:

○ *Significant turnover in the top tier of executive management could be expected to result in an impairment of value 5% to 10% (or $15 to $30 million).*

○ *It is estimated that 10% turnover in the sales group in the three months following the announcement of the divestiture could result in a loss of from 4% to 6% of annual revenue, a potential negative impact of $12 to $18 million on valuation..*

○ *Timely introduction of new products under development is anticipated to result in $7 million in current year sales (or $14 million in value). The loss of key product management personnel would put this revenue stream at risk.*

4. Identify key personnel.

Identify the specific individuals attached to each of the exposures noted and their annual salaries. The salary information can then be used as a basis for characterizing bonus awards.

Example: 39 key employees with aggregate annual salaries of $3.6 million have been identified. They fall into these categories:

○ *Executive management consists of these 5 individuals: CEO, CFO, SVP of Sales & Marketing, SVP of Product Development, and VP of R&D. Their aggregate base annual salary totals $1 million.*

○ *Sales management and sales staff account for 28 individuals with aggregate salaries totaling $1.8 million.*

○ *Key product development staff consists of 6 developers with aggregate salaries of $800,000.*

5. **Determine type and magnitude of incentives.**
   Establish the types of incentives to be employed and the
   magnitude. Incentives generally fall into three categories: (1)
   retention bonuses that are awarded to designees who remain
   employees in good standing until the transaction is completed;
   (2) performance bonuses that are awarded to designees if sales,
   revenue, or profitability thresholds are attained; and (3) success
   bonuses that are awarded to designees if the enterprise is sold
   or sold at or above a predetermined price. Awards typically are
   expressed in terms of percentage of annual salary.

   *Example: Executive managers will be eligible for bonuses
   of 140% of annual salary, subject to the conditions described
   in their retention agreements and broken down in this way:
   retention (40%), performance (50%), and success (50%). Sales
   management and sales staff will be eligible for bonuses of 60%
   of annual salary, broken down in this way: retention (30%)
   and performance (30%). Product development staff will be eligible for retention bonuses equal to 40% of annual salary.*

6. **Determine reasonableness of incentives.**
   The reasonableness of the incentives should be tested. This can
   be accomplished by comparing the value of the awards to the
   exposures they are designed to insure against and to the gross
   proceeds anticipated from the divestiture.

   *Example: Aggregate exposure, using the most conservative
   estimates, exceeds $34 million and gross proceeds from the
   sale are estimated at $300 million. Incentives total $2.8 million
   or approximately 8% of the exposure and less than 1% of gross
   proceeds. By these measures, it would appear that the incentives are aligned with the risk.*

WEEKLY ACTION ITEM CONTROL

This tool is provided for illustrative purposes. It embodies the key components of a process management tool, namely, the clear identification of tasks to be completed, the assignment of responsibility for those tasks, and the specification of deadlines for their execution. Although this illustration covers only the first eight weeks of the process, it can be used through the finalization of the transaction.

ACTION ITEM	RESPONSIBILITY	COMMENTS
Week 1		
Draft divestiture plan	Core team	Complete by end of week 1
Draft communication plan	Human resources	Complete by end of week 1
Week 2		
Approval of communication plan	Human resources	Obtain approval from CEO and investor relations
Approval of divestiture plan	Team leader	Obtain approval from CEO
Week 3		
Select and engage broker	Team leader, finance	Obtain approval from corporate headquarters

Action Item	Responsibility	Comments
Select and engage accounting firm	Finance	Obtain approval from corporate headquarters
Week 4		
Start developing offering document	Core team, broker	Provide guidance and set deadline
Week 5		
Identify potential buyers	Core team, broker	Review list of those who will be contacted by broker
Begin preparation of data room	Business unit executives, finance, legal, broker	Kickoff meeting to provide guidance to business unit executives
Start developing management presentations	Core team, broker	Provide guidance and set deadline
Initiate disentanglement process	Core team	Assign project leader and establish guidelines
Week 6		
Review first draft of offering document	Core team, broker	Provide recommendations and edits
Announce divestiture	Human resources, investor relations	Coordinate announcement
Week 7		
Send out teaser	Broker	Distribute to approved list
Week 8		
Review responses to teaser	Core team, broker	Evaluate responses, determine if further follow-up is needed
Distribute confidentiality agreements	Broker, legal	Confidentiality agreements to qualified potential bidders
Finalize offering document	Core team, broker, legal, corporate headquarters	Obtain sign-offs for distribution to potential bidders

COMMUNICATION PLAN OUTLINE

This outline identifies key elements of a communication plan.

EXECUTIVE SUMMARY
- An expression of the intent to sell the subject properties
- A brief description of the properties being sold
- A statement of the strategic rationale for the divestiture

COMMUNICATION PLAN OBJECTIVES (BY CONSTITUENCY)
- **Shareholders and investment community.** Convey the positive impact that the divestiture will have on shareholder value.
- **Employee populations.** Ensure stability of operations.
- **Customers.** Assure that their interests will be unaffected.

MESSAGING (BY CONSTITUENCY)
- **Shareholders and investment community.** Emphasize strategic rationale and long-term benefit.
- **Employees of parent/seller.** Reinforce management's commitment to the business and that no other major changes are currently anticipated.

- **Employees of unit being sold.** Reinforce the fundamental strengths of the business and the fact that the divestiture decision was based solely on a lack of strategic fit.
- **Customers.** Emphasize that superior customer service remains the organization's paramount objective.

DELIVERABLES

- **Shareholders and investment community.** Press release and analyst briefings, if appropriate
- **Employees of parent/seller.** Memo and speaking points for senior management
- **Employees of unit being sold.** Speaking points for senior management and communications package consisting of announcement memo and anticipated questions and answers.
- **Customers.** Letter, speaking points for face-to-face and phone discussions, and direction to customer-facing personnel for routing of customer questions

ASSIGNMENTS

- Assignment of deliverable to those responsible for their development
- Description of review process
- Identification of those who will execute the elements of the plan

EXECUTION TIMELINE

- Time frame for final review of each deliverable
- Timing of plan execution

ISSUES AND RESOLUTION CONTROL

This document can be used to capture all issues/items identified by those involved in the transaction that require resolution before it can be completed. Eventually, there will be project teams working on various aspects of the transaction (e.g., the disentanglement process), and issues/items relevant to those teams can be handed off (see item 2). This tool is useful to ensure that all unresolved issues/items are documented, assigned, and tracked to the point of resolution.

ITEM	SUBJECT	ISSUE	OWNER	DUE DATE	RESOLUTION	RESOLUTION DATE
1	Corporate discounts on vendor contracts	Ensure that contracts are reviewed to determine financial impact on Divestco.	VP Operations	xx/yy/10		
2	Corporate discounts on vendor contracts	Ensure that this items is transferred to disentanglement team to resolve all associated issues.	Disentanglement team leader	xx/yy/10		

CHAPTER 4

PREPARING FOR
THE TRANSACTION

4.1 INTRODUCTION

(a) OVERVIEW   Although some aspects of the divestiture's preparation phase are initiated during planning (as we discussed in section 3.7(d) and illustrated in Exhibit 3.7), all major preparatory activity starts subsequent to the planning phase. Preparation, as we define it, consists of those measures necessary to position the business for sale, and it has two components: preparation for the selling process and preparation for the separation of the business being sold from that of the seller. We discuss the former in this chapter and the latter, the disentanglement process, in Chapter 5.

(b) IMPORTANCE OF TIMELY PREPARATION   Close attention to transaction preparation is critical to the efficient, and often successful, execution of a divestiture. Early engagement of the appropriate external resources, specifically financial advisors and outside accountants, is extremely important since these organizations provide services that are essential to getting the business unit to market. Financial advisors play a pivotal role in validating the seller's approach to the market and in creating a competitive environment and an orderly and efficient process for the transaction. Similarly, an accounting firm's services are generally integral to the presentation of the business unit's financial statements in the form necessary to meet the requirements of many buyers. Accordingly, any delay in the engagement and employment of these resources will impede the progress of the selling process. Therefore, it is important that the seller position itself to engage these service providers and initiate their efforts as soon as possible after the divestiture plan has been put in place.

4.2 PREPARATION PHASE PROCESS STEPS

The steps involved in preparing for the selling process are discussed in detail in the sections that follow and are illustrated in Exhibit 4.1. They are:

- **Selection and engagement of external resources.** The necessary external resources typically engaged by the seller include: a financial advisor (a business broker or investment banker) to advise and represent the seller and to manage certain aspects of the selling process; an accounting firm to validate the financial statements of the business being divested; and other professionals or consultants, such as attorneys or other advisors to the transaction, if needed, to assist in the process. These professionals should be engaged as early as possible in the preparation phase.

- **Validate transaction structure.** Once the seller has engaged its financial advisor, it will want to elicit the advisor's input on the planned structure of the transaction to ensure that the structure optimizes the objectives of the seller.

- **Development of selling materials.** The seller and its financial advisor will initiate the development of documents to support the selling process once they have agreed on how they will approach the market. If the seller elects to sell the business unit via an auction process, the selling or marketing materials include

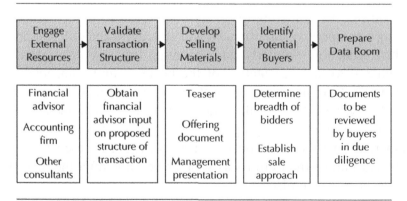

EXHIBIT 4.1   ELEMENTS OF TRANSACTION PREPARATION PROCESS

a teaser, an offering document, and a management presentation. These documents, to varying extents, describe the business and its attractiveness as an investment to potential buyers.

- **Identification of potential buyers.** The seller and the financial advisor will jointly identify the market for the business unit being divested and determine the approach to be used in the selling process (i.e., an auction or an alternative approach).
- **Preparation of a data room.** This stage of the preparation process involves the creation of a site (physical or virtual) to house documents to be reviewed by potential buyers as part of their due diligence.

4.3 ENGAGEMENT OF EXTERNAL RESOURCES

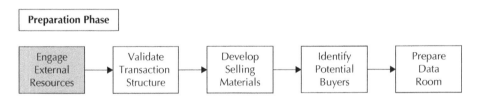

(a) **INTRODUCTION**   The key external resources generally required for the effective execution of a divestiture are a financial advisor and an accounting firm. In addition, it may be desirable to engage other resources, such as regulatory or transaction-related legal expertise, to assist in the process. Also, for transactions involving smaller organizations with limited resources and expertise, it may be desirable to outsource major aspects of the deal, so long as the seller retains control over the decision-making process. The nature and extent of the assistance that might be outsourced are discussed in the next sections. It is also worth noting that there may be a need to engage other consultant/professionals to assist in the preparation for the separation of the businesses. This contingency is discussed in Chapter 5.

(b) **EVALUATION OF A FINANCIAL ADVISOR**   Sellers may engage either a business broker or an investment banker as financial advisor for a divestiture transaction. The distinguishing characteristics of each are discussed in detail in section 3.6(d). Generally, there is a strong relationship between the size of the transaction and the type of advisor used. Business brokers usually are engaged for small to midsize transactions where niche market knowledge may be of particular importance. In contrast, bankers generally are engaged for larger transactions where financial expertise and capabilities are needed. However, this choice is ultimately influenced by the particulars of the transaction and the needs and preferences of the seller.

The financial advisor is engaged for two general reasons: to advise the seller on various aspects of the transaction and to manage and facilitate the transaction. The advisor would provide input on the structure of the transaction, on the seller's approach to the market (i.e., an auction or alternative approach), and on the targeting of potential buyers. It will also assist with the management of certain aspects of the transactions, such as the development of selling materials and the orchestration of the selling process. As noted, the selection of a financial advisor, whether broker or banker, is dictated by the nature of the specific transaction in play. That choice is also influenced by the relative weight placed on these criteria:

- **Transaction experience.** The seller should evaluate the breadth and depth of the advisor's experience in the divestiture process. As we discuss in section 4.6(b), there are a variety of types of sales, ranging from preemptive bids to public auctions. The advisor should have demonstrable skills and experience in assisting with and advising on transactions where these various approaches have been employed.
- **Market knowledge.** It is extremely desirable for the advisor to have in-depth knowledge of the market served by the business being divested. This knowledge would include an understanding of the size, growth potential, and dynamics of that market as well as its composition (i.e., the size and reputation of major competitors within it).
- **Knowledge of and access to specific potential buyers.** This quality is closely related to, but different from, market knowledge. It is a by-product of an advisor's familiarity with the market but relates more to relationships the advisor has with *individual companies* in the market as well as an understanding of the strategic interests of those companies.

- **Quality of the advisor's valuation of the business.** Advisors will prepare a range of valuations of the property being sold, generally based on revenue and earnings multiples from recent comparable sales and on other valuation approaches, such as discounted cash flow (DCF) analysis. This exercise should provide further evidence of the advisor's knowledge and understanding of the market. The seller will also have developed valuations as part of its assessment process, and any significant variations from the seller's valuation should be explained by the prospective advisors, and their rationales for such variations should be critically assessed.
- **Capabilities to execute the type of transaction contemplated.** The transaction can take a number of forms, from the outright sale of the stock or assets of the business to more complex options, such as spin-offs or equity carve-outs. As noted, choice of the financial advisor can be strongly influenced by the size and nature of the transaction. More complex transactions, which often involve the sale of larger businesses, may require the resources and capabilities of an investment banker. This could include the ability to manage an initial public offering (IPO), the need for a fairness opinion (a letter assuring stockholders of the selling company opining on the fairness of the purchase price, form of payment, and other aspects of the transaction), or access to financing for the transaction. In such cases, it is unlikely that a business broker will have the requisite capabilities; thus, an investment banker would be engaged instead of, or in addition to, a broker.

(c) SELECTION OF A FINANCIAL ADVISOR The selection process frequently involves the evaluation of several possible advisors. In larger corporate organizations, selection may also be influenced by relationships the corporation has established over time. These relationships may be with advisors who have satisfactorily represented the corporation in past merger and acquisition (M&A) transactions or may be with financial institutions (banks and brokerage houses with investment banker operations) that have assisted the corporation in such activities as debt or equity financing. As previously noted, the choice of candidates will also be influenced by the size of the prospective transaction and the specific needs associated with it. The larger the transaction, the more attractive it will be to a broader range of potential advisors, because of the substantial size of the fee, and the more likely the corporation will be to engage a more prestigious representative, because of the comfort doing so may provide corporate management, the board of directors, and shareholders.

Frequently, the candidates competing for the engagement make presentations to a selection team made up of senior corporate management and members of the core divestiture team to demonstrate their expertise and capabilities as well as to explain how they would approach this specific transaction. Although the final decision may be made by corporate management, typically the core divestiture team has an influence on that choice. The divestiture team's input should reflect the desire to best match the needs of the transaction with the capabilities of the candidates. Ultimately, though, a choice will most likely be made based on all of the factors noted (i.e., need, capability, and relationships). Although cost is generally not a major variable in the decision-making process, it may come into play if the candidates are comparable in all other respects and fee structures are not. (Fee structures are discussed in section 3.6(d).)

(d) ENGAGEMENT OF FINANCIAL ADVISOR   Once the seller has chosen a financial advisor, the advisor is engaged. Terms of the engagement typically include the identification of specific services to be provided, the length of the engagement, and the basis of compensation. The engagement terms will generally also reference exclusivity, termination, and indemnification. An annotated outline of an engagement letter appears in Exhibit 4.2. It is important to note that language dealing with indemnification very clearly places the burden for any representations in marketing materials circulated to potential buyers, such as the offering document, on the seller and that any claims made against the advisor related to errors or omissions will be indemnified by the seller. Therefore, the divestiture team leader should impress on the team the need to take ownership in these documents and to ensure that the team realizes that the organization is responsible for any misrepresentation contained in them.

Services to Be provided

- Advice regarding the structure of the transaction
- Assistance in the search and identification of potential buyers
- Assistance in the preparation of the offering document and management presentation
- Initiation of the transaction
- Assistance with negotiations

Term

- Fixed period generally ranging from 6 to 12 months

Compensation

- Monthly retainer credited toward the transaction
- Transaction fee based on a graduated scale with a guaranteed minimum if the transaction is completed

Definition of Transaction Consideration

- Basis for calculating the advisor's commission (e.g., consideration equals cash paid plus any debt assumed by the buyer)

Exclusivity

- Advisor will be the sole representative of the seller for the term of the agreement

Termination

- Agreement can be terminated with a stated number of days notice by either party
- Advisor is entitled to its fee if a transaction is completed with any party identified by the broker within a stated number of months (usually 6 to 12) after the termination

Indemnification

- Advisor will be indemnified by the seller for any claim for false, untrue or incomplete statements

Confidentiality

- Seller may want to include a confidentiality provision if there is no separate NDA

EXHIBIT 4.2   FINANCIAL ADVISOR ENGAGEMENT LETTER OUTLINE

(e) ENGAGEMENT OF ACCOUNTING FIRM   Potential acquirers may request audited financial statements for a divested business unit for any of several reasons, including requirements of lenders providing financing for the acquisition, due diligence objectives of the acquirer, or, in certain circumstances, the acquirer's Securities and Exchange Commission (SEC) reporting requirements. However, most corporations do not routinely have each of their business units individually audited. Although there are exceptions, such as divestitures of freestanding subsidiaries that have been audited annually or non-U.S. business units that require audits by local statute, most divestitures involve businesses whose operations or infrastructure have been merged to some degree with that of the parent/ seller organization. As a result, any audits that have been conducted will have been for the financial statements of the larger, combined entity.

Typically, the financial statements of the business being divested will be internal-use statements that have been generated for operational reporting and management purposes and may not meet all of the reporting and disclosure requirements of generally accepted accounting principles and will not have been subject to a dedicated audit. Under these circumstances, before the business unit is put on the market, the seller will normally need to engage an accounting firm to perform an audit of the unit, referred to as a carve-out audit. The next sections elaborate on the nature and scope of a carve-out audit as well as situations in which such an audit is not required.

- **Nature and scope of a carve-out audit.** As noted, carve-out audits are performed to comply with lender requirements, acquirer due diligence requirements, or, under certain circumstances, SEC reporting requirements. Although an acquirer can sometimes achieve its internal due diligence requirements without an audit, its lenders will not normally finance the acquisition without having audited financial statements for the business. Many lenders will, in fact, require audits of up to three previous years' statements, although audits for the previous one or two years may be acceptable depending on the size of the transaction and the flexibility of the lender. SEC regulations will come into play if the divested unit is large enough to have a material effect on the consolidated financial statements of the acquiring company. If applicable, the acquirer postacquisition will be required to restate its prior three years financial statements, inclusive of the acquisition's audited results, to comply with SEC Regulation S-X.

Carve-out audits involve the validation of internal-use statements of the business unit being divested; they can be very transaction-test intensive and protracted. For such audits, the accounting firm may establish materiality thresholds that are dramatically lower than those employed in the audit of the financial statements of the seller as a whole. That, in turn, is likely to result in extensive transaction testing, multiple adjustments, and a lengthened audit process. If multiple-year audits are required, the process can easily take several months to complete and can be a gating factor in getting the business to market. As a result, the carve-out engagement should be initiated as soon as reasonably possible after the decision to sell has been made.

- **When a carve-out audit may not be necessary.** There are situations in which a carve-out audit may not be necessary or desirable. These would include transactions involving a small business unit, such as a small subsidiary, a product line, or even an individual product that will be self-financed by the buyer. However, even in these situations, it may be advisable for both seller and buyer to engage an accounting firm to perform agreed-on procedures to establish buyer confidence in the validity of the financial statements and to forestall potentially avoidable disagreements on valuation. Typically, such services would be mutually agreed on once a buyer has been confirmed, and the scope of the work to be performed will generally not have a significant impact on the duration of the sales process.

Also, as previously noted, the need for an audit may be precluded, or the amount of audit work to be performed may be substantially reduced, under certain circumstances. This would be the case if the unit being sold was a stand-alone business that had been subjected to annual audits or if the divested business or a segment of that business was a foreign affiliate that had been audited annually in compliance with local law.

(f) SELECTION CONSIDERATIONS There are practical limitations affecting the choice of an accounting firm to perform a carve-out audit, if it is needed. Buyers and their lenders will generally prefer that one of the four largest national firms is engaged, for reasons real (their extensive resources) and perceived (their superior reputation). It is also very likely that the seller's independent accountant is one of those four firms, since those organizations with the most active business portfolios are large, publicly traded corporations that typically have national firms as their auditor. If the seller's auditor is a national firm, it will generally prefer to use that firm for the carve-out audit, to satisfy both the preferences of potential buyers and its desire to complete the audit as quickly and efficiently as possible. The use of the seller's firm will reduce the start-up time associated with pre-engagement particulars, since existing lines of communication can be easily accessed. More important, the firm's familiarity with the business should reduce the slope of the learning curve associated with the execution of the audit. Although there is no requirement for a firm to engage its existing auditor for the carve-out, the factors noted will generally have a significant influence on that choice.

(g) AUDITED CARVE-OUT VERSUS STAND-ALONE PRO FORMA FINANCIAL STATEMENTS   Performance of the carve-out audit, any associated adjustments to the financial statements, and the issuance of its opinion end the accounting firm's involvement with the statements of the business unit. However, it is important to note that these carve-out financial statements present the business as it is owned and operated by the selling corporation, and do not reflect the results of operations of the business unit as if it were on a stand-alone basis, an important aspect of the preparing the business for sale. The seller will, therefore, want to develop pro forma financial statements that reflect the impact of certain adjustments—many of which will be identified as part of the disentanglement process—so that potential buyers are presented with a view of the business as a fully costed, stand-alone entity. These adjustments would generally include items such as:

- Removal of cost allocations from the carve-out financials for services provided by the corporate parent that do not reflect actual stand-alone costs
- Addition of estimated expenses that would be incurred to put the business on a stand-alone footing

- Elimination of nonrecurring or unusual items in the carve-out financials in order to normalize the business unit financials

Although buyers will undoubtedly closely scrutinize these adjustments, the seller is well advised to create such a standalone view as a point of departure for buyers' valuation analysis. If these adjustments are reasonable, the credibility of the seller will be enhanced, as will the efficiency of the negotiating process. While the development of pro forma statements is a topic that is more appropriately discussed in the context of the disentanglement process in Chapter 5, it is briefly noted here to dispel any notion that the carve-out financial statements, although often necessary, are an adequate representation of the business and to emphasize the importance of presenting the divested business on a stand-alone basis to potential buyers.

(h) DETERMINING THE NEED FOR OTHER SPECIALISTS   The need for additional external expertise is largely dependent on the availability of internal resources. Frequently, additional transaction-related legal resources are needed to prepare the business for sale and to manage the selling process. Within most corporations, internal M&A legal expertise is a relatively rare commodity, and, if the selling corporation has an active portfolio, competition for that resource can be intense. As a result, the lead attorney may delegate certain aspects of the transaction to a firm that specializes in M&A transactions. Those activities that would typically be delegated are assistance in data room preparation and contract and related document preparation and review. The lead attorney may also find it necessary to draw on legal experts who specialize in areas such as employment, intellectual property, real estate, tax, or environmental law. The need for such expertise will be particularly acute if the transaction involves business operations outside the United States.

As previously noted, smaller companies with limited M&A experience and expertise may find it especially necessary to engage external resources to fill capability gaps. In such situations legal support and certain aspects of transaction and financial management may be entirely outsourced. Law firms that specialize in M&A transactions can play a major role in managing all of the legal aspects of the transaction. Similarly, large accounting firms with transaction service departments or M&A consultants with transaction expertise can provide advice and support in managing the preparation and negotiating processes. These types of resources, in concert with the seller's financial advisor, can fill virtually all gaps in seller expertise. However, the seller must recognize that, while it can draw on a substantial reservoir of expertise, *it cannot outsource responsibility* for the transaction. It must have a team leader or small core divestiture team actively involved to direct the process and retain overall accountability for making the key decisions related to the transaction.

4.4 VALIDATION OF THE TRANSACTION STRUCTURE

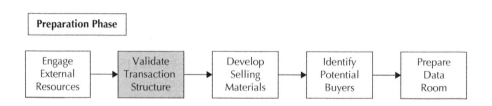

(a) **OVERVIEW**   Once chosen, the financial advisor will initiate a number of activities, including the staging of the selling process, the development of the selling materials, and the creation of a data room. However, before proceeding with these activities, the advisor and seller should review and validate (or challenge) the anticipated structure of the transaction. The discussion that follows places that review in the context of the seller's overall decision-making process regarding transaction approach and structure.

Analytical activities related to deal structure follow a logical progression throughout a transaction's life cycle, beginning in the assessment phase and continuing through the planning, preparation, and negotiation phases. Reevaluation of the seller's position on transaction structure by its financial advisor is an important step at this point in the process.

The seller will have initially considered alternative courses of action to address the disposition of the business during assessment phase of the process and, again, in the development of the approval document in the planning phase. As discussed in Chapter 2, preliminary decisions will have been made during the assessment phase regarding the *approach* to addressing strategic concerns about the subject business. At that time, approaches to the disposition of the business would include consideration of retaining and investing, liquidating, or divesting. Once the organization has fixed on divestiture, some consideration may then be given to the *structure* of the transaction. Doing this requires an evaluation of the advantages and disadvantages of specific transaction structures, such as the outright sale of the shares or the assets of the business or, possibly, the creation of a spin-off or carve-out entity (options described in section 2.4(b)).

The development of the approval document, described in section 3.3, will have caused the seller to focus more intensely on the transaction structure. That document will articulate a preliminary position on the seller's preferred form of the transaction. When the financial advisor is engaged in the preparation phase of the process, the structuring of the transaction should be revisited so that the seller can draw on its advisor's expertise and knowledge to validate or challenge its own position. The final step in this progression will occur in the structuring phase of the transaction (discussed in Chapter 7), when the seller negotiates the specific details of the final structure of the transaction with the buyer. This ongoing evaluation process is illustrated in Exhibit 4.3, highlighting the dynamics of the evaluative and decision-making processes in the preparation phase.

(b) REEVALUATION OF TRANSACTION STRUCTURE   After the financial advisor is selected, the seller should make full use of the advisor's knowledge of the industry and of the condition of financial markets as well as its perspective on the relative interest and preferences of potential buyers. The advisor will generally have insights, some of which may have surfaced during the selection process, that complement those of the seller. These insights should serve to confirm the seller's position on structure or cause the seller to adjust that view, if there are factors that have not been adequately considered. These factors could include such things as the receptivity of the public market to a carve-out transaction, the potential for an asset swap with a competitor, or the established positions of significant potential buyers on structure (e.g., strong preferences for asset versus stock deals).

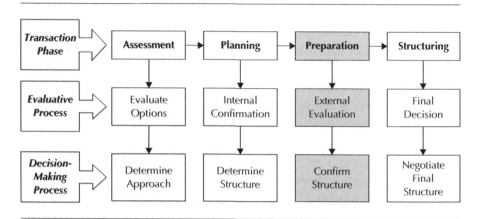

EXHIBIT 4.3   TRANSACTION APPROACH AND STRUCTURE EVALUATION CONTINUUM

This is an important stage of the transaction process because the *seller's* predisposition for a certain structure will have to be firmly established, in light of all relevant variables, before the business is put on the market. Although it may be subject to modification in the negotiation process, this is the time at which the seller's position on the basic form of the transaction will be established and eventually communicated to potential buyers.

4.5 DEVELOPMENT OF SELLING MATERIALS

(a) INTRODUCTION   Once a financial advisor has been engaged, the seller will also work with it to develop selling materials that will be delivered to potential buyers. These selling materials typically consist of a teaser, an offering document, and a management presentation. A teaser will generally be developed and distributed in situations where the seller has decided to put the business on the market via a public auction. It is a document that contains a brief discussion of the business along with abbreviated financial information. The offering document describes the major aspects of the business, presents historical and projected financial performance, and discusses the strategic potential of the business. The management presentation usually takes the form of a PowerPoint slide show and is the basis for a live presentation to selected potential buyers by the executive management of the business unit being sold. It mirrors the content of the offering document but also provides a forum for elaboration on the themes presented and for interaction with those being presented to.

In developing these materials, the roles of various elements of the team will generally be established along the lines described next. The business unit executives should provide the basic body of knowledge of the history of the business and its potential going forward. The financial advisor, along with the business unit executives, should help shape the discussion of strategic potential of the business. The other members of the core divestiture team should ensure that the content of the documents is consistent with the messaging in the communication plan (i.e., that it conveys the inherent value of the business being sold and, if appropriate, reflects the seller's strategic rationale for the divestiture). The objective of this collaboration should be to balance accuracy, salesmanship, and consistency with the seller's messaging to its constituencies (see section 3.8). These selling materials are discussed individually and in detail in the next three sections.

(b) TEASER If the seller chooses to market the business through a public auction, it would work closely with its financial advisor to develop a brief document for distribution to a broad cross-section of potentially interested parties. The teaser would contain a short description of the business, its major products and/or services, a description of the market it serves, and the strategic qualities that would make it an attractive investment. It would also contain summary historical financial information, such as revenue, earnings before interest, taxes, depreciation, and amortization (EBITDA), profit margins, and growth rates. The teaser should also invite expressions of interest that would be responded to with copies of the offering document, once nondisclosure agreements (NDAs) had been executed with its recipients. (The NDA is described and discussed in detail in Chapter 6.)

(c) OFFERING DOCUMENT   The offering document (OD), also referred to as the offering memorandum, confidential information memorandum, or prospectus, is a paper that presents a detailed picture of the business being sold. It is usually prepared by the financial advisor, based on detailed input (sometimes called broker due diligence) from the business unit executives, and subject to critical review by the core divestiture team.

Once approved by the seller, the OD is distributed to selected potential buyers, subject to the above-noted NDA. (See section 6.4 for a thorough description of the management of the selling process.) The OD should be designed to enable these potential buyers to determine whether they wish to proceed with the pursuit of a transaction while minimizing disclosure of proprietary data to those competitors who may simply be trolling for competitive information. Accordingly, the OD should contain sufficient information for the recipient to refine its understanding of the business and its potential and to perform an analysis the business's financial performance, including a preliminary valuation.

The OD will generally contain these elements, which are also illustrated in Exhibit 4.4:

- **Introductory statements regarding *disclaimers* of representations and warranties and notice of *confidentiality* of the information provided.** Although the offering document will be distributed under the name of the financial advisor, it will clearly indicate that the information provided is that of the seller and, while believed to be accurate, neither seller nor financial advisor make any representations or warranties as to its accuracy, completeness, or attainability (in the case of forward-looking financial estimates). Despite these standard disclaimers, it is important that the seller take great care in ensuring that the document contains accurate information and projections that are based on reasonable and defensible assumptions. Otherwise, the seller risks exposure to doubts about the credibility of the document or, worse yet, to claims of damages by affected parties. This section of the document will also reference the operative confidentiality agreement that will have been negotiated in advance of distribution (see section 6.4(a)).

- An *executive summary* containing a brief overview of the business and an indication of the terms of the sale required by the seller. Terms of sale would include items such as the requirement of an all cash transaction (if applicable), a description of what is and what is not included in the sale, and a requirement for evidence of financial capacity of the bidder to consummate the transaction.
- A discussion of *investment considerations.* Investment considerations are those strategic qualities of the business that would generate enthusiasm among potential buyers. They may include such characteristics as product quality, market position, brand recognition of the products or the company, superior financial model, and the quality of management. This section of the document is a vehicle for the seller to highlight opportunities for potential buyers to leverage the business unit's strengths for future growth and profitability.
- A description of the *industry or market* within which the business operates. This section should contain a description of industry characteristics, such as size, market drivers, and growth potential, as well as a discussion of how the property being sold is positioned to exploit those dynamics. To the extent possible, the seller should utilize third-party information about market size and growth to provide an objective view of market potential. If the transaction is large, it may want to obtain legal/regulatory advice from antitrust experts.
- A description of the *product portfolio* of the business. This section should describe the business, its major product and/ or service lines, and all individual products/services of note. Specific attention should be paid to differentiating characteristics, such as products and services that have superior market position or brand recognition. However, care should be exercised in how these characteristics are expressed, avoiding the use of any terms that may imply a potential restraint of competition.
- A discussion of the *organization and administration* of the business. This section should include instructive views of the organization of the business. This may include a functional

organization chart, a presentation of headcount by function and/or a presentation of headcount by product/service line. This section should also profile executive management, highlighting relevant experience and expertise, and it should describe important aspects of the facilities that support the operation as well.

- **A presentation of a *financial overview* of the business as if it were a stand-alone operation, absent operational support of the selling corporation.** This section would generally include historical pro forma income statements for the three most recently completed years and estimated statements for the current year. These statements typically are based on high-level estimates that will be further refined by results of a carve-out audit and by the results of the disentanglement process (described in Chapter 5). This overview will generally also include a discussion and analysis of significant trends and anomalies as well as major issues such as the treatment of shared services, the underlying assumptions affecting the development of the pro forma statements, and any significant accounting policies.

- **A discussion of the *development potential* of the business.** It can be useful to include a discussion of significant potential or untapped opportunities that the executive management of the business unit consider important. Such a discussion must be approached carefully, since it will generally be tied to investment opportunities that the seller may not have exploited. Therefore, it should focus on opportunities that would result from combining the business with potential buyers' complementary assets and within a portfolio that would yield unrealized synergies.

The OD is distributed under the name of the financial advisor to those potential buyers mutually agreed on by seller and advisor, typically with instructions not to contact the seller directly and to communicate only through the advisor. The number of recipients will be dependent not only on the size of the market but also the selling approach (an auction or alternative approach) employed. The OD is generally distributed as soon as it is available, since a month or months

Introductory Comments

- Disclaimer of representations and warranties for information provided
- Reference to governing confidentiality agreement

Executive Summary

- Brief history and description of the business
- May include terms of sale, usually requiring all cash for transaction, a description of what is included and what is not, and evidence of financial capacity

Investment Considerations

- Listing and description of strategic capabilities that can be leveraged by new owner for enhanced growth and profitability

Industry Overview

- Description of the market
- Discussion of market dynamics to include size, growth, and market drivers

Organization and Administration

- Description of the business's organizational structure with organization charts
- Various views of the organization, such a headcount by function or by product line
- Profiles of senior executives
- Descriptions of major facilities
- Real property ownership or lease terms

Development Potential

- Discussion of organic growth potential
- Description of new or untapped strategic opportunities

Financial Overview

- Historical and projected pro forma financial summary
- Discussion and analysis to include adjustments made to arrive at pro forma statements, treatment of shared services, and significant accounting policies

EXHIBIT 4.4   OFFERING DOCUMENT OUTLINE

usually pass between the time the decision to divest is made and the OD is drafted. In most cases, the major gating factor in the finalization of the OD is the seller's comfort with the pro forma financial statements contained in the document. This, in turn, is dependent on the results of the carve-out audit and the identification of all material adjustments resulting from the disentanglement process. These factors are discussed in more detail in Chapters 5 and 6.

(d) MANAGEMENT PRESENTATION   The management presentation, also developed jointly by the advisor and the divestiture team, is generally drafted after the OD has been completed and closely tracks the content of the OD. However, it is much more than a simple rehashing of the same information contained in the OD. The presentation will be given to a limited number of bidders, those that have survived a pruning process designed to capture only the most attractive bidders that have advanced to preliminary due diligence. Sections 6.4 and 6.5 provide a thorough description of the bidding process, but suffice it to note here that those bidders that will advance to the preliminary due diligence phase will have demonstrated a willingness and capability to meet seller valuation requirements.

The management presentation, a live presentation typically supported by a PowerPoint slide show, is a format that presents an opportunity for interaction between the bidders that have advanced to this phase of the process and the management team of the business unit being divested. The presentation enables the management team to elaborate on and emphasize key themes, such as strategic growth opportunities and the development potential of the business. Across the table, it will enable the bidders to challenge and discuss important assumptions embedded in the data contained in both the OD and the management presentation. In addition, it will enable these bidders to evaluate the business unit management.

While the management presentation is an opportunity for the bidders to evaluate both the business and its management, it is also a forum for business unit executives to showcase their knowledge and themselves. It should be impressed on these executives that this presentation, among other things, is an audition with their prospective owners. Therefore, it is important that they project *command* of all relevant aspects of the enterprise being sold. This includes a thorough knowledge of the business, an in-depth understanding of the market, and perhaps most important, a clearly articulated strategic vision for the company going forward.

To get the best results of the management presentation, the team and its advisors should prepare for it relentlessly. Such preparation should be thorough and ensure:

- **Quality of the presentation document.** As noted, the supporting document for the management presentation is usually a PowerPoint slide show. The state of presentation quality has progressed substantially in recent years, which has raised the level of expectations of those on the receiving end of formal presentations. The divestiture team should ensure that the quality of the presentation meets those expectations. It should be crisp, well structured, complete, and visually appealing. The development of the presentation should be supported by an individual, whether employee or consultant, with strong PowerPoint skills and a keen eye for graphic illustration. Such an individual can make a significant contribution to the document and, ultimately, the presentation.
- **That the presenters have factual command of business and market information.** Factual command is the bedrock of the presentation. It projects credibility. Presenters should have a comprehensive and shared knowledge of the business and the market. Accordingly, they should be sensitized to the fact that contradictions or inconsistencies among the team will undoubtedly have a deadening impact on the attitudes of potential buyers.
- **That the presenters share a strategic vision for the business.** Factual command must be supplemented by strategic vision. Presenters, particularly the most senior executive, should be able to present the business in the context of market drivers and trends and its ability to exploit those dynamics. The presenting team must be keenly aware of the fact that potential buyers will be focused first and foremost on the future of the business and

its potential going forward. Therefore, the team's main goal is to clearly demonstrate the growth opportunity for the business, around which buyers can build their investment thesis.

- **That the presentation is exhaustively rehearsed.** Effective group presentations take coordination and practice. The presentation should be rehearsed as often as necessary to ensure that it flows naturally and tells a consistent and positive story. To optimize its impact, the team should simulate the presentation environment to the greatest extent possible.
- **That key questions are anticipated.** The divestiture team should critique and challenge the presenters during their rehearsals. Most of the questions that potential buyers will ask can be anticipated. Those questions should be asked and responded to in the context of the presentation. The team should critique the quality of the responses and work with presenters to ensure that they project confidence, command, and credibility.
- **That presentation skills are optimized.** Most executives can significantly improve their presentations with the input of professionals who specialize in presentation skills and techniques. Presentation consultants are readily available and should be engaged, particularly if those presenting do not have polished skills. This is a relatively inexpensive way to improve the quality of the end product.

The combination of the measures just described can have a significant impact on the persuasiveness of the presentation, which in turn can help to optimize the value of the business. It should also be noted that those organizations being presented to are not all equal. The seller should confer with its financial advisor to orchestrate the best possible sequencing of presentations. For example, after one or two presentations, the team will gain confidence, work through rough spots, and generally raise the level of presentation quality. Similarly, if there are six or eight presentations to potential buyers, the team may get stale in later presentations. It is therefore worth rating the attractiveness and purchase probability of candidates and sequencing them accordingly (i.e., presenting to the most attractive and likely buyers in the middle of such a group).

4.6 IDENTIFICATION OF POTENTIAL BUYERS

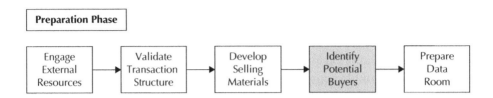

(a) **INTRODUCTION** The identification of potential buyers is generally a joint effort of the core divestiture team and the financial advisor. It is a product of the parties' knowledge of the buying market and the goals and objectives of the seller.

With regard to market, the seller usually will have an informed view of the range of potential strategic buyers by virtue of its understanding of the competitive landscape. The advisor may supplement that view with knowledge of an interested company or companies in adjacent markets, but, more important, the advisor will generally have relationships with potential financial buyers that may have an interest in entering or expanding into the relevant market. Together, seller and advisor will be able to assemble a comprehensive list of potential buyers that can be segmented and rated based on characteristics such as perceived interest and ability to finance the transaction.

Insofar as its goals and objectives are concerned, the seller will generally be driven by the desire to maximize after-tax sales value. This fact would suggest that the largest number of potential buyers should be provided the opportunity to bid on the property. However, there may be situations in which the seller will be influenced by additional considerations, such as a desire to close the transaction quickly and confidentially. The desire for speed and confidentiality may be driven by concerns about management distraction and/or the susceptibility of the business to impairment, if the business is particularly fragile or is small in size. Therefore, the seller must weigh the benefits of competition against the disadvantages of a protracted and potentially disruptive process. Consideration of these various factors will influence the type of sales process that will be employed.

(b) DETERMINING THE TYPE OF SALES PROCESS   Based on the factors just noted, the seller can choose among four options to bring the business to market. Those options are:

1. Acceptance of a preemptive bid involving a single buyer
2. Negotiated sale involving a small number of potential buyers
3. Limited auction involving a controlled number of bidders
4. Broad, public auction involving all interested and qualified buyers

The benefits and disadvantages of each of these approaches to the market are discussed in detail next.

(i) Preemptive Bid.   A preemptive bid by a single buyer has several advantages. It can reduce the time to market substantially and can result in a favorable purchase price if the seller can extract a significant premium for exclusivity. It also eliminates or sharply reduces the potential for leakage of information about the impending sale, since by definition it limits the number of parties privy to that information and reduces the amount of time that confidentiality has to be maintained. This situation has the residual benefit of minimizing disruptions to the business and the potential impairment that can result. However, the absence of other bidders eliminates the element of competition and can reduce the likelihood of the seller realizing full value for the property being sold, if the buyer is not locked into paying a significant premium. If a preemptive bid is entertained, the seller should maintain as much leverage and flexibility as possible. Leverage should be maintained by not granting exclusivity to the presumed buyer until the seller is confident of closing the deal on an acceptable basis. Doing this implies a high level of confidence that the valuation range the seller has projected is a good representation of market value and that this value, along with other terms of the deal, is attainable. In addition, the seller must keep its options open (such as proceeding to an auction if negotiations deteriorate) until it is reasonably certain it will close a deal under acceptable conditions or run the risk of a failed transaction, or one that does not realize the full value of the business being sold.

(ii) Negotiated Sale.   The negotiated sale option involves parallel negotiations with two or three potential buyers. It has the benefits

of introducing an element of competition into the process and an increased likelihood of completion. In addition, it may be able to be executed quickly and confidentially. However, parallel negotiations add a level of complexity to the process that can make the management of a negotiated sale quite challenging. It may require the involvement of multiple transaction teams as well. This approach also does not fully test the market value of the property being sold. Two conditions should be present for this approach to be adopted. The bidders should be credible, known quantities that represent the most likely finalists regardless of approach used, and the seller must place a premium on a rapid and/or confidential process. Otherwise, the seller is strongly advised to consider a limited or a broad-based (public) auction, discussed next.

(iii) Limited Auction.   The limited auction approach employs an auction process, but preselects a fairly narrow field of bidders based on criteria agreed on by the seller and the financial advisor. These criteria would include characteristics such as size, market position, perceived ability to finance the transaction, and the competitive relationship of the bidders to the seller. By narrowing the field, the seller presumes that the process will be relatively efficient and, because of the competitive nature of the approach, that full value will be realized. It is unlikely that confidentiality can be maintained because of the number of organizations and individuals that will be involved in the process. A limited auction can be an effective approach if all potential, competitive bidders can be identified and included in the process. Doing this requires in-depth familiarity with the market and, even then, runs the risk of eliminating strong but unexpected bidders from the process.

(iv) Public Auction.   A public auction will limit bidders only insofar as they are unintentionally not reached in the announcement and invitation process (described in section 6.4). The attempt to attract all potential bidders that might reasonably be expected to bid on the business makes this approach logistically challenging and protracted. It also requires a public acknowledgment of the sale. These characteristics generally result in a level of management distraction, and potential business erosion, that is substantially greater than that experienced

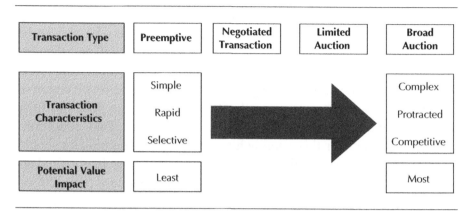

EXHIBIT 4.5   SALES METHOD CONTINUUM

in the other approaches described. However, if it is efficiently and effectively managed, a public auction will generally yield a transaction with optimal terms for the seller.

The relative advantages and disadvantages of these four types of approaches are illustrated in Exhibit 4.5.

The approach to the market should be dictated by the goals and objectives of the seller. While conventional wisdom suggests that a public auction is generally the best vehicle for optimizing value, other factors may influence the seller to adopt another approach. These factors might include a desire to close the deal quickly if the business is particularly vulnerable during the selling process.

4.7 PREPARATION OF A DATA ROOM

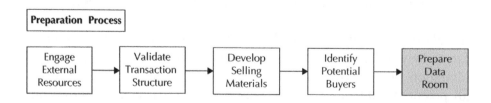

(a) INTRODUCTION A data room is a site that contains extensive documentation of key aspects of the business that is being sold. That information is generally organized and indexed by the team into the listed information categories (see Appendix 4A for a more granular listing of information generally provided in a data room):

- Financial
- Product/Service
- Intellectual Property
- Legal Matters
- Insurance
- Sales and Marketing
- Customer Service
- Employee Matters
- Information Systems
- Research and Development

Review of the data contained in the data room is a critical aspect of buyer due diligence. It is an opportunity for potential buyers to assess the data underlying representations that have been made by the seller in the offering document, the management presentation, and discussions with business unit executives. Furthermore, key elements of this information will support representations and warranties that will be incorporated into the purchase and sale agreement in the form of schedules to that contract, and data room access will be the first opportunity for buyers to scrutinize this information.

(b) PHYSICAL VERSUS VIRTUAL DATA ROOM Historically, data rooms have been dedicated physical sites where a large volume of documents is housed for review by potential buyers. In recent years, as technology has facilitated electronic housing and distribution of data, sellers have increasingly utilized virtual data rooms for this purpose. Both types of sites have advantages and disadvantages for the seller. The basic trade-off between these two approaches is cost and control. Virtual data rooms provide a high degree of control but at a substantially greater cost. These factors are discussed in detail in section 6.5.

(c) DATA ROOM MANAGEMENT Management of the data room, whether physical or virtual, is an important and resource-consumptive task. It requires planning, coordination, and the dedicated efforts of managers with strong process management skills. The creation of the data room is a dynamic process that occurs over an extended period. Often multiple bidders are given access to the data room during a first round of due diligence and before a winning bidder has been determined. Prior to this first, or preliminary, round of review, the data room is extensively populated with documents, but certain aspects of highly proprietary information may not be revealed. For example, customer names on contracts or the identity of employees on employee rosters containing compensation information may be redacted. In addition, bidders may ask for additional clarifying information that then must be trafficked through the system by the seller and financial advisor. Once a winning bidder has been determined, any blinded or redacted information will be revealed and additional more sensitive, proprietary information may be added to the data room. Finally, information in the data room that will appear in schedules to the sale and purchase agreement will have to be identified, reviewed, and, in some cases, updated. Consequently, data room maintenance is a task that can continue up until the close of the transaction.

It is generally advisable to assign a single individual from the seller's team to assemble and transfer documents to the data room (whether physically or electronically), subject to the review and approval of the legal team and the appropriate business managers. This individual should generally be an operations manager with a thorough understanding of the business and its information base (i.e., where the various types of information is housed internally and how it can be accessed most efficiently). In addition, an individual from the financial advisor's engagement team will typically be assigned responsibility for receiving, indexing, and housing this information in the data room. During the data room assembly process, the divestiture team should also establish rules of access as well as how those rules will be enforced and who within the team will be the point of contact for bidder questions and requests.

4.8 OVERVIEW OF THE PHASED DISCLOSURE PROCESS

Throughout the various aspects of the transaction—from initiation through confirmatory due diligence—the seller is faced with decisions about how much information should be disclosed at each stage of the process. It is important for those managing the transaction to understand the relationship between data availability and the number and quality of bidders that are given access over the course of the selling and negotiation phases. This section provides an overview of the disclosure process and a description of where access to the data room fits within that process.

Access to the data room is pivotal in a process that entails increasing disclosure and a decreasing number of potential buyers. When access to the data room is granted, the amount of information provided increases dramatically while the number of bidders is sharply reduced. The data provided document representations made in early-stage materials, such as the offering document, and provide detailed support for representations and warranties made in the final agreement. Exhibit 4.6 illustrates this relationship as well as the last stage in the information access process, the final contract.

Understandably, there is an inverse relationship between the volume and granularity of information provided to bidders and the number

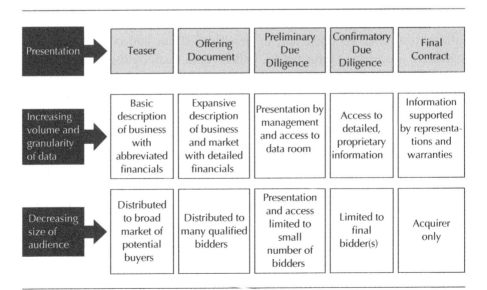

Presentation	Teaser	Offering Document	Preliminary Due Diligence	Confirmatory Due Diligence	Final Contract
Increasing volume and granularity of data	Basic description of business with abbreviated financials	Expansive description of business and market with detailed financials	Presentation by management and access to data room	Access to detailed, proprietary information	Information supported by representations and warranties
Decreasing size of audience	Distributed to broad market of potential buyers	Distributed to many qualified bidders	Presentation and access limited to small number of bidders	Limited to final bidder(s)	Acquirer only

EXHIBIT 4.6   PHASED DISCLOSURE PROCESS

and quality of the bidders getting that information. As illustrated, when employed as a selling mechanism, the teaser is distributed to a large number of potential buyers (dozens or even scores of organizations) and contains abbreviated information. If there is an especially large population receiving the teaser, it may be blinded (i.e., not even contain the name of the business unit being put up for sale). Those organizations that proceed to the next stage, the receipt of the offering document, are a substantially reduced subset of those that have received the teaser and, significantly, are also bound by an NDA. Although the information provided in the OD is much richer in detail, the probability that a substantial number of those receiving the OD are doing so to obtain competitive intelligence is high, so there should be a conscious effort to keep as much proprietary information as possible out of the document.

Those bidders allowed into the first phase of due diligence are generally few in number (typically less than 10 and very often half that number) and have gone through a qualification process that provides a high degree of confidence that they are truly interested in the acquisition and are willing and able to meet the basic requirements of the seller. However, only one of these bidders will emerge as the owner; the remainder will be reduced once again to the status of competitor. Therefore, information is often presented in generic fashion and certain detailed, sensitive, proprietary information will be held back by the seller.

The organization(s) permitted to advance to final confirmatory due diligence will be provided detailed information that was redacted, or perhaps not provided in any form, in preliminary due diligence. More often than not, the final or winning bidder will be the lone organization allowed to advance to this stage. However, if the seller has reservations about its ability to close with that organization, it may allow another firm to participate to maintain leverage and to have a backup if negotiations with the lead organization fall apart. Finally, the winning bidder will be provided with access to information and to representations and warranties regarding its validity in the form of the final agreement and associated schedules.

Specific aspects of phased disclosure of information are discussed in greater detail in Chapters 6, 7, and 8.

KEY POINTS

1. Close attention to transaction preparation is critical to the efficient, and often successful, execution of a divestiture. Early engagement of the appropriate external resources is extremely important since these organizations provide services that are essential to getting the business unit to market. (Section 4.1(b))

2. Arguably, a financial advisor—a business broker or investment banker—will be the most important resource the seller will engage. To optimize the use of this important resource, the seller should make every effort to match the capabilities of the advisor with the needs of the specific transaction involved. (Section 4.3(b)–(d))

3. A carve-out audit of the business being divested often is required to satisfy the needs and preferences of potential buyers. Because such audits can be protracted procedures, once the decision to sell has been made, the seller should engage an accounting firm for this purpose as soon as possible. (Section 4.3(e)–(f))

4. Final determination of the structure of the prospective transaction is a gating factor in the critical path of the transaction process. The seller should elicit input from its financial advisor regarding the form of the transaction to ensure that all relevant aspects of the market environment are considered and that the transaction structure chosen will optimize value. (Section 4.4)

5. The management presentation is a pivotal event because it is a forum for interaction between the management team of the business being divested and the field of qualified, potential buyers. The divestiture team should leave no stone unturned in its efforts to prepare for this event. (Section 4.5(d))

6. Data room preparation and management are dynamic and resource-consumptive activities. To ensure efficient and effective assembly and management of the site, the divestiture team must clearly define roles and responsibilities for creating the site as well as ground rules for its management. (Section 4.7(a)–(c)

ILLUSTRATIVE DATA ROOM INFORMATION LISTING

This document is provided for illustrative purposes. It is not meant to be comprehensive. It identifies the major categories of potential data room documents, but the actual data provided in the data room is dependent on the specifics of the transaction being executed, particularly the nature of the business being divested.

FINANCIAL DATA
- Historical financial statements
- Managerial financial statements (monthly, quarterly, and annual)
- Accounting policies
- Budgets
- Budget versus actual reports and analysis
- Tax returns
- Bank statements and reconciliations for major bank accounts
- Accounts receivable and aging information
- Inventory records
- Fixed asset records
- Carve-out audit
- Bridge schedules

PRODUCT/SERVICE INFORMATION
- Product/service descriptions
- Product/service sales histories
- Product and product line profit and loss statements

INTELLECTUAL PROPERTY INFORMATION (ACTUAL AND IN PROCESS)
- Copyrights
- Trademarks and service marks
- Patents
- Internet domains

LEGAL MATTERS
- Customer agreements
- Supplier agreements
- Lease agreements and amendments
- Contractor agreements
- Agent agreements
- Employee agreements (employment, severance, and incentive)
- Proof of ownership of material assets
- Resolved, threatened, or pending litigation
- Any communication regarding noncompliance with laws or governmental regulations

INSURANCE INFORMATION
- Details of insurance coverage
- History of insurance claims
- Workers' compensation reports

SALES AND MARKETING INFORMATION
- Description of sales and marketing process
- Description of sales and marketing department (headcount and responsibilities)
- Documentation of agreements with agents, resellers, and distributors

- Monthly sales by product (units and dollars)
- Reports on sales by channel
- List of top XX customers
- Analysis by sales by geographic region
- Descriptions of pricing and discounting policies
- Marketing budgets for last three years

CUSTOMER SERVICE INFORMATION

- Customer information and order system description
- Customer inquiry and complaint database
- Customer surveys for the last X years

EMPLOYEE MATTERS

- Current organization chart
- Copies of position descriptions
- Salary, bonus, profit-sharing, and merit increase information
- Sales compensation plans
- Details of employee benefits and retirement plans
- Company policies for vacation, sickness, bereavement, work schedules, and performance reviews
- Quantification of accrued leave time
- Terminations for cause within the last five years
- Retention agreements

INFORMATION SYSTEMS INFORMATION

- Listing of major information system providers and vendors
- Detailed description of phone system
- Detailed description of all major information systems (e-mail, network, accounting, customer service, production, sales, and customer information management systems)

RESEARCH AND DEVELOPMENT INFORMATION

- Major research projects for the last X years
- Products/services presently under consideration for development
- Product plans and designs currently under development
- Competitive tracking information

CHAPTER 5

DISENTANGLEMENT

5.1 DISENTANGLEMENT: PREPARING THE BUSINESS TO BE SEPARATED

The divestiture's preparation phase consists of two distinct components. Chapter 4 focused on the first component, preparing for the selling process, when the divestiture team retains advisors, creates marketing documents, and assembles supporting information. Here we turn our attention to the second component, preparing the divested business to be separated from the selling corporation, a process we call disentanglement.

Over time, most business units become interdependent in some way with other units of the parent organization. These interdependencies may exist in organizational functions ranging from the front office (e.g., offering bundled products and services or sharing a combined sales force), to the back office (e.g., occupying common facilities or sharing operational infrastructure or services). The process of disentanglement requires the divestiture team to identify all such interdependencies and to plan and implement a controlled termination of each of these connections with the selling corporation. The form of termination may differ for each interdependent function, depending on factors such as the divestiture approach, the capabilities of the acquirer, and the requirements of the selling corporation. In some cases, a function supported by the selling corporation may be transitioned to the support of the acquirer, while in other cases, the selling corporation may develop a stand-alone capability for the divested business.

Although disentangling a divested business from its parent organization may appear to be analogous to integrating an acquired business, it is generally more demanding, because it entails more complexity and must be executed within substantially tighter time constraints.

In an acquisition, the team starts with an open integration agenda and, ordinarily, an abundance of detailed information about the target business obtained from the due diligence process. The acquisition team can choose to prioritize certain areas, where rapid integration creates the highest value, and recommend a gradual integration of less important areas. Integration plans normally envision an implementation time horizon that spans one to two years *after* the close of the transaction. Consequently, the preclose integration planning is done at a relatively high level, and most of the detailed planning and operational execution occurs following the close.

In contrast, the divestiture team must consider and address *every* area of interdependency, necessitating significant advance planning and operational execution as well as contractual agreement and logistical coordination with the acquirer. Often many areas of interdependency exist, as functions of the divested business are intertwined with other business units over a period of years, if not decades, of ownership. Additionally, these interdependencies may not be well recorded, as shared business functions often evolve in a logical, but undocumented, manner over time. This means that the divestiture team must conduct a substantial information-gathering effort, just to identify the interdependent areas, before meaningful disentanglement planning can take place.

Additionally, the disentanglement of a divested business tends to be an extremely condensed process, because the selling corporation usually desires to sever all operational connections with the divested business as soon as practicable following the close. While the specific time frames can vary, most interdependent functions must be disentangled and transitioned within a period of several months. Many functions, in fact, may actually have to be separated by the time of the close. As a result, divestitures require most of the operational planning for disentanglement, and certain implementation steps, to occur *prior* to the close of the transaction.

Despite its complexity and time constraints, disentanglement is an area that is given insufficient attention in many organizations because of the competing demands of preparing for the divestiture transaction. Yet, if disentanglement planning is neglected and left to the last minute, it can cause major problems for the selling corporation. For this reason, an effort focused on the *operational* preparation for disentanglement should be organized and mobilized early in the preparation phase, as described in this chapter.

5.2 DISENTANGLEMENT PROCESS STEPS

The disentanglement phase starts with the assembly of a cross-functional group of internal managers. This group identifies each area of interdependency, develops a plan for disentanglement, and then oversees the implementation of the plan. The disentanglement phase consists of five key operational steps.

Step 1. Gathering information: inventory of interdependent functions. As mentioned in section 5.1, the areas of interdependence between business units may be numerous and poorly documented, especially if the divested business has been part of the selling corporation for a long time. As a result, the divestiture team must start disentanglement planning with an information-gathering process, by assembling a cross-functional group of internal managers with knowledge of the operations of the divested business. These managers should identify and describe all areas where interdependency exists, and then manage the disentanglement of these areas.

In section 5.3, we discuss who should be included in this cross-functional group and how they should be directed. We also discuss the information-gathering process and stress the importance of thoroughness in this first step.

Step 2. Determining the required end state: will a function need to stand alone? Once the divestiture team has identified the interdependencies, it knows which business functions must be disentangled. The next step is to determine what must be done with each of these functions. Does the divested business need to have stand-alone capabilities, or is the plan to rely on the acquirer to provide the required support following the close?

The answer to this question is dependent on several factors, including the divestiture structure, the capabilities of potential acquirers, and the particular requirements of the selling corporation. Each of these factors can impact the actions required by the selling corporation in disentangling the divested business.

In section 5.4, we discuss the factors that affect the scope of the disentanglement plan. We also present a framework for establishing the required end state of the disentanglement, a determination that the team makes for each interdependency.

Step 3. Developing the disentanglement plan: detailing the operational steps. At this point, the divestiture team has decided where it needs to take each interdependent function, for example, whether to transition it to the support of the acquirer or to create a stand-alone capability. The next step is to determine *how* to transition each function to its required end state by preparing a detailed disentanglement plan. Timing is the most critical factor to be considered in this step. The team must act immediately on some functions, especially if they are to be transitioned to a stand-alone state; other elements of the plan may be deliberately left open until the acquirer is known.

We present an outline for the disentanglement plan in section 5.5 and discuss each component of the plan, such as the responsible parties, the operational steps to be taken, their timing, and the costs to be incurred.

Step 4. Quantifying the impact of the disentanglement: one-time costs versus run-rate expenses. An important component of the disentanglement plan is the financial impact on the parties to the divestiture transaction. We consider two essential financial aspects of disentanglement in section 5.6.

First, we discuss one-time costs. As it prepares the disentanglement plan for each function, the team quantifies the one-time costs associated with the plan and, based on the projected timing, determines whether the costs will be borne by the selling corporation before the transaction closes or by the acquirer afterward.

Second, we address how the ongoing, or "run-rate," operating expenses of the divested business are impacted by its separation from the selling corporation. A key element of the offering memorandum, and of the management presentation, is the financial representation of the divested business absent the operational support of the selling corporation, as discussed in section 4.3(g). These pro forma financials enable potential acquirers to properly value the business by comparing its profitability to similar (stand-alone) businesses, and they are initially developed by the selling corporation based on high-level estimates. Once the detailed disentanglement plan is prepared, the financial estimates are refined and updated, in order to support their validity during the due diligence process.

Step 5. Executing the plan: disentangling. Once the identity, capabilities, and integration strategy of the acquirer are known, plans for the transition of each interdependent area can be finalized and implemented. Doing this involves reaching agreement with the acquirer concerning which activities will terminate immediately with the close, which ones will continue for a limited period to facilitate a controlled transition, and which activities will continue for a longer period. In some instances, the disentanglement of a function may also require agreements with third parties.

In section 5.7, we discuss the types of arrangements that are typically established with the acquirer, such as the transition services agreement for short-term services and the commercial services agreement for services that are intended to survive beyond the initial transition. We also present and discuss several operational considerations for the team as it implements the disentanglement plan.

Exhibit 5.1 illustrates the disentanglement phase steps, which are discussed in detail in the remaining sections of this chapter.

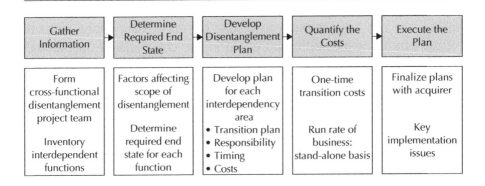

EXHIBIT 5.1 DISENTANGLEMENT PHASE PROCESS

5.3 GATHERING INFORMATION

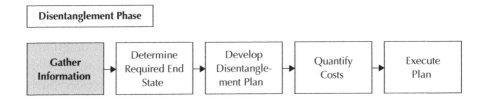

(a) ASSEMBLING A CROSS-FUNCTIONAL DISENTANGLEMENT PROJECT TEAM As discussed in section 1.4, there are certain stages of the divestiture process that necessitate an expansion of the team to address particular requirements of the transaction. In the disentanglement stage, a cross-functional project team of internal managers is needed to identify the areas of interdependency between the divested business and the selling corporation and to manage the disentanglement of those functions.

The exact composition of this group of internal managers is dependent on the degree of interdependence, which is different for every organization. Some business units have sufficient scale to warrant their own dedicated support functions or are part of an organization that operates in a highly decentralized manner. These organizations have few interdependencies to consider and do not require a large effort to manage the disentanglement. More commonly, however, the divested business is not large enough to justify having a stand-alone support infrastructure, or the selling corporation has consolidated operational functions across its businesses over time. In these situations, the disentanglement is more complex, requiring a greater level of participation from internal managers.

The cross-functional project team's first task, therefore, is to understand the existing level of operational interdependence between the divested business and the selling corporation, so that it knows how much effort is required and can bring in additional resources if needed. Several necessary characteristics of the cross-functional project team and how the team should be managed are discussed next.

(i) Cross-Functional Team Should Be Assembled Early in the Divestiture Process.   The divestiture team takes its first look at disentanglement issues when it prepares the organization plan in the planning stage, as discussed in section 3.4. The organization plan calls for the team to perform a high-level analysis of the business operations and infrastructure, primarily for employee assignment (i.e., to determine which employees will stay with the selling corporation and which will comprise and manage the key operating functions for the divested business after its separation). This employee assignment, particularly the selection of the individuals who will lead formerly shared infrastructure functions, helps to create the initial nucleus of the disentanglement team. The individual selected to manage an operating function for the divested business may come from one of several sources, depending on the disentanglement approach and the availability of resources:

- Managers having some prior involvement with the function under the selling corporation's ownership, who are assigned to manage the function for the divested business following the sale
- Managers newly hired to assume responsibility for the function on a stand-alone basis
- Contract resources retained to manage the function on a temporary basis until it is transitioned to the acquirer

Because of the time pressure involved, the earlier managers can start to focus on the disentanglement process, the better. Ideally, this group should meet immediately after the employee assignment is completed and bring in any additional resources as soon as the need is identified. As mentioned in section 5.1, the disentanglement planning is best managed as an activity parallel to the transactional preparation.

(ii) Disentanglement Effort Should Be Led by a Member of the Core Divestiture Team.   An executive from the core divestiture team should be placed in charge of the cross-functional disentanglement project team. This executive could be a senior executive from finance or operations or be a member of line management, depending on the organization structure and on the individuals comprising the core team. To be successful in this role, however, the leader must have several key attributes:

- Broad-based understanding of the business operations and the financials of the selling corporation and of the divested business
- Ongoing involvement with the divestiture transaction, so that disentanglement issues can be appropriately incorporated into the divestiture agreements
- Sufficient organizational influence to direct a cross-functional project and make key decisions

(iii) Team Should Represent All Major Operating Functions.   The cross-functional project team should be composed of managers representing all of the major operational functions, from revenue-producing activities, to back-office infrastructure. Individuals responsible for managing any known shared infrastructure functions should specifically be included in this group (e.g., information technology operations, real estate, product or service production and delivery, accounting and finance, human resources, or customer services).

These individuals, with their day-to-day knowledge of the business operations, are critical to the information-gathering part of the disentanglement planning. This is especially the case in situations where the interdependencies between the corporation's business units are not adequately documented.

(iv) Team Should Include Representatives from Selling Corporation and from Divested Business.   The team needs to include the individuals responsible for managing shared functions of the selling corporation,

in addition to the employees assigned to manage those functions for the divested business, because both perspectives are needed, and each has separate tasks to perform. By definition, each group will be looking at the process from different viewpoints, depending on whether it is terminating the interdependency or assuming the operational responsibility.

These individuals should be made jointly responsible for the successful disentanglement and transition of the function under their responsibility, to ensure that there is a smooth handoff as each interdependent service is terminated.

(v) Team Should Continue to Meet and Communicate Regularly.   The team should conduct regularly scheduled meetings (at least semimonthly), to review the status and progress of the plans for each interdependent function, and to identify and respond to any major issues that arise. The team will likely uncover new information and learn things as it goes along, and must be in a position to make rapid decisions and midcourse adjustments, to ensure that timetables do not slip. Additionally, a close linkage should be maintained with the divestiture transaction team to ensure that any disentanglement issues affecting the deal (e.g., costs or timing) are communicated and coordinated with the acquirer.

(b) PREPARING THE LIST OF INTERDEPENDENT FUNCTIONS   Once the cross-functional disentanglement project team is assembled, its first task is to gather as much information as possible about the operational relationship between the divested business and the selling corporation. This is performed by methodically reviewing all available documentation and by using the team members' knowledge of the business to fill in gaps. The team reviews each business function, categorizing it as either dedicated to the divested business or interdependent. Interdependent functions are then listed and described, creating the agenda for the disentanglement plan. The next points elaborate on each step.

(i) Gathering Details: Where to Look for Information.   Several sources of information can help the team document the full extent of operational interdependency between the divested business and the selling corporation. As mentioned, and as described in section 3.4, the organization

plan is the obvious starting point, because it represents the most recent effort taken by management to identify the key organizational areas that are operationally interdependent.

In order to add to the information gleaned from the organization plan, the team should methodically review the income statement and organizational chart of the divested business. Starting with revenues, and working through cost of sales, selling, general and administrative costs, the team should account for the major categories of revenue and expense flowing through the income statement. Team members should then relate the major revenue and cost categories to the people, products and services, operational functions, assets, and business processes that generate those revenues and incur those costs, incorporating their day-to-day knowledge of the business into the review. Performing this type of analysis will ensure the review is thorough, and it will also help team members to anticipate issues that may arise in the due diligence, as the acquirer will likely employ a similar analytical process.

Depending on the organization, internal control documentation may be of some use to the team. Also, in some cases, intercompany services may be documented by service-level agreements or other formal arrangements. These agreements will help the team immensely, to the extent they exist. Additionally, if the business being divested had been acquired within the last several years, the acquisition integration plan would be an invaluable resource.

(ii) Distinguishing Dedicated from Interdependent Functions. As the team reviews each business process, it will find that a number of functions of the divested business are essentially resident within the activities of the employees and supported by the assets that will transfer to the acquirer. For purposes of this discussion, these are referred to as dedicated functions. Conversely, other functions involve some level of interdependence between the divested business and the selling corporation. These will be referred to as interdependent functions, and comprise the areas requiring disentanglement planning. This distinction between dedicated and interdependent functions is illustrated in Exhibit 5.2.

An example of a dedicated function is a sales force that represents only product lines of the divested business, of which all sales

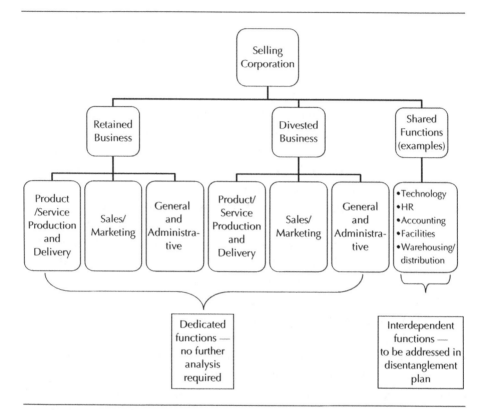

Exhibit 5.2   Illustration of Dedicated versus Interdependent Functions

employees, along with supporting sales management systems and customer/prospect databases, will transfer to the acquirer upon the close of the transaction. Dedicated functions such as this require no further analysis by the cross-functional team.

An example of an interdependent function is a shared regional distribution center that is responsible for managing the inventory of multiple business units, which the selling corporation intends to retain control of after the divestiture, to support its remaining business units. After the close of the transaction, the divested business's access to this distribution center is no longer a given. This situation creates a capabilities gap within the divested business that needs to be filled, either by the selling corporation or by the acquirer. A number of questions logically arise, such as whether the selling corporation would be willing to provide this service to the acquirer following the divestiture and, if not, how it envisions winding down support for the divested business, and over what period of time. The cross-functional team will include areas such as this on its list of interdependent activities for further analysis and disentanglement planning.

(iii) Interdependence Can Be a Two-Way Street.   Many of the operational dependencies the team is likely to identify will be cases where the divested business is dependent on assets or services of the selling corporation. In these cases, the selling corporation effectively controls the transition, deciding, for example, whether or for how long it is willing to continue to provide services after the close of the transaction. However, some dependencies work the other way—the divested business has assets or provides services that are important in some way to the selling corporation. This means that the selling corporation will become dependent on the willingness of the acquirer to provide access to these assets or services, unless a plan is created to become self-sufficient in this area by the time the transaction closes. Therefore, it is important that the cross-functional team looks for interdependencies in both directions as part of its review.

(iv) Many Business Processes Have an Underlying Technology Component.   The information technology (IT) manager assigned to the disentanglement team should play a broad role, reviewing each area along with the respective functional manager to ensure that any underlying IT systems dependencies have been considered. As examples, in human resources (HR), the HR information system needs to be considered, and in accounting, the general ledger system must be included in the review. These types of IT dependencies can easily be overlooked.

(v) Identify Ownership of the Assets that Underlie Business Functions, and Look for Any Key Third-Party Dependencies.   The team should not just look at business processes when it performs its review. It also needs to make sure it understands the ownership and use of any assets that are foundational to revenue generation or to the performance of a business function.

For example, if the divested business's products incorporate certain intellectual property (IP, such as a patented technology), then the team needs to find out several things: which legal entity within the selling corporation owns the IP, whether any other business of the selling corporation also utilizes the IP, and whether ownership of the IP will transfer to the acquirer. If the selling corporation does not own the IP but has acquired rights to it from a third party, then the team needs to understand whether these rights can be contractually assigned to the acquirer. If not, then the disentanglement plan should be to obtain the third party's consent to the assignment of the rights or to identify and secure a viable alternative, before the divestiture transaction closes.

(vi) Conduct Initial Review as Thoroughly as Possible.   It is entirely possible that some areas of interdependence will not be identified in the initial review but at some time along the way as the disentanglement plan is prepared. Identifying a large, complex interdependency late in the deal process puts undue pressure on both the business operation and the transaction team. To mitigate this undesirable but real possibility, the team should apply sufficient diligence in the initial review to ensure it has identified all of the largest and most complex interdependency areas, particularly those that need the most lead time to plan for and implement.

(vii) Questions for the Team to Ask.   To help identify areas of interdependence that may not be initially obvious, the team should ask these types of questions in its review of the divested business:

- Does the divested business provide all of the services (i.e., people resources, business processes and functions) and own all of the assets (i.e., tangible and intangible assets, contractual rights and permissions) it needs to generate the revenues reported in its financial statements?
- Does the divested business provide all of the services and own all of the assets it needs for the conduct of the business functions comprising the costs and expenses reported in its financial statements?
- Will all of the personnel performing the services and the underlying assets be transferred to the acquirer, or is the selling corporation planning on retaining any?

- In which specific areas is the divested business reliant on a service or asset of the selling corporation to generate revenue or conduct a business function?
- In which specific areas is the selling corporation reliant on a service or asset of the divested business to generate revenues or conduct a business function?

Additionally, functional managers must ask more targeted questions to identify the interdependencies for their area. For example, IT managers must look deeply into the technical details of the business, not only to identify the services provided but also to clearly document which legal entities within the selling corporation actually own the underlying technology that those services are based on, as discussed in the example just given. These managers would ask questions such as:

- Which operating units provide what types of functional services to the divested business?
- What technology platforms do they utilize?
- What hardware and software components are incorporated into those platforms?
- Which legal entities own the rights to that IP (and which of those entities are part of the sale)?
- Are the rights to any key components obtained from third parties?

Likewise, other functional areas will have their own sets of questions to ask. As another example, HR will ask questions about the compensation and benefit plans covering the employees of the divested business:

- What are the compensation and benefit plans that cover employees of the divested business?
- Are these plans dedicated to the divested business, or are they part of corporate plans?
- What are the terms of these plans, especially concerning any changes in ownership of the divested business?

(viii) Assembling and Documenting the Details.   The team should assemble and document the relevant details for all interdependent functions: a description of the function or service, the terms of any

applicable intercompany service agreements, and the basis for any intercompany charges, cost allocations, or third-party costs for these services. While some interdependent functions will be formally documented with an intercompany service-level agreement that specifies activity-based pricing, other areas may not be documented at all, and perhaps may not involve any intercompany charges. It is important for the team to document what is known about the actual function or service performed and to analyze how each function is reflected in the income statement. In particular, the team should understand the basis of any cost allocated to the divested business and whether it approximates the cost the divested business might incur on a stand-alone basis for similar services.

Exhibit 5.3 is an illustrative list of some of the types of interdependent areas that may be identified by the cross-functional team. Note that the list identifies the business units providing and utilizing each service (i.e., whether the divested business relies on a unit of the selling corporation, or vice versa), since this impacts the disentanglement plan for the function.

5.4 DETERMINING THE REQUIRED END STATE

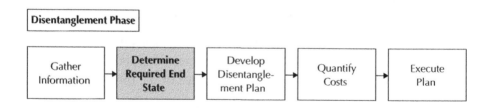

(a) WILL A FUNCTION NEED TO STAND ALONE? Once the list of interdependencies is developed, the team knows which functions need to be disentangled, but it does not yet know what must be done with these functions. The next step, therefore, is to decide whether it is in the selling corporation's interest to manage the transition of the interdependent functions toward operational self-sufficiency, or whether it makes more sense to do as little as possible before the close of the transaction and allow the acquirer to assume the burden of providing operational support to the divested business.

Function	Description of Service or Asset	Business Unit Providing Function	Business Unit Utilizing Function	Terms of Inter-Company (or Third-Party) Service Agreement	Amount and Basis of Service Charges or Cost Allocations
Sales	Cross-selling activities				
Marketing	Bundled products/services, joint marketing activities				
Product or Service Production and Delivery	Shared manufacturing and warehousing facilities				
Real Estate	Shared office facilities, phone systems				
Technology	Shared data center operations, network support, desktop support, e-mail Shared (or licensed) IP				

Exhibit 5.3 Illustrative List of Interdependent Functions (Continued)

Function	Description of Service or Asset	Business Unit Providing Function	Business Unit Utilizing Function	Terms of Inter-Company (or Third-Party) Service Agreement	Amount and Basis of Service Charges or Cost Allocations
Back-Office Operations	Shared customer service				
Accounting	Shared general ledger, general accounting, accounts payable, accounts receivable, billing				
Human Resources	Shared HR information systems, payroll, compensation benefit plans, recruiting				
Treasury	Shared banking, cash/currency management				
Corporate Staff Services	Shared tax, legal, corporate purchasing				

EXHIBIT 5.3 Illustrative List of Interdependent Functions

The answer to this question depends on the divestiture structure, the capabilities of potential acquirers, and any particular requirements of the selling corporation. These three factors determine how much disentanglement work needs to be set in motion, and when.

(i) Creating More Alternatives for Divestiture, or a Bigger Competitive Auction, Can Make Disentanglement More Complicated. There are only a certain number of potential strategic acquirers for a given divested business, firms that have synergistic operations of sufficient scale that can readily integrate the divested business into their various support services. If the selling corporation chooses to restrict the sale process to these strategic acquirers, it may or may not assemble a large enough competitive group to ensure a robust auction process. For this reason, selling corporations are often advised to expand the field to include financial acquirers, organizations such as private equity groups, which have ample financing and which tend to be very aggressive bidders for investment opportunities they find of interest. Some selling corporations go one step further in expanding their options, evaluating whether value can be optimized by tapping the public equity markets by spinning off the divested business in a public offering, or possibly viewing a public offering as a fallback in case an auction does not result in the desired value. This process of determining the structure that will optimize the value of the divestiture is described in section 3.1.

From the perspective of the disentanglement, expanding the number of divestiture options considered or the field of potential acquirers increases the likelihood that the divested business will need to stand alone. To illustrate, consider the range of available divestiture options as existing along a continuum, as shown in Exhibit 5.4.

If the divested business is sold to a strategic acquirer with operations of sufficient scale, there is no need for it to become self-sufficient. The disentanglement plan will be to transition the divested business from being dependent on the selling corporation for certain services to being dependent on the acquirer for those services. While this is the most straightforward and lowest-cost option, it may not be the option that optimizes value if the field of bidders is small.

As the selling corporation expands the field of bidders to include organizations such as financial acquirers whose portfolio companies

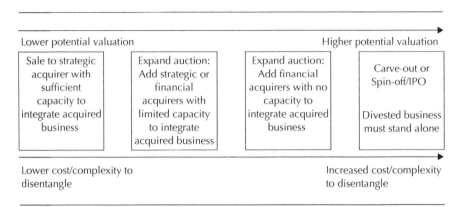

Lower potential valuation			Higher potential valuation
Sale to strategic acquirer with sufficient capacity to integrate acquired business	Expand auction: Add strategic or financial acquirers with limited capacity to integrate acquired business	Expand auction: Add financial acquirers with no capacity to integrate acquired business	Carve-out or Spin-off/IPO Divested business must stand alone

Lower cost/complexity to disentangle

Increased cost/complexity to disentangle

Exhibit 5.4   Divestiture Scenarios and Implications for the Disentanglement Plan

may have less operational capacity, it is more likely that the divested business will need to become operationally self-sufficient at least in some respects. The disentanglement plan in this case will be for the selling corporation to determine what it takes for the business to become self-sufficient, then decide which elements of this plan to initiate prior to the sale and which elements to leave for the acquirer to assume based on its particular capabilities and plans. If the field is further expanded to include financial bidders that have no other relevant operational holdings, the selling corporation will need to help the acquirer transition the divested business to a completely stand-alone basis over some period.

If a public offering is considered, there is little doubt and less transitional flexibility; the divested business will have to become a separate stand-alone corporation, with its own operational infrastructure, administration, and staff functions. In particular, the administrative and staff functions would need to become sufficiently capable to meet the regulatory and compliance burdens of a publicly traded company. This route is by far the most complicated and expensive to undertake from a disentanglement perspective.

Therefore, in deciding on the divestiture structure, the implications for the disentanglement should be considered along with the potential upside in valuation, so that the selling corporation can consider the potential cost of options along with the benefits. Selling corporations may be understandably ambivalent in choosing a sale structure that requires a complicated disentanglement. However, they may find that expanding the sale options materially increases value and justifies the additional effort.

(ii) Selling Corporation's Particular Requirements also Affect Disentanglement.   In certain cases, the selling corporation will have firm views about what it is willing to do, or not do, to accommodate the divestiture of one of its businesses. It is critical for the team to understand the selling corporation's preferences and constraints up front because this has an obvious impact on the disentanglement plan.

Regardless of the earlier discussion concerning the expansion of sale options, the selling corporation may take the position that it is not worth spending any energy creating stand-alone capabilities for the divested business, even if the valuation is not optimized. This might be for any of several reasons: perhaps the business is small and the valuation upside potential is not material, or operational management is needed for other activities deemed more strategically important, or the divested business's performance is deteriorating and the corporation would like to sell it as quickly as possible. Any of these reasons could cause the selling corporation to opt for the most expedient disentanglement approach and forgo the prospect of a higher valuation.

Another possibility is the selling corporation may have specific views about what postclosing transition services it is willing to provide to the acquirer, and for how long. For example, for security reasons, a corporation may want access to its internal networks terminated immediately upon the sale of a business unit. That situation would dictate to the disentanglement team that for this specific function, a postclosing transition is off the table and that whatever is done to disentangle this function, it must be completed before the closing of the sale.

(b) DETERMINING THE REQUIRED END STATE FOR EACH INTERDEPENDENT FUNCTION   Having listed the interdependent functions, and understanding how the divestiture structure and any corporate requirements impact the disentanglement, the team is now in a position to make operational decisions about what it will do for each function.

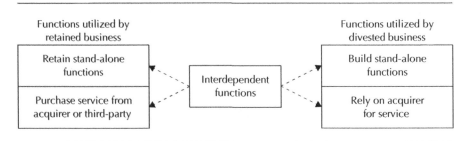

EXHIBIT 5.5   ESTABLISHING THE REQUIRED END STATE FOR INTERDEPENDENT
FUNCTIONS

The team should establish a specific end state for each interdependent function, choosing to pursue one of several actions:

- Retain a stand-alone function for the selling corporation
- Purchase a service for the selling corporation from the acquirer or from a third party
- Build a stand-alone function for the divested business
- Rely on the acquirer to provide a service to the divested business

These options are illustrated in Exhibit 5.5 and are explained in the discussion that follows.

Functions Utilized by the Divested Business

- **Build a stand-alone function for the divested business.** For these functions, the selling corporation provides a service to the divested business that it will retain following the divestiture and plans to replace the service by building a similar stand-alone function within the divested business.

   For example, the selling corporation may manage a single corporate-wide e-mail system and have a technology security policy requiring the immediate separation of a divested business from its shared network servers. As a result, it might be unwilling to provide e-mail service to the divested business following the sale, even for a transition period. Further, the sale process may indicate that a financial acquirer with no current operational capacity will prevail in the bidding. In this instance, the selling corporation may decide to build and implement a stand-alone e-mail capability within the divested business that is separate and operational by the time the sale closes.

- **Rely on the acquirer to provide the service.** For these functions, the selling corporation provides a service to the divested business that will be retained after the divestiture and plans to let the acquirer assume responsibility for integrating the function following the close of the transaction (either providing the service itself or obtaining it from a third party).

For example, all business units of the selling corporation may be supported by a consolidated general accounting function. The selling corporation might be willing to provide, if needed, accounting services to the divested business for a reasonable transition period following the close. Additionally, the auction process may point to an acquisition by a sizable strategic acquirer, making it likely that the acquirer could easily provide accounting services to the divested business. In this case, the selling corporation may decide to do nothing with this function before the sale, providing accounting services until the acquirer integrates the function following the close.

Functions Utilized by a Retained Business Unit of the Selling Corporation

- **Purchase the service from the acquirer or from a third party.** For these functions, the selling corporation relies on a service or assets of the divested business that will be transferred to the acquirer following the divestiture, and would prefer to acquire the service from the acquirer on a commercial basis after the close of the transaction. Not knowing whether the acquirer would be interested in providing the service, the selling corporation must also consider alternative ways of obtaining this service from other third parties.

For example, the selling corporation may incorporate products created by the divested business as components of bundled products or services offered to customers, and sees value in continuing these bundled offerings. The selling corporation's plan may be to approach the acquirer at some point in the sale process and inquire about its willingness to enter into a value-added reseller agreement that incorporates mutually beneficial revenue-sharing terms. As an alternative, the selling corporation may also plan to investigate whether products of third parties could potentially be substituted into the bundled offering.

5.5 DEVELOPING THE DISENTANGLEMENT PLAN

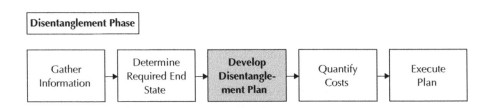

(a) **TIMING AND ITS IMPACT**   Once the selling corporation has decided directionally where it needs to take each interdependent function, it tasks its cross-functional team with determining exactly how to accomplish this. Timing is the key consideration in the questions asked by the team as it formulates the detailed plan. Does the disentanglement plan for a function need to be initiated before the close? Does it need to be completed before the close? Is the selling corporation willing to provide postclosing transition services for a function, and if so, for how long? What steps can or should be taken now versus what should await input from the acquirer? (On this last question, it may be advisable to seek regulatory advice concerning what activities the acquirer should, or should not, be allowed to influence before the deal closes. See the related discussion on preclosing covenants in section 7.5(a)).

The central consideration for preparing the detailed plan, therefore, is timing, as discussed next.

- **Building stand-alone functions generates most of the preclose planning and implementation activities.** If the required end state for a function is a stand-alone capability within the divested business, the team needs to decide when this capability needs to be up and running. In the example discussed earlier concerning a stand-alone e-mail system, the project team would be instructed to make this system operational by a specific date on or before the anticipated close of the transaction. If the capability will not be operational until some time after the close of the sale, then the team needs to plan to provide existing services for a defined transition period, something that must be negotiated and subject to a formal agreement with the acquirer.

- **Relying on the acquirer requires up-front planning for the disentanglement and postclose transition services.** If the required end state for a function is integration by the acquirer, the team needs to know the acquirer's specific integration strategy before it can take meaningful action on the disentanglement. In the example discussed earlier concerning accounting services, the team would have little implementation work to perform until it understands exactly what the acquirer's integration plan is for the accounting function. However, the team should use the time prior to closing to think about how long it might take to disentangle the accounting function based on its own considerations and constraints (e.g., so that it can manage through quarterly or year-end reporting periods), and for how long following the close it might be willing to provide transition services, since these factors need to be known in order to negotiate the terms of a transition services agreement with the acquirer.

- **Purchasing the service from the acquirer requires preparing for negotiation of terms.** If the scope of the disentanglement plan for a functional area is to purchase a service from the acquirer, the team's preclosing focus is to establish the terms under which it desires to purchase these services, since any such arrangement will have to be agreed with the acquirer as part of the overall deal negotiations. In the example of bundled products and services discussed earlier, the team should use the time before close to develop a term sheet for a proposed reseller agreement, ideally so that it can be included in the data room for the acquirer's examination during due diligence.

(b) DEVELOPING THE DETAILED DISENTANGLEMENT PLAN   Exhibit 5.6 reflects an illustrative framework for the disentanglement plan, the key elements of which are described in the points that follow.

Function	Description of Service or Asset	Responsible Individual: Providing Organization	Responsible Individual: Utilizing Organization	Required End State	Migration Approach/ Alternatives	Timing	Disentanglement Costs		Status/ Issues to Be Resolved
							P&L Expense	Capital Expenditure	
				(e.g., build stand-alone function or rely on acquirer to integrate)	(i.e., actions/ steps to get to end state, and consideration of alterna-tives, any key third-party dependencies)	(e.g., complete prior to close, plan for postclosing transition)			

EXHIBIT 5.6 ILLUSTRATIVE DISENTANGLEMENT PLAN FRAMEWORK

- **Function and description of service or asset.** The disentanglement plan should address all functions identified in the List of Interdependencies (i.e., Exhibit 5.3).
- **Responsible individuals.** This section identifies the individuals from the business unit providing the service and the unit utilizing the service (i.e., the selling corporation and the divested business) who are accountable for the function's successful transition. As discussed in section 5.3(a), each function should be jointly owned, since the divested business and the selling corporation need to coordinate a number of parallel activities in order to smoothly transition a function to its required end state. The selling corporation focuses primarily on disentangling the elements of the divested business from its remaining activities, while the divested business focuses on assuming responsibility for managing the separated function, either on a stand-alone basis or as part of a function integrated with the acquirer.
- **Required end state.** As discussed in section 5.4(b), one of four approaches is determined for each interdependent function. For functions utilized by the divested business (which normally represent most of the interdependencies), the team will decide to build a stand-alone function or rely on the acquirer to integrate the activity. For functions utilized by business units retained by the selling corporation, the team will decide to retain a stand-alone function or purchase it from a third party after the divestiture closes.
- **Migration approach/alternatives.** Once end states are established for each function, a specific plan is prepared detailing exactly how the function will be disentangled. Some complex areas may require separate supporting plans outlining the specific steps to be taken and the required sequence of activities. It is important for the team to think through possible alternative approaches, especially in cases where it decides to rely on the acquirer to integrate the service, since it will have to adapt to the acquirer's integration plan, or in cases where there is a key dependency on a third party.
- **Timing.** As discussed in section 5.5(a), timing can fall into one of three categories: (1) complete the disentanglement before

the close; (2) plan for a short-term transition following the close (via a transition services agreement); or (3) plan for a longer-term relationship with the acquirer (via a commercial agreement).

- **Disentanglement costs to be incurred by the selling corporation.** Disentanglement costs represent one-time expenditures the selling corporation makes to develop stand-alone capabilities or to otherwise separate functions from its ongoing operations. The team should distinguish whether the item is a capital expenditure (i.e., an asset is being built that will be on the acquisition balance sheet) or an operating expense to be incurred by the selling corporation (e.g., consulting services).
- **Status and issues to be resolved.** Responsible managers should report to the cross-functional team regularly to update it on the status of activities, and report, on a timely basis, any issues that need to be decided and resolved.

5.6 QUANTIFYING THE DISENTANGLEMENT COSTS

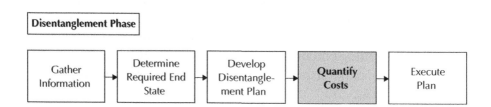

As discussed in section 5.2, an important part of the disentanglement is its financial impact on the parties to the transaction. There are two essential financial aspects to be considered: the one-time costs incurred prior to the transaction and the ongoing run-rate expense implications for the divested business after disentanglement.

(a) ONE-TIME COSTS
(i) Placing Disentanglement Costs in Context of Total Divestiture Costs. For those members of the team working on the disentanglement plan, it is important to keep in mind that the selling corporation wants to keep close track of all divestiture costs, of which the disentanglement

is just one component. Cost expectations of the selling corporation are normally set when it approves the board paper (see section 3.3(c)), initially as a percentage (e.g., 5% to 10%) of the estimated proceeds. During the preparation stage, the divestiture team engages advisors and starts incurring professional fees relating to the transactional preparation, as discussed in section 4.3. Once the disentanglement plan is prepared, as discussed in section 5.5, the team begins incurring costs relating to the organizational separation. By this point, the selling corporation is spending a material amount of money on the transaction and wants to ensure that the divestiture costs stay within its expectations. To help manage and communicate this spending activity, the team should prepare a comprehensive summary of all estimated transaction costs, such as shown in Exhibit 5.7, and update it regularly throughout the course of the transaction. The disentanglement team, in particular, should communicate on a timely basis any change in assumptions, or in approach, that impacts the projected costs.

In addition to the total expenditure, the classification of divestiture costs in the financial statements is also important to the selling corporation (i.e., whether costs will be charged to the income statement or to the balance sheet). Only certain costs are allowed to be incorporated into the gain or loss calculation; the remainder must be treated as either operating expense or capital expenditures. The team should consult the divestiture transaction's accounting subject matter experts in making these financial reporting distinctions. (See the discussion of financial reporting considerations in section 7.4(b).)

(ii) One-Time Disentanglement Costs Incurred by the Selling Corporation.   As discussed in sections 5.4 and 5.5, the selling corporation may decide to initiate disentanglement activities for certain operational functions prior to the close. In so doing, it is choosing to bear the related one-time transition costs, since the actions are undertaken unilaterally. The key, in such instances, is to clearly identify and communicate the specific projects to the acquirer during the due diligence, so it is clear to both parties what operational capabilities will be in place, by when, and precisely which project costs will be borne by the selling corporation. The parties may have to formalize this understanding in the purchase agreement for any projects that are under way, but not yet completed, at the time of the close.

	Operating Expenses	Selling Costs (include in gain/loss on sale)	Capital Expenditures	Total Costs
Direct Transaction Costs:				
Financial advisors (e.g., broker)		$x		$x
Legal advisors		$x		$x
Accounting services (e.g., carve-out audit)		$x		$x
Tax advisors		$x		$x
HSR filing fees		$x		$x
Disentanglement Costs:				
Consultants	$x			$x
Hardware			$x	$x
Software	$x		$x	$x
Severance/ outplacement	$x			$x
Facilities decommissioning costs	$x			$x
Lease buyout costs	$x			$x
Other Divestiture Costs:				
Deal-related employee bonuses (retention, performance, success)	$x	$x		$x
Accruals for liabilities (e.g., litigation, contracts)	$x			$x
Asset impairment charges	$x			$x
Totals	$x	$x	$x	$x

EXHIBIT 5.7 ILLUSTRATIVE DIVESTITURE COST SUMMARY FOR THE SELLING CORPORATION

(iii) One-Time Costs Incurred by the Acquirer: Transition Services.   If the disentanglement plan for a function is to rely on the acquirer to assume responsibility, the selling corporation is normally expected to offer transition services until the acquirer can complete its integration. The cross-functional team should create an itemized list of the services required to support a function through the transition period, which of those services it is willing to provide, for what period of time, and at what cost to the acquirer. These elements of service, term, and cost will be negotiated along with the other elements of the transaction and documented in a transition services agreement (TSA). The service element, in particular, should be defined precisely so that there is no misunderstanding about what level of service will be provided and what specific steps will occur as the service is terminated. The more complex a divested business is to disentangle, the more extensive a TSA the acquirer is likely to expect. This agreement is discussed in more detail in section 7.5(c).

(b) PRESENTING THE "RUN RATE" OF THE BUSINESS ON A STAND-ALONE BASIS: PRO FORMA FINANCIALS   When it prepares to put the business up for sale, as discussed in section 4.5, the divestiture team develops income statements, balance sheets, cash flow statements, and a variety of financial analyses for incorporation into the offering document and management presentations. Potential acquirers spend a lot of time analyzing and understanding these financials in detail, so that they can compare the acquisition target to comparable businesses, and arrive at a proper business valuation in support of their bidding strategy.

When an acquisition target is a business unit carved out of a larger organization, potential acquirers often suspect that the internal expenses allocated to the target's income statement for shared services have little resemblance to what these services would cost on a stand-alone basis. As a result they tend to zero right in on the allocated costs in their financial diligence. If they become convinced that costs would increase upon a change in ownership because too little expense was allocated to the divested business, it would have a direct negative bearing on the valuation and bidding, a situation that the selling corporation would prefer to avoid.

To address these concerns, selling corporations often include a set of financials, often referred to as the pro forma financials, which represent their best estimate of what the divested business might look like on a stand-alone basis. In the pro forma financials, cost allocations for shared operational functions are replaced with estimates of expenses those functions would incur absent the support of the selling corporation. As discussed in section 4.3(g), these pro forma financials often are based on high-level estimates, which the selling corporation should refine as its disentanglement planning progresses. The team can refine the stand-alone cost estimates in several ways:

- Utilizing published functional cost benchmarks based on businesses of similar size
- Comparing functional costs of the divested business to other units within the selling corporation that have stand-alone capabilities for those functions
- Utilizing the day-to-day operational knowledge of the cross-functional team

Although potential acquirers will be understandably skeptical, and will form their own opinion about what the postdivestiture business will look like based on their particular integration strategy, the pro forma financials remain a good starting point for the due diligence. The pro forma financials are also an opportunity to present the selling corporation as having given the disentanglement a good amount of careful thought and planning based on their operational experience, which builds credibility and confidence with the potential acquirers.

(c) TYING THE PRO FORMA INCOME STATEMENT TO INTERNALLY REPORTED RESULTS: BRIDGE SCHEDULE   If pro forma financials are the basis of presentation of the divested business in the offering materials, the selling corporation should prepare a "bridge schedule" that allows potential buyers to see the adjustments that have been made to the reported financial results. This bridge schedule should be in the data room along with the other financial materials, with the adjustments clearly explained and documented, as it will be an important aspect of the financial due diligence. The bridge schedule typically begins with the income statement as internally reported, to present the

	Revenues	Expenses	Operating Income
Income statement as internally reported	$x	$x	$x
Add or Subtract: Carve-out audit adjustments	+/− $x	+/− $x	+/− $x
Subtract: Internal cost allocations for services provided by other business units		− $x	+ $x
Add: Estimated costs to provide services on a stand-alone basis		+ $x	− $x
Add or Subtract: Nonrecurring or unusual items	+/− $x	+/− $x	+/− $x
Pro forma income statement on a stand-alone basis	$x	$x	$x

Exhibit 5.8   Illustrative Bridge Schedule

divested business "as management views it," and then makes a series of adjustments to arrive at the pro forma income statement. The types of adjustments often seen are presented in Exhibit 5.8 and are described in the points that follow.

- **Income statement as internally reported**. The starting point for the bridge schedule is revenues, expenses, and operating income from the income statement used for internal financial reporting. In the financial due diligence, the acquirer will normally start by looking at the same income statement that management uses to run the business. The acquirer will often tie this income statement to the general ledger to ensure what is presented truly comes from the selling corporation's internal reporting process. As a result, any financials presented to the acquirer that deviate from the general ledger should be reconciled on a step-by-step basis through a bridge schedule.
- **Carve-out audit adjustments.** As discussed in section 4.3(g), acquirers often require a carve-out financial statement audit of

the divested business covering the most recent two or three years. Although most selling corporations have an annual audit of their consolidated financial statements, having an audit done of the specific business being divested is an extra step, one that can have a major impact on the timing of the transaction. (It also can be a costly step. The team should ensure the estimated carve-out audit expenses are included in the divestiture cost summary discussed in section 5.6(a).)

The carve-out audit also results in a set of financial statements different from the ones used for internal reporting. For example, the carve-out audit involves a much more detailed level of scope, so the auditors can find and recommend adjustments that were not identified in the course of normal reporting. Additionally, in preparing the carve-out financial statements, it is possible that a different methodology for allocating shared corporate service costs to the divested business may be utilized.

- **Internal cost allocations.** The purpose of this adjustment is to remove the internal cost allocations for shared services and replace them with the estimated stand-alone costs.
- **Estimated stand-alone costs.** As discussed earlier, the estimated stand-alone costs are initially developed for purposes of the offering document and management presentation based on high-level estimates. As the disentanglement plan is more fully developed, these costs should be periodically updated to ensure that the ballpark figure given to acquirers still holds up after detailed plans have been formulated. It is especially important, when the transaction involves a financial acquirer, that the selling corporation update its stand-alone cost estimates based on the informed opinion of its cross-functional team.
- **Nonrecurring or unusual items.** The income statement may include income or expenses from unusual one-time events, such as costs related to the sale of the business, restructuring charges, or insurance claims, which will not recur. In preparing the pro forma income statement, the seller is usually advised to normalize the financials to exclude these items, since they do not represent the normal run rate of the divested business. This step also allows the selling corporation to frame how the

acquirer will approach its quality of earnings analysis in the financial diligence.

- **Pro forma income statement on stand-alone basis.** The result of the bridge schedule represents the selling corporation's best thinking about the run rate of the business if it were audited and on a stand-alone basis, with no unusual or nonrecurring aspects. This will be the jumping off point for the valuation and discussions of valuation multiples. While the acquirer will seek to develop its own view of the appropriateness of these adjustments, it is much better to have the acquirer check and validate the selling corporation's bridge schedule than to have each reconciling item discovered in due diligence raised as a surprise. Preparing the bridge schedule can also help keep the acquirer's efforts honest, ensuring, for example, that the acquirer does not propose adjustments in only one direction, that of seeking to lower the purchase price.

5.7 EXECUTING THE DISENTANGLEMENT PLAN

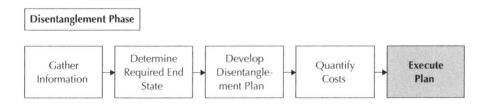

(a) **POSTCLOSING STATE: KEY AGREEMENTS** Once the identity, capabilities, and integration strategy of the acquirer are known, plans for the transition of each interdependent function are finalized and implemented. For certain functions, the plan will be to terminate support with the close. In these cases, the selling corporation has chosen to build stand-alone capabilities or to rely on the acquirer to assume them immediately. For other functions, there is a transition services agreement, an agreement to provide postclosing support for a limited period. And for other functions, the parties may reach a commercial agreement to continue service for a longer period. This postclosing state is illustrated in Exhibit 5.9.

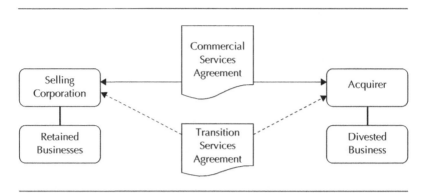

EXHIBIT 5.9   POSTCLOSING RELATIONSHIPS

(b) OPERATIONAL CONSIDERATIONS IN IMPLEMENTING THE DISENTANGLEMENT PLAN Depending on the particular circumstances and plans of the selling corporation, the implementation of the disentanglement plan can become an extraordinarily complex and time-consuming task. Several suggestions may be worth considering as the team embarks on this phase of the divestiture.

- **Complexity and change requires ongoing communication.** Regular communication is critical to the success of any significant corporate activity, and the disentanglement plan is no exception. The cross-functional project team needs to meet regularly, and those who are accountable for disentangling each function need to raise any issues or new information on a timely basis. As the teams look deeply into each function, they inevitably come across new or unexpected aspects of the disentanglement, for which timely decisions need to be made. The team will be most successful if it is organized to be reactive, responsive, and fluid within a complex and changing environment.
- **It is never too early to start the disentanglement planning.** In the first meeting of the cross-functional team, a comment often heard is "We need to wait until we know more about the acquirer until we can do anything." Only when prodded to think through the various areas and issues relating to disentanglement will team members begin to see the areas where certain

actions should be planned for, initiated, or even completed regardless of the acquirer's identity or plans. Starting disentanglement planning early takes a lot of pressure off the entire process and reduces the possibility of something material being overlooked.

- **Have backup plans ready.** In the best case, the team will think through what it might do for each major function if the acquirer's integration strategy requires a change in the disentanglement approach or timing. This applies not only to areas where the selling corporation plans to purchase services from the acquirer but also to any element of the disentanglement plan where the acquirer will be relied on. The cross-functional team needs to maintain awareness that the disentanglement and transition is just another element of the divestiture that gets negotiated. The operational executives might have a preference for how a particular function is best disentangled, but that approach will happen only if both parties to the transaction agree to it. Flexibility and adaptability to change and modify plans may well be required.

- **Be aware that management of the divested business and the selling corporation may have conflicting objectives.** The team should be aware that there may be conflict between the managers remaining with the selling corporation and those going with the divested business, as these two groups seek to agree on the details of the disentanglement strategy. The managers of the divested business may feel distracted about their personal job situation during this time, which may create tension between individuals. Additionally, the business interests of the two organizations may diverge: The approach best for the divested business may not be the one that is best for the selling corporation.

    The core divestiture team leader will serve as the arbiter of any such disagreements, and should ensure that the resolution of these items is clearly documented and communicated to the broader team to avoid confusion once a particular solution has been determined.

KEY POINTS

1. Disentangling a divested business is more arduous than integrating an acquired business, because it usually entails more complexity and imposes tighter time constraints on the divestiture team. Most of the operational planning, and certain implementation, steps, therefore, must occur prior to the close of the transaction. (Section 5.1)

2. Identifying a large, complex interdependency late in the deal process puts undue pressure on both the business operation and on the transaction team. To mitigate this undesirable but real possibility, the team should apply sufficient diligence in the initial review, employing a cross-functional team. The focus should be on both business processes and on the assets that underlie those processes. (Section 5.3)

3. Is it in the selling corporation's interest to transition interdependent functions toward self-sufficiency, or does it make more sense to do as little as possible before the close of the transaction, and allow the acquirer to assume the burden of integrating the function? The answer depends on the divestiture structure, the capabilities of potential acquirers, and the particular requirements of the selling corporation. (Section 5.4)

4. Timing is the key consideration for the team as it formulates the detailed disentanglement plan. (Section 5.5)

5. There are two essential financial aspects to be considered: the one-time costs and the run-rate expense implications for the divested business. (Section 5.6)

6. For certain functions, the plan will be to terminate support with the close. In these cases, the selling corporation has chosen to build stand-alone capabilities or to rely on the

acquirer to assume them immediately. For other functions, there is a transition services agreement, an agreement to provide postclosing support for a limited period. And for other functions, the parties may reach a commercial agreement to continue service for a longer period. (Section 5.7)

CHAPTER 6

MANAGING THE SELLING PROCESS

6.1 SELLING PROCESS: SHOW TIME

Thus far, we have detailed an extensive process for planning and preparing for the divestiture transaction. In Chapter 3, we discussed planning activities such as the development of the board paper, organization plan, retention plan, and communication plan. We covered transactional preparation, which includes retaining advisors, drafting marketing materials, and preparing for due diligence, in Chapter 4. We then turned our focus to preparing for the operational separation of the divested business from its parent organization in Chapter 5. Here, in Chapter 6, planning and preparation culminate with the initiation of the selling process.

The public announcement of the selling corporation's intent to divest one or more of its business units signals the start of "show time" for the divestiture team. Leading up to the announcement, virtually all of the preparatory activities have been performed by a small team in a highly confidential setting. However, once the public announcement is made, the environment changes dramatically. Most of the process will now occur on a stage. From this point forward, the divestiture team's words and actions will be subject to scrutiny by an audience, and this audience's reaction can significantly increase or decrease the value of the deal.

As discussed in section 3.8, the audience of parties interested in the divestiture actually consists of several constituent groups, each having unique concerns. In order to inspire the enthusiasm and confidence of these groups, the selling corporation must adapt its messages to address each set of concerns.

For example, shareholders pay close attention to what is said about the selling corporation's strategy. This group wants to understand how the divestiture fits into the corporation's long-term plans. The shift in focus away from the divested business is expected to be accompanied by an indication of which segment(s) of the business will receive greater emphasis for future growth. Put succinctly, shareholders want to know how the divestiture will increase the corporation's value.

Potential buyers, however, are more interested in what is said about the divested business. They want to know why this is an attractive investment opportunity for them and may need to be convinced that the selling corporation is not just trying to rid itself of a troubled business.

Employees of the selling corporation, particularly those who are part of the divested business, have their own set of concerns. They will have many questions about how the divestiture will affect them personally, and the announcement may provoke a strong emotional reaction from them. As a result, employees of the divested business unit need both information and reassurance, delivered with empathy and respect. The divestiture team should not underestimate how quickly and easily employees of the divested business can become distracted after the public announcement.

Not only will the selling corporation's words be studied and evaluated, but so will its behavior following the announcement. The best way to continue to send a positive message about the divestiture is to follow the initial announcement with an efficient sale process, with speed and certainty of closing being the most important factors. Once the divestiture is announced, an extended period with no news from the selling corporation is likely to portend a problem. Knowing that the divestiture process is observed closely, the team needs to manage the sale process in a way that sustains momentum. A capable broker will make a major contribution toward this goal, utilizing its experience and savvy to shepherd potential buyers through a well-defined sale process and holding participants to tight timelines. The divestiture team will also see its extensive planning and preparation contribute significantly to a smooth selling process.

The public nature of the selling phase of the divestiture significantly raises the stakes for the transaction. An organization that delivers a positive initial message to its stakeholders and sustains momentum with a well-managed sale process has a much better chance of optimizing shareholders' value than one that suffers from a lack of attention, planning, and discipline. Consequently, we will emphasize two critical success factors in this chapter: effective, tailored communications, and an efficient, disciplined sale process.

6.2 SELLING PROCESS STEPS

In section 4.6(b), we discussed the typical options for approaching the sale of a business unit. These options range from a preemptive process involving a single buyer, to a public auction, which could attract a large number of participants. While these approaches differ in the number of potential buyers involved, they are similar in terms of how the selling process is conducted. Specifically, most sale processes tend to follow a two-step format. In the first step, potential acquirers are solicited to submit an initial valuation, or valuation range, based on preliminary information that has been provided. If the valuation is directionally acceptable, the selling corporation invites the potential acquirer(s) to proceed to the second step, which consists of a closer look at the business leading to a definitive offer.

Even if the field of potential acquirers consists of a few organizations, or only one, a two-step process still makes sense because it prevents wasted time. Neither buyer nor seller wants to engage in an expensive and time-consuming due diligence process only to find that the parties' respective views about the valuation of the business are not even in the same ballpark. By providing for a preliminary offer based on summary-level information, both parties can quickly determine whether there is a basis for proceeding. If the discussions do move forward, the parties will enter the second stage confident that a successful deal is attainable and worth the additional effort. Conversely, if the valuation is not mutually acceptable, participants can walk away from the discussions without having expended significant time or money.

Since many sales follow this type of approach or some variant of it, we have modeled this chapter to follow a two-step sale process, which typically includes 10 elements:

1. **Final preparation.** Before publicly announcing the prospective divestiture, the team ensures certain key things have happened, namely: (a) approval of final marketing materials and communications plans, (b) completion of audits, (c) signing retention agreements with key staff, and (d) coordination of the timing of the announcement with corporate management.

2. **Making the announcement.** When the selling corporation announces its intention to sell one or more of its business units, it implements its communications plan, directing targeted messages to specific internal and external stakeholder groups.

3. **Contacting potential buyers and distributing marketing materials.** This activity, when the broker approaches prospective acquirers and distributes offering materials, initiates the first step of the two-step selling process.

4. **Soliciting and evaluating initial indications of interest.** At a time specified by the broker, potential acquirers submit initial bids, usually in the form of nonbinding indications of interest. The broker evaluates the bids and reviews them with the selling corporation.

5. **Inviting bidders into the second round.** In this stage, the second step of the two-step selling process, a select group is invited to conduct due diligence, where prospective acquirers are provided access to more detailed information and then asked to make final, definitive offers for.

6. **Due diligence.** The due diligence process normally includes a management presentation, access to a data room, and the ability to ask follow-up questions, providing potential acquirers a level of access to the details of the business that is intended to be sufficient to enable them to finalize their valuations.

7. **Distributing the draft purchase agreement.** Sometime during the course of due diligence, the broker distributes a draft of the purchase agreement to the second-round participants. This draft agreement specifies the terms under which the selling corporation would be willing to close the transaction. Bidders are directed to mark up this draft with their proposed changes.

8. **Evaluating definitive offers.** In this step, the selling corporation uses the competitive nature of the auction to optimize offers, not only in terms of price but also in terms of proposed changes, or mark-ups, to the purchase agreement. Assuming two offers have a similar valuation, the offer containing fewer mark-ups to the agreement will be viewed more favorably by the selling corporation.

9. **Negotiations.** In speaking to the bidders about their offers, the broker will normally focus mainly on the valuation. Although bidders usually are asked to submit their best and final offer, the broker can, and often does, ask them to improve their offers, especially if several are in the same price range. If a bidder has an attractive financial offer but an onerous contract mark-up, it is conceivable that it could also be asked to revisit its mark-up in certain areas. At this point, one or possibly two players are selected to perform the remainder of their diligence and to begin to negotiate the purchase agreement.

10. **Confirmatory due diligence.** Simply stated, confirmatory due diligence includes any activities the potential acquirer needs to complete in order to close the transaction. Brokers distinguish this element of the diligence as "confirmatory" because this work is expected to confirm or validate information that has already been factored in to the bidder's valuation. Accordingly, offers are not expected to change as a result of confirmatory diligence findings.

These steps can be categorized into four major groups of activity, which are discussed in detail in this chapter and are summarized in Exhibit 6.1.

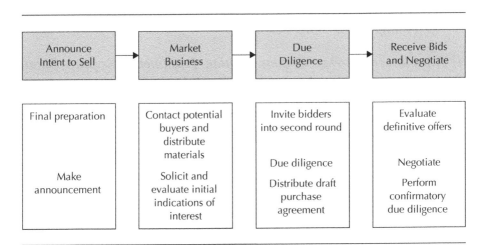

EXHIBIT 6.1 SELLING PROCESS STEPS AND CONSIDERATIONS

6.3 ANNOUNCING THE INTENTION TO SELL

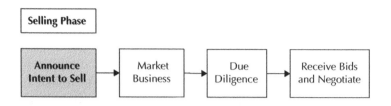

(a) FINAL PREPARATION   Once the corporation announces its intention to make the divestiture, the deal will begin to take on a life of its own. In the days and weeks following the initial announcement, the team's time can be dominated by interaction with various process participants and stakeholders, requiring its efforts to be largely reactive. This level of distraction is inevitable. Knowing this, the team should make sure its full attention is available for the postannouncement period. One good way to accomplish this is to methodically conduct a final review, designed to ensure that these key preparatory activities have been addressed before the announcement takes place:

- Announcement-day communication documents
- Marketing materials
- Audits
- Employee retention agreements
- Timing of the announcement

(i) Announcement-Day Communication Documents Require Final Corporate Approval.   As discussed in section 3.8, the communications planning process generates a number of deliverables. Each of these deliverables, such as the internal and external announcements, question-and-answer documents, PowerPoint slides and scripts for live presentations, and employee information packages, should be reviewed and formally approved to ensure consistency with the core messages developed for the divestiture. Reviewers of the communications documents should include corporate communications, investor relations, executive management, employment counsel, and human resources. There will likely be many things going on across the corporation that may affect strategic positioning, requiring this group to place the

divestiture announcement into the context of the overall public story the corporation wants to tell about its strategy and initiatives.

An important internal deliverable that the team should also include in this review is the employee information package, which details how employees' compensation and benefits will be impacted as a result of the divestiture. This package should include an individualized statement (e.g., calculations of vested retirement benefits, accrued vacation benefits, etc.) along with a question-and-answer document, which explains what is currently known about how employee benefits will be impacted by the divestiture and also noting items that cannot be determined until the acquirer is identified. Distributing such a package immediately after the announcement, even if some of the details cannot be finalized until later in the divestiture process, will go a long way toward alleviating employee concerns. Without such a proactive approach, the human resources group can expect to be besieged with employee compensation and benefit questions.

(ii) Final Marketing Materials Should Be Reviewed and Signed Off. The marketing materials (i.e., the teaser and offering document) form the divested business's first impression with potential buyers. As such, the marketing materials must have a persuasive, motivating effect. They should portray the business in the best possible light, demonstrating the upside opportunity of ownership to potential buyers.

At the same time, the marketing materials constitute the initial fact base against which due diligence activities will later be performed, and for certain transactions they will be examined by regulators as well. So the materials need to be both *persuasive* and *factual*. In order to achieve both objectives, the team should ensure that the marketing materials are positively positioned and have been reviewed and approved, and that the accuracy of all key facts have been verified.

The divestiture team should complete the review of the teaser and offering document before the announcement is made. Otherwise, team members may feel pressured to rush through their review, so that potential acquirers are not kept waiting once they start asking the broker for a copy of the "book."

While it is beneficial for the entire divestiture team to review and comment on the marketing materials, the most important reviewers are from the executive management, legal, and finance functions.

- **Executive management.** Executive management should review and approve the offering document's rationale for the divestiture to ensure consistency with its planned announcement messages and that the document sufficiently highlights the value of the business (especially the Investment Considerations and Development Potential sections, described in section 4.5(c)). Management should also closely review how the market is defined and how competition is characterized, as this is the section that may receive regulatory scrutiny for transactions above a certain size. (See section 7.7(b) for further discussion of antitrust regulations.)

  As discussed in section 4.8, another area requiring management's judgment and concurrence is the amount of proprietary information divulged. Even in a limited auction, numerous parties will ask for and receive copies of the offering document, some with the objective of attaining a competitive advantage from the information revealed about the divested business. Although recipients are bound by confidentiality agreements, the selling corporation should nevertheless explicitly determine the level of information it is comfortable including in the offering document, withholding the most sensitive information (e.g., identity of customers, key employees, pricing) until a later stage in the process.

- **Legal.** As mentioned, transactions above a certain size are subject to regulatory review, making it essential in these instances for the internal and/or external legal advisors to examine all of the marketing materials before they are finalized. Even for smaller transactions, it is still prudent to have the appropriate members of the legal team review all key documents related to the divestiture, as they provide useful context and sometimes flag issues for later consideration when the contracts and agreements are being negotiated and structured. Moreover, while the offering document and teaser are essentially marketing pieces, and despite their inclusion of disclaimers, the legal team may still want to vet the supportability of certain statements made in these materials so that the selling corporation does not unwittingly create a credibility gap.

- **Finance.** The finance representatives on the divestiture team can be useful as a quality control monitor for the marketing materials. Finance has primary responsibility for the accuracy of the historical results and forecasts as well as any financial facts quoted in the narrative sections of the document. Additionally, given its knowledge of the operations and relationships across the organization, finance can also serve as a liaison to managers within the divested business, having these managers verify information or operating statistics for areas within their responsibility. This review will minimize the possibility of any inconsistencies or conflicts between information potential buyers will see in the offering documents and the supporting information that will be in the data room.

(iii) Carve-out Audit Should Be Complete, or Nearly So.   It is preferable for the carve-out audit to be completed before the announcement so that the audited financial statements can be incorporated into the marketing materials.

This, however, can create a timing problem, with the completion of the audit being the single event holding up the announcement of the divestiture. Consider a typical timeline. If brokers and accountants are engaged at approximately the same time, the broker usually can complete its information gathering and draft the offering document within a four- to eight-week time frame. A carve-out audit, however, normally requires a *minimum* of 12 weeks to complete, possibly much longer if the audit covers two or three years or if it does not proceed smoothly. This means that all other preparations for the announcement can be in place, ready to go, and then the team might have to wait for an additional month or more for the audit to be completed. This is the reason for our recommendation, in section 4.3(e), that the team arrange to have the audit initiated at the earliest possible moment—as soon as approval to divest the business is received.

If the audit is still in progress when the corporation is otherwise ready to make the announcement, the broker, in its zeal to get the selling process started, may recommend releasing the marketing materials using unaudited numbers and providing the audited accounts to potential buyers later in the process. This is because the audit does not technically have to be completed until later in the process, usually in order for the acquirer's financing to be finalized. However, the divestiture team should consider using unaudited financials in the marketing materials only if several conditions are satisfied:

- The team should be *highly* confident there will be no material audit adjustments. The existence of significant audit adjustments after distribution of the offering document can undermine bidders' confidence and potentially alter their valuation of the business. There is usually a point in the fieldwork when the auditors can inform the divestiture team that they have identified most of the major adjustments. The team should avoid publishing the marketing materials before this point.

- The team should be reasonably certain about how much additional time is required to complete the audit. If the audit is still in progress when the selling process starts, the audit's completion suddenly becomes a deliverable that will be monitored closely by potential acquirers. Any delay in the completion of the audit is likely to erode the confidence of the bidders, causing them to extend their other due diligence efforts and further slowing the sale process.

- The team must be comfortable with its capacity to support the remaining audit activities while also accommodating the potential acquirers' due diligence requirements. Once the offering document is completed, ideally all of the accounting and finance teams' energy should be focused on supporting the soon-to-come buyer diligence process. A financial staff that remains distracted by the completion of the carve-out audit has significantly less capacity to support the preliminary diligence, which could hamper the selling process.

(iv) Key Employee Retention Arrangements Should Be in Place.   Key employees, typically the senior managers of the divested business who will be offered retention/incentive plans, should be signed up before the announcement is made. These managers must be counted on for their leadership, and they will be positively motivated by the knowledge that they are being treated fairly by the corporation. Other employees of the divested business will look closely at this group for signs of their support, or lack of support, for the divestiture transaction. Another reason this team needs to be signed before the announcement is they will be put to work on the divestiture immediately. Consequently, they should not be distracted and potentially demotivated by concerns about their own situation.

(v) Timing of the Announcement Should Be Coordinated with Corporate Management.   Once the communications documents, offering materials, audits, and retention agreements are reviewed, approved, and completed, the final preparatory matter is coordinating the timing of the announcement with the parent corporation. Corporations normally prefer to orchestrate their public agenda, so there will likely be a specific viewpoint on the timing of the divestiture announcement. For example, there may be other acquisitions or disposals planned or under way, and the corporation may want to combine the several transactions into one narrative that emphasizes the execution of its strategy.

Another possibility is the corporation may wish to include the divestiture announcement into its scheduled release of quarterly earnings, utilizing an already-established mechanism for delivering the corporation's results and key messages to many of the same stakeholders (e.g., investors, analysts, and media). Doing this ensures that all investors hear the same message at the same time, and in the context of the corporation's broader narrative. Additionally, if the disposal is recorded as a discontinued operation (see related discussion in section 7.4(b)), the end of a quarter is a very convenient time to make the announcement and simultaneously disclose the operating results of the corporation's continuing operations, separated from the divested business.

(b) MAKING THE ANNOUNCEMENT   Beginning with the announcement, the divestiture process transforms from a tightly controlled and confidential effort to one that is conducted in full view of a number of stakeholder groups. The divestiture team should think of its management of the logistics of the announcement as the first public demonstration of the corporation's ability to conduct a well-planned and smoothly run divestiture process.

(i) Managing the Announcement Logistics.   A member of the divestiture team should be responsible for managing the logistics of the

announcement and coordinating the involvement of executive management, corporate communications, investor relations, and human resources. This coordinator should prepare an announcement logistics schedule, specifying the timing of meetings, presentations, and release of the announcement documents. The schedule should cover relevant activities leading up to the announcement, those occurring on announcement day itself, and those planned for the days following. An illustrative announcement logistics schedule is shown in Exhibit 6.2.

In the several-week period leading up to the announcement, the primary tasks include securing venues and planning the communications logistics, such as webcasts or conference calls. Additionally, as discussed in section 6.3(a), the coordinator should ensure that all communications documents have received the required corporate approvals.

Announcement-day activities are divided between the external announcement to the public and internal communication with employees. The public announcement is fairly straightforward. If the transaction is small, the corporation can announce its intent to divest by issuing the press release. For a larger deal, the announcement can be made in a live meeting, often combined with other corporate announcements as discussed earlier.

The employee announcement, however, may require more detailed logistical planning. It is strongly preferable for employees of the divested business to hear the announcement directly from a senior executive. Employees' sensitivities will be quite high at this time, and they may take personally or misread what may well be innocent oversights in the announcement meeting logistics. While the employees may not be happy to hear the announcement initially, they will appreciate an executive traveling to their location and directly explaining to them the rationale for the divestiture. If it is not possible to have an executive present at every location affected by the sale, all employees, including those who are not in the office, should have the opportunity to connect to the live announcement through a conference call, video conference, or webcast. The divestiture team should not allow its members to become so busy with the transaction that they overlook the details that can shape employee perceptions.

Date/Time	Task	Responsibility	Key Documents	Comments
X weeks prior to announcement	Arrange for venues, webcast, and/or video conference for external and internal announcement meetings	Corporate communications, operating management	Vendor contracts	
X days prior to announcement	Obtain all necessary corporate approvals of announcement documents	Corporate communications, HR management	All communications documents	
1 day prior to external announcement—late in day	Make internal announcement to employees of divested business	Senior executive	PowerPoint slides and scripts	Ideally, employees of the divested business should be informed prior to the public announcement by a senior executive, in person (if not prohibited by SEC or other guidelines)
Announcement day—at opening of business	Make internal announcement to employees of selling corporation	Senior executive	Internal announcements	Internal announcement to unaffected employees may be via a written communication

Exhibit 6.2 Illustrative Announcement Logistics Schedule (Continued)

Date/Time	Task	Responsibility	Key Documents	Comments
Announcement day	Make external announcement	Senior corporate management, investor relations	Press release, PowerPoint slides and scripts	May be live or written, depending on size and importance of business
Announcement day	Follow-up meetings with employees of divested business	Business unit management, HR management	Question-and-answer documents, employee benefits packets	Departmental meetings and group meetings with HR, as required.
Postannouncement	Calls/visits with key customers and vendors	Business unit management	Customer and vendor communications	
Postannouncement	Receive external inquiries	Broker, investor relations, corporate communications	Question-and-answer documents	Potential bidders routed to broker: others to investor relations or corporate communications
Postannouncement	Receive internal inquiries	Business unit management, HR	Question-and-answer documents	

EXHIBIT 6.2 ILLUSTRATIVE ANNOUNCEMENT LOGISTICS SCHEDULE

Postannouncement activities include both outbound communications, such as outreach to important customers and vendors, and inbound communications, such as handling inquiries from potential bidders, or from employees. Clear accountability should be assigned for each area, and communications materials such as question-and-answer documents should be distributed to the relevant parties to ensure that the team's messages are consistent. It should be made clear in the various announcement-day materials where internal and external inquiries ought to be directed.

(ii) Delivering a Consistent Message: Message Triangle.   Once the written communications are completed and the logistical details are in place, all that remains is to deliver the announcements. As mentioned earlier, the external announcement may or may not be done through a live presentation, depending on the size and importance of the business, while the internal announcement should be a live event. Even if the external announcement is done by means of a press release, however, the selling corporation should prepare its team to field follow-up questions.

An effective enabling mechanism for the corporation's spokespeople to deliver a consistent message and reinforce it after the announcement (whether in live question-and-answer sessions following the presentations, in interviews, or in follow-up conversations) is to use a well-established media training tool, the message triangle. A message triangle is a useful visual aid and an extremely shorthand way to distill the corporation's intended message about the divestiture into a few points on one sheet of paper. It normally contains three core messages, with supporting points aligned to support one of these messages. This allows the corporation's representatives to stay on message rather than get sidetracked by questions, which will hit them from a number of different perspectives. Separate message triangles should be developed for external audiences and internal audiences.

The key external audiences consist of shareholders, potential acquirers, customers, and vendors. Shareholders are fundamentally concerned with how the divestiture will increase the corporation's value, so they will want to know the selling corporation's strategic rationale for the deal and how the proceeds will be used (e.g., to make

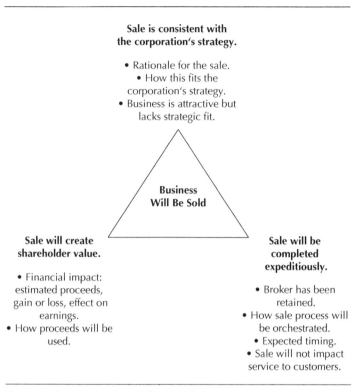

Sale is consistent with
the corporation's strategy.

- Rationale for the sale.
  - How this fits the
  corporation's strategy.
- Business is attractive but
  lacks strategic fit.

Business
Will Be Sold

Sale will create
shareholder value.

- Financial impact:
  estimated proceeds,
  gain or loss, effect on
  earnings.
- How proceeds will be
  used.

Sale will be
completed
expeditiously.

- Broker has been
  retained.
- How sale process will
  be orchestrated.
- Expected timing.
- Sale will not impact
  service to customers.

EXHIBIT 6.3   ILLUSTRATIVE MESSAGE TRIANGLE FOR AN
EXTERNAL AUDIENCE

other acquisitions, pay down debt, pay dividends, or fund share repur-
chase programs). If the divested business is presented as unaligned
with the corporation's strategy, shareholders will also expect the sale
to be completed quickly so that the selling corporation can focus on
its growth strategy. Potential acquirers, conversely, want to hear less
about the selling corporation's strategy and more about the divested
business, and whether this is a good investment opportunity for them.
Customers and vendors mainly want assurance that the sale process
will not cause an interruption or result in a change in the level of service to which they have grown accustomed.

A message triangle for external audiences, as illustrated in
Exhibit 6.3, might address these concerns and interests through several
core messages:

- The sale is consistent with the corporation's strategy.
- The sale will create shareholder value.
- The sale will be completed expeditiously.

Note how the supporting points reinforce the core messages while addressing particular concerns, such as the attractiveness of the divested business and the expectation that customer service will not be interrupted.

The internal audience consists of the employees of the selling corporation, with the employees of the divested business being most centrally involved. The employees of the divested business are likely to receive the announcement of the intent to divest as a blow to their organizational pride, wondering if the sale signals a problem with the business. They will also have many concerns about their jobs and their benefits. In contrast to the external audiences, employees' questions about the divestiture will be much more personal in nature.

Another internal group not to be ignored is employees of the retained business units of the selling corporation. Although senior executives who are involved in the corporation's strategic portfolio analysis know whether any additional business units are being considered for disposal, most employees probably do not. Employees seemingly unaffected by the divestiture, therefore, will listen closely to the corporation's rationale for hints about whether other units might be considered for sale.

A message triangle for internal audiences, as illustrated in Exhibit 6.4, might address these concerns by developing core messages directly aimed at the employees' likely questions:

- Why is the business being sold?
- How will the employees be affected?
- What will the next steps be?

Note that the main message themes are similar to those for external audiences, but are framed in a much more personal way, addressing more directly what the internal audience really wants to hear. The corporation should point to the potential benefits of being owned by an enthusiastic acquirer, but should also be honest about the fact that many questions cannot be answered until the acquirer is identified.

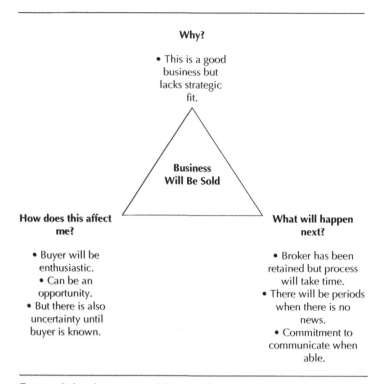

Why?

• This is a good business but lacks strategic fit.

Business Will Be Sold

How does this affect me?

• Buyer will be enthusiastic.
• Can be an opportunity.
• But there is also uncertainty until buyer is known.

What will happen next?

• Broker has been retained but process will take time.
• There will be periods when there is no news.
• Commitment to communicate when able.

EXHIBIT 6.4: ILLUSTRATIVE MESSAGE TRIANGLE FOR AN INTERNAL AUDIENCE

Another critical aspect of the message is to shape employee expectations about when and how they will receive updates about the sale as the process proceeds. Employees should receive a commitment that the corporation will keep them informed, but should also be told that the corporation will not be at liberty to speak to them during certain periods, as is usual during the sale of a business.

6.4 MARKETING THE BUSINESS

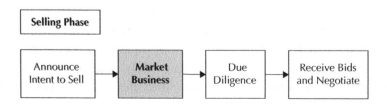

Selling Phase

| Announce Intent to Sell | **Market Business** | Due Diligence | Receive Bids and Negotiate |

(a) CONTACTING POTENTIAL BUYERS AND DISTRIBUTING MATERIALS The selling corporation and its broker normally develop a list of potential acquirers during the preparation stage. Once the announcement is made, the broker immediately approaches these prospective acquirers to gauge their level of interest. The broker and the selling corporation may also field inquiries from other interested parties who become aware of the availability of the business, supplementing their outbound marketing efforts.

Once an organization expresses interest, the broker sends out the first component of the marketing materials, the teaser, which is described in section 4.5(b). The teaser is a very brief document containing just enough information to generate interest, but which includes nothing that the selling corporation judges to be sensitive or proprietary. If the teaser accomplishes its objective and generates continued interest from the potential acquirer, the next step is for the organization to execute a confidentiality agreement, often referred to as a nondisclosure agreement (NDA). The NDA must be executed in order for the potential acquirer to receive more detailed, proprietary information upon which to base an initial offer.

(i) Nondisclosure Agreement. The selling corporation, depending on the scale of the process, may execute several dozen NDAs with potential acquirers as it seeks to establish a competitive auction. By definition, every one of these organizations except for one will not acquire the divested business. So there is a need to establish legal protection against the damage an unsuccessful acquirer can create by disclosing this information or by using the information or access to employees to compete with the divested business.

The NDA is the first legally binding agreement executed by the selling corporation and the potential acquirer. It requires the potential acquirer not to disclose any information deemed to be confidential as well as the existence and the contents of the deal discussions, and also prevents the potential acquirer from hiring or soliciting employees of the selling corporation (known as the no-poach provision.) These restrictions may endure for several years. Exhibit 6.5 includes an outline of the typical elements of the NDA agreement. Most of the terms of the NDA (such as the definition of, and the limitations on, what is

Purpose

The purpose for disclosing the confidential information is the consideration of a possible transaction between the parties.

Information

The information being disclosed is nonpublic, confidential, and proprietary.

Access

The information shall be kept confidential and transmitted only to representatives on a need-to-know basis.

Return

Recipient agrees to keep a record of the location of the information, and to return it on request, destroying any analyses that incorporate the information.

Limitation

The confidential information does not include information that: (1) is or becomes public knowledge; (2) becomes available through a third party that is not bound to confidentiality; or (3) is independently developed.

Disclosure

A process is described for disclosing the information if the recipient is legally compelled to do so.

Confidentiality

This section specifies what is not to be disclosed. For example: (1) the existence of the contents of the agreement; (2) the fact that the information exists and has been made available; (3) the fact that discussions are taking place; and (4) any term, condition, or other fact related to the potential transaction.

No Liability or Obligation

The recipient recognizes that the disclosing company will conduct the selling process at its sole discretion and has no liability or other obligation as a result of signing the NDA.

Specific Performance

Monetary damages may not be adequate in case of a breach of the agreement and that the disclosing company is entitled to relief by way of injunction or specific performance.

EXHIBIT 6.5   NONDISCLOSURE AGREEMENT (NDA)—ILLUSTRATIVE OUTLINE (CONTINUED)

No Contract

No contracts exists until, and unless, there is a definitive agreement.

No Representation

The disclosing company is making no representation or warranty about the accuracy or completeness of the information.

Governing Law

A specified state will have jurisdiction over the agreement.

Severability

If one provision of the NDA is invalid or unenforceable, it will not affect any other provision.

No Poach

The party receiving the confidential information will not solicit or hire [any, or a specified group] employees of the [disclosing company, or a specified division] for an [agreed period] of time.

Counterparts

Each party can sign a separate copy of the NDA, and each copy will be deemed an original.

Entire Agreement

The NDA represents the entire understanding between the parties.

EXHIBIT 6.5   NONDISCLOSURE AGREEMENT (NDA)—ILLUSTRATIVE OUTLINE

deemed confidential information, the restrictions on the parties, and the procedures if discussions terminate) are fairly noncontroversial. Where the difficulty usually comes is in the no-poach provision.

The no-poach provision is normally the first item that the potential buyer and seller have to negotiate. From the selling corporation's perspective, the no-poach provision should be written as broadly as possible—for example, covering any employee, whether involved in the sale or not, for as long as possible. From the potential bidder's perspective, the fact that it has entered into potential acquisition discussions should not impair its hiring practices, so it prefers as narrow a no-poach provision as possible—for example, covering only employees it meets or becomes aware of during the diligence, and for a short period of time. Also, the potential acquirer may want to provide for an exception, or carve-out, in case employees come to its attention as a result of normal, broad-based solicitations, such as job advertisements or company Web sites. Negotiations of no-poach provisions can become a significant impediment for some potential acquirers, especially for large organizations that may find such agreements cumbersome to internally administer.

(ii) Distributing the Offering Document and the Preliminary Process Letter.   Once the NDA is executed, the potential acquirers can begin to receive what is classified as confidential information about the divested business. The first piece of confidential information is the offering document (described in section 4.5(c)), which is also known as the confidential information memorandum to underscore that this information is covered by the terms of the nondisclosure agreement.

The broker usually distributes a letter along with the offering document, the preliminary process letter, which describes the first round of the bidding process for the participants. In the preliminary process letter, the broker establishes a specific time deadline and other requirements for the initial round of bidding and describes how the remainder of the sale process will be conducted for the parties that are invited to participate in the second round. Exhibit 6.6 contains an illustrative outline of a preliminary process letter.

(b) SOLICITING AND EVALUATING INITIAL INDICATIONS OF INTEREST   At the time specified, the broker will receive initial bids for the business. These bids are normally received in the form of a nonbinding indication of interest (IOI), which states the valuation (or range) at which the bidder would be willing to acquire the business. The IOI is signed by the bidder but is not countersigned by the selling corporation, since at this point there is no legal agreement between the parties, other than the nondisclosure agreement, which covers the confidential information evaluated in making the bid.

The exact form of the IOI can vary, since it usually is shaped to be responsive to the requirements contained in the bid instructions. Thus, IOIs can differ greatly in terms of how much detail they contain.

Invitation

Broker has been retained as financial advisor to Selling Corporation for the potential sale of _____ business unit and is inviting recipients to submit a preliminary, nonbinding Indication of Interest (IOI), outlining the terms under which they would propose acquiring the business. IOIs should be submitted [when] [how] [to whom].

Indications of Interest—Required Contents

IOIs should address specific aspects of the offer:

- *Purchase price and consideration.* Provide an estimate (or range) of purchase price on a cash-free and debt-free basis and include the proposed form of consideration (e.g., cash or shares)
- *Financing sources.* Describe sources of funding, any commitments received, and any conditions to financing.
- *Due diligence requirements.* Selling corporation will conduct management presentations and provide a data room with customary information. Bidders are requested to identify any specific anticipated diligence issues.
- *Required approvals and consents.* Identify any required approvals (e.g., shareholders, board of directors) or consents (e.g., government) required to complete the transaction.
- *Timing.* Estimate the time frame within which due diligence will be completed, financing obtained, and any required approvals and consents secured.
- *Other.* Bidders may be asked to identify their specific plans for the business (e.g., management, employees, operating locations).

Description of Transaction Process

After receipt and review of IOIs, a group of potential acquirers will be selected and then allowed to perform additional due diligence and submit final bids. The selected parties will be provided access to due diligence materials and sent a draft purchase agreement to enable them to formulate their final proposals. Due diligence will include meetings with management and access to a data room which will contain customary financial, operational and legal information. [At the end of a defined time period], potential acquirers will be asked to submit final proposals including a copy of the draft purchase agreement marked up to show requested changes. A final procedures letter with further details will be sent to potential acquirers participating in this phase of the process.

EXHIBIT 6.6   PRELIMINARY PROCESS LETTER—ILLUSTRATIVE OUTLINE (CONTINUED)

Caveats

Broker and Selling Corporation may change or terminate the process at any time, for any reason. There is no obligation to accept or reject any offer. Selling Corporation can negotiate with multiple parties and enter into an agreement with one without prior notice to the others.

Exhibit 6.6   Preliminary Process Letter—Illustrative Outline

If any items are left open or are unclear, the broker will contact bidders for clarification before reviewing any offers with the selling corporation. An outline of points addressed in a typical IOI is shown as Exhibit 6.7.

(i) Indication of Interest versus Letter of Intent—Avoiding Exclusivity. Bidders customarily prefer that the preliminary offers they make to acquire the business be nonbinding, meaning that they are not legally obligated to pay the price they are quoting and they reserve the right to walk away from the transaction at any time. This is prudent because due diligence may reveal reasons to alter the valuation or to terminate discussions. As discussed, the document typically seen in bid situations is the IOI.

Sometimes bidders will choose to submit their offer in the form of a letter of intent (LOI). An LOI is similar to an IOI in that it is a nonbinding offer for the business subject to stated conditions. But the key differences are that an LOI typically provides more detail and

---

Purchase price [range] and terms
Sources of financing
Due diligence process envisioned
Necessary approvals
Plans for the business (e.g., whether there are plans for employees, operating locations)
Material conditions (e.g., signing key executives to employment agreements)
Advisors (identity of bidder's financial and legal advisors)
Timing (how long does bidder anticipate to complete diligence and obtain required approvals)

Exhibit 6.7   Indication of Interest—Illustrative Outline

asks the selling corporation to provide a stated time period during which the potential acquirer can pursue the acquisition on an exclusive basis; during this period the selling corporation agrees not to hold discussions with any other party. The exclusivity provision is legally binding, so both parties would execute an LOI.

From the bidder's point of view, it would be preferable to pursue an acquisition without the pressure of a competitive auction. Therefore, sellers should not be surprised to be asked for exclusivity. However, the selling corporation should approach this decision with extreme caution, since agreeing to exclusivity with one bidder can effectively undermine the leverage that might be gained from the auction. By putting the competitive dynamics of the auction on hold for the duration of the exclusivity period, the selling corporation loses leverage and may actually lose the option of selling to the alternative players if this one deal conversation breaks down.

Ideally, the selling corporation should not agree to exclusivity; instead, it should conduct negotiations with several organizations and sign a deal with the organization that can complete the transaction first. Competitive leverage would thus be employed to optimize speed as well as terms. If the selling corporation does agree to exclusivity, it should be done late in the sale process, when the probability of reaching a satisfactory agreement with one organization is judged to offset the loss of negotiating leverage.

(ii) Qualifying the Offers.   Once IOIs are received, the broker qualifies the bids, evaluating the credibility of the bidders and weighing their ability to execute the transaction. Many bidders, especially those that are active acquirers, tend to develop reputations for certain patterns of behavior, and savvy brokers are well informed about these kinds of things. Some organizations are thought to be tire-kickers, looking at a lot of businesses but rarely pursuing acquisitions in earnest; others are believed to be finishers, being more selective, making bids only if they are seriously interested, and having a track record for closing transactions. Reputations are also considered when it comes to the valuations. Some bidders are known for submitting high valuations and then reducing them after due diligence, while others are known for presenting a more dependable initial valuation.

The broker will also look at the sources of financing to determine the bidders' capability to close the transaction. An all-cash offer with no financing contingency is of course optimal but is usually unrealistic for larger transactions. In many cases then, the deal will be contingent on financing. If so, the broker must determine whether bidders have lined up specific financing sources, whether they have received preliminary financing commitments, and what types of conditions are connected to the financing. Opining on the financing arrangements is a critical aspect of the broker's role in the evaluation of the bids.

The bid is also scrutinized for conditions that might affect the certainty of the valuation, such as a stock (versus cash) offer, an earn-out, where part of the consideration is made contingent on future results, or conditional, based on a multiple of historical or forecasted results that are subject to due diligence scrutiny.

The broker will summarize the bids and their evaluation in a bid summary such as shown in Exhibit 6.8.

(iii) Selecting the Participants for the Second Round. The broker presents the bid summary to the selling corporation and recommends a certain number of qualified bidders based on agreed decision criteria, normally including price and financing. In making its decision about which bidders to invite into the second round, the selling corporation may apply some additional criteria to rule certain bidders into or out of the process, including:

- **Speed.** The more quickly the acquirer can complete its due diligence, the more confident the seller can be that there will be a transaction. The evaluation of a bidder's ability to move quickly through the acquisition process is based on what is said in the IOI but also on its reputation. As discussed, organizations develop reputations and track records, and brokers tend to be aware of them.
- **A good home for the business.** This is admittedly a far less tangible consideration than something like price, but it can be a real consideration for the selling corporation in forming the field of potential acquirers. The selling corporation, especially if it has owned a business for a long time, may be comfortable with an acquirer (this is especially the case for strategic

BIDDER	VALUATION	FINANCING	DEAL STRUCTURE	CONDITIONS	DUE DILIGENCE	TIMING	OTHER
	• Bid (or range) • Multiples of revenue/EBITDA	• Sources (equity, debt) • Financing contingency • Sources • Conditions	• Specific form of transaction (e.g., cash for assets) • Tax assumptions (step-up) • Balance sheet assumptions at closing (cash, debt, working capital)	• Necessary approvals (e.g., board, shareholder) • Specified level of preclosing results • Employment agreements with management	• Subject to customary business, legal, tax, financial, and accounting reviews • Any specific requirement (e.g., management meetings customer/vendor interviews, site visits) • Due diligence/information request list	• Expect to be able to complete diligence review in [ ] days	• Plans for the business (employees, locations)

EXHIBIT 6.8   Bids Received—Illustrative Summary

acquirers) that has similar standards for integrity, quality, and customer service. The selling corporation, if concerned that the actions of the acquirer would impact its own reputation, might want at least some comfort that bidders invited into the second round will be a good home for the divested business.

6.5 DUE DILIGENCE

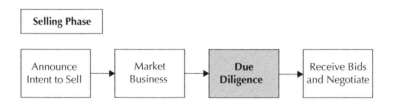

(a) INVITING BIDDERS INTO THE SECOND ROUND   Once the broker and the selling corporation reach consensus on which organizations to include, the selected bidders are invited to participate in the second round of the sale process: performing due diligence, and then making final, definitive offers to acquire the business.

The broker normally lets participants know if they have made it to the second round by a phone call to the bidders' principals, so that the selling corporation's rationale can be explained. Also, the broker may see these parties on either the buying or selling side of other transactions. Therefore, it is in the broker's interest to maintain good relationships with all of the bidders, delivering messages personally and in a way that demonstrates that the auction has been conducted in good faith. The broker may also choose, while inviting bidders into the second round, to inform them (without violating confidentiality) where they generally stand in the process. If, for example, a bidder has been invited into the second round but its valuation is significantly below other bids, the broker may say that to be competitive in the second round, the offer must be improved.

The call is then followed up by the final process letter, which clearly describes the process for the second, final round of bidding. Exhibit 6.9 illustrates a final process letter.

Invitation

Broker is inviting recipients to participate in the second and final round of the process for the sale of [Selling Corporation's] _____ business unit.

Description of Transaction Process

The selected parties will be provided access to due diligence materials and sent a draft purchase agreement to enable them to formulate their final proposals. Due diligence will include meetings with management and access to a data room, which will contain customary financial, operational, and legal information. [At the end of a defined time period], potential acquirers will be asked to submit final proposals including a copy of the draft purchase agreement marked up to show requested changes. Final offers should be submitted [when] [how] [to whom].

Guidelines for Final Offers

- *Best and final offer.* Offers should be best and final. Bidders should not expect to have an opportunity to revise the offer, though the Broker may contact them to seek clarifications or revisions to the offer.
- *Purchase price.* Fixed price for 100% interest in the [assets or stock].
- *Purchase agreement mark-ups.* Offers should be accompanied by a copy of the purchase agreement that was distributed by the Selling Corporation, marked up to show any requested changes.
- *Financing.* State sources and confirm that the deal has been financed without any remaining contingencies.
- *Due diligence.* Identify any remaining confirmatory diligence to be completed. Any open items should not have an impact on the purchase price.
- *Conditions.* Specify whether there are any conditions to the offer (e.g., execution of employment agreements with key employees, receipt of key consents).
- *Authorization and approvals.* Confirm that all internal approvals have been obtained. Indicate any (external) approvals or consents to be obtained and timing expectations.
- *Timing.* Specify when bidders expect to be in a position to close the transaction.
- *Expiration.* How long the offer will remain open.

Caveats

Broker and Selling Corporation may change or terminate the process at any time, for any reason. There is no obligation to accept or reject any offer. Selling Corporation can negotiate with multiple parties and enter into an agreement with one without prior notice to the others.

EXHIBIT 6.9 FINAL PROCESS LETTER—ILLUSTRATIVE OUTLINE

(b) PRELIMINARY DUE DILIGENCE   Second-round participants normally receive a management presentation and access to a data room containing detailed information about the business. Additionally, depending on the number of bidders involved, the broker may allow bidders to request additional information or have follow-up meetings with management. These activities, collectively referred to as preliminary due diligence, are usually scheduled to occur within a fixed period of time established by the broker. After the time allotted for preliminary diligence is completed, potential acquirers are asked to submit final offers. The opportunity to conduct final, or "confirmatory," diligence is offered only to the bidder or bidders with which the selling corporation decides to pursue a definitive agreement, after consideration of the final offers.

There are two primary reasons why the selling corporation allows a fixed time for preliminary diligence and establishes a confirmatory diligence stage. First, it maintains momentum and efficiency in the sale process. By establishing a specific time when second-round bids are due, the seller forces bidders to look primarily at information that allows them to finalize their valuations and place a lower emphasis on all other diligence work, which by definition would not create additional value for the seller. Second, as discussed in section 4.8, the selling corporation can then withhold the disclosure of the most sensitive and proprietary information (e.g., customer lists, pricing details and strategy, employee-identifiable data) until confirmatory diligence, allowing only one or two organizations to see this information.

Despite these constraints imposed on the process, potential acquirers will often push to obtain as much information as they possibly can during the preliminary diligence phase. The acquirer's diligence objectives are much broader than simply finalizing the valuation, including, for example:

- Determining whether to proceed with the acquisition
- Validating key representations made about the business by the selling corporation
- Identifying any material exposures, liabilities, or vulnerabilities in the business
- Validating integration assumptions and formulating a high-level approach

- Validating the historical financial results (e.g., audit work paper review)
- Legal review of key contract terms (e.g., assignability or change in control provisions)
- Discussions with key customers to ensure that there are no underlying problems or intent to cancel

Although several of these objectives are clearly confirmatory in nature, the potential acquirer needs to complete a good portion of this work in order to know the full extent of required mark-ups to the draft purchase agreement. For example, if a bidder becomes aware of a potential litigation exposure during diligence, it may want to ask for indemnification from the selling corporation. This may not be a headline valuation issue, but bidders will want to identify as many of these types of items as they can so that they can be incorporated into the contract mark-up. Therefore, many potential acquirers would be uncomfortable leaving major confirmatory steps incomplete until the last stage of the process.

The contrasting objectives can create a tension between the potential acquirers, which are trying to extract as much information as possible, and the broker, which is trying to enforce the preliminary diligence time limitation. This is an area where a good broker can bring the experience and sound judgment required to achieve the best balance, allowing bidders a sufficient level of access to the business while maintaining momentum and sale process discipline.

(i) Management Presentation: Focus on Salesmanship.   The preliminary due diligence typically includes a presentation by the management team, which is intended to showcase both the business and the management team. It is a delivery of facts, but it is also a sales pitch with the objective of increasing bidders' enthusiasm. A lot of value can be created by a good management presentation, so the selling aspect of the presentation cannot be overemphasized.

In many cases, the management team that will go with the divested business may not have been part of a business that has been sold before. So, while the team may have strong knowledge about the markets, competitors, and operations of the business, its inexperience with divestiture transactions might lead it to approach the management presentation the same way it would an internal operating plan meeting. Buyers such as private equity groups, in contrast, are used to listening to road shows given by visionary entrepreneurs. In such a case, the divested business's management may come across as a bit conservative by comparison.

Consequently, in preparation, management should be coached to emphasize its vision for the business and the corresponding upside potential. It helps to keep in mind that the management presentation is in effect a job interview; that management will be measured not just on its factual command of the business, but also on its vision, energy, and enthusiasm. A fundamental objective of the presentation, therefore, is to convince the buyer to invest *in the management team* as well as in the business.

(ii) Approaching the Management Presentations as a Learning Process.   As discussed in section 4.5(d), the best results are obtained if the management team is thoroughly prepared for the presentation. The presentation is typically scripted to ensure the message is delivered consistently and all key points are addressed by each speaker. Dry runs allow the speakers to internalize their notes so that they are not simply reading their scripts to buyers but are speaking naturally. These practice sessions also help the team to prepare for questions. The broker can be particularly helpful here because of its experience with the selling process; it can act as the bidder and help prepare the team by asking pointed questions. The team can then discuss and agree on the best way to approach these questions.

As the actual presentations approach, the broker can further assist the presenters by preparing a briefing document covering each of the organizations that will be in the second round. In this way, the team will be able to customize comments to point to the strategic fit with each potential acquirer. The broker should schedule the presentations thoughtfully, starting with a less important bidder or two to allow the team to refine its pitch. Presentations to the most important bidders should be reserved for the middle of the process, far enough along for the presentations to be smooth but not so far in that the team is liable to be fatigued and stale.

Typically the management presentation is a two- or three-hour meeting, with the presentation followed by a question-and-answer session or functionally organized break-out meetings. If break-out meetings are scheduled, the broker should coordinate them and get a list of the bidder's questions or agenda in advance. The broker should also attend every meeting to ensure it is aware of any issues that emerge, especially any that might impact the valuation.

The selling corporation may want to have a representative attend the management presentations, but this individual would not normally be very active in the discussion. There might be a question or two that are best answered by the selling corporation, such as why the business is for sale or what postsale transition services the selling corporation is prepared to offer. However, even if only as an observer, the representative from the selling corporation might be helpful in providing feedback to the presenting group.

No matter how much the team practices, it will face something unexpected during each presentation. Questions may be asked during the meetings that were not anticipated, or points may not come across as intended in tone or tenor. The team should conduct a debriefing session at the end of each presentation to review what went well and what didn't. This feedback should be used to make adjustments for the next day, to the presentation slides, the script, or the prepared answers. These adjustments can significantly improve successive presentations as well as the team's level of self-confidence as it interacts with the bidders.

(iii) Data Room.   The other key element of preliminary due diligence, along with the management presentation, is the data room, which was discussed in section 4.7. Those with experience in mergers and acquisitions still visualize the data room as an actual room filled with attorneys and accountants, boxes of contracts and other documentation, and a junior broker or attorney sitting at the door logging people in and photocopies out. This scene is changing dramatically with the advent and increased use of electronic, or "virtual," data rooms over the last several years. Some estimates place use of electronic data rooms at 20% of all U.S. mergers and acquisitions.[1]

Although virtual data rooms are quickly becoming the norm, the team should still make an active decision as to whether a traditional

---

1   "The Data Room,"*Boston Globe*, January 23, 2006.

or a virtual data room makes more sense for its particular transaction. Some of the advantages of electronic data rooms from the standpoint of the selling corporation follow.

- **Ability to run concurrent sessions**. An unlimited number of individuals from multiple organizations can review documents simultaneously, resulting in a faster due diligence process. This allows for more bidders to be involved, removes geographic/travel constraints, and lowers venue costs.
- **Ability to measure usage.** The selling corporation can see metrics on which documents have been reviewed or which search terms bidders are using to search for documents. These metrics can act as a barometer of the process, both to gauge which bidders are most active and, therefore, most interested and to identify issues that might be potential areas of concern to buyers.
- **Control over access to documents**. The selling corporation can restrict certain documents from being seen by certain organizations or even individuals, allowing a level of control over access. This would be useful, for example, if the selling corporation wanted to restrict access to certain highly sensitive documents until a later stage in the selling process.
- **Security.** Most electronic data rooms are password-protected, encrypted, and offer other protective features to enhance security.

Conversely, there is only one major disadvantage to using a virtual data room: the effort and cost to set it up. The divestiture team will have to electronically scan any paper documents, plus pay the electronic data room provider a fee, which is normally based on the number of documents posted online. Therefore, a virtual data room may not be cost-effective in a process involving a small business unit or only a few bidders. But for a larger transaction, especially in an auction, the advantages are increasingly seen by many organizations as worth the effort and the cost of setup.

One last decision the selling corporation needs to make is when to open up the data room: before or after the management presentation. While opening the data room may seem like a way to accelerate the sale process, it can have an unintended consequence: derailing the management presentations. If bidders have been through the contracts and documents before hearing the overall strategy and direction of the business, they do not have a context within which to place the details. They may then be tempted to drag the presenters into detailed questions during the management presentation, obscuring the bigger picture. Anticipating this pitfall, the broker usually announces the opening of the data room at the end of each management presentation. This is actually in the bidders' interest as well; understanding the business fundamentals and strategic direction can help bidders better understand and interpret items in the data room.

(c) DISTRIBUTING THE DRAFT PURCHASE AGREEMENT   During the preliminary due diligence, the broker will distribute a draft of the purchase agreement to the second-round participants. This draft agreement contains the terms under which the seller would be willing to close the transaction; and bidders are invited to mark it up with their proposed changes. There will almost always be changes, because in an auction, the seller usually distributes a seller-friendly agreement, which it fully expects bidders to mark up. We discuss the structuring and negotiation of the purchase agreement in greater detail in Chapter 7.

6.6 BIDDING AND NEGOTIATIONS

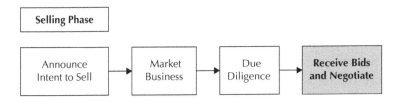

(a) EVALUATING DEFINITIVE OFFERS   At the time specified, the broker receives final bids for the business. These bids are normally received in the form of an offer letter, which fully addresses all items requested in the final process letter, such as:

- **Final valuation and form of consideration.** Bidders should not expect to have an opportunity to revise the offer, though the broker may contact them to seek clarifications or revisions to the offer.

- **Financing arrangements.** This would include sources, conditions, and confirmation that the deal has been financed without any remaining contingencies.
- **Confirmatory due diligence items remaining to be completed.** Any open items are expected to have no impact on the purchase price.
- **Conditions to the offer** (e.g., execution of employment agreements with key employees, receipt of key consents).
- **Confirmation that all internal approvals have been obtained.** Additionally, this section would include indication of any (external) approvals or consents to be obtained and timing expectations.
- **Expected timing to close the transaction.**

Additionally, the final offers are accompanied by a copy of the purchase agreement marked up to show the bidder's requested changes.

The selling corporation, in evaluating the offers, certainly considers the price, but also looks very closely at any conditions the buyer is requesting and how extensively it has marked up the draft contract. Given a similar valuation, the offer containing fewer conditions and contract mark-ups will be viewed much more favorably by the selling corporation because it signals that the party will be less difficult to negotiate the contract with.

(b) NEGOTIATIONS The final process letter typically sounds one-sided: Bidders are told that they cannot expect to make another bid and, therefore, are asked to present best and final offers, but the broker and the seller reserve the right to go back to bidders to ask them to increase, or "clarify," their offers. This ability to dictate the terms of the process to bidders is the result of the negotiating leverage that an auction affords the seller. If only one bidder was involved, negotiations would proceed quite differently.

In speaking to the bidders about their offers, the broker will normally focus mainly on the valuation. However, if a bidder has an attractive financial offer but an onerous contract mark-up, it is conceivable that a bidder could be asked to revisit the mark-up in certain areas. This is a particularly important time during the sale process, and good brokers can create substantial value for the selling corporation if they artfully exploit the auction process to extract full value from the bidders.

At this point, one or possibly two players are selected to perform the remainder of their diligence and to negotiate the purchase agreement, which the seller will execute with one of the parties. While it may be viewed as simpler to select one bidder with whom to move forward toward a close, some negotiating leverage is surrendered once the competitive field is eliminated. For this reason, some sellers choose to keep two bidders in the process, right up until they sign the purchase agreement with one of them. Ideally, a bidder should never feel that it is alone in the process; there should always be a sense that there are other players involved.

Once the selling corporation and bidder reach concurrence on price and the contract mark-up, they are far from finished negotiating. Despite having submitted a mark-up, the terms of the offer made by the bidder are normally subject to the completion of confirmatory due diligence, which will likely raise additional issues the acquirer will want to incorporate into the purchase agreement. This has the practical effect of keeping the purchase agreement open for further negotiations. Additionally, in structuring the acquisition transaction and creating the final contracts and agreements, there are normally many details yet to be addressed by the parties, with one example being the finalization of agreements for transition services. We discuss the negotiations of the contracts and agreements further in section 7.6 because this activity tends to occur as a separate and much more detailed step after the total valuation and summary-level terms of the acquisition are agreed on.

(c) **CONFIRMATORY DUE DILIGENCE**   As discussed in section 6.5(b), the bidder(s) with whom the corporation chooses to negotiate a definitive agreement are allowed to perform confirmatory diligence. Brokers refer to it as "confirmatory" because this work is expected to confirm or validate information that has already been factored in to the valuation; valuations are not expected to change as a result of confirmatory diligence. However, as mentioned, confirmatory diligence often does have an impact on the bidder's proposed mark-up to the purchase agreement.

A common element of the confirmatory diligence is a meeting between the accountants representing the buyer and the auditors who performed the carve-out audit for the selling corporation. This is equivalent to a peer review, where the buyer's accountants review the audit work papers to ensure that appropriate audit standards were applied in the audit: sample sizes, audit procedures performed, materiality thresholds, results attained, and, in particular, understanding the resolution of proposed audit adjustments. Additionally, the reviewers can determine the detailed approach and application to any accounting areas subject to judgment, such as revenue recognition, so the work paper review can be quite useful for the acquirer. If any part of the purchase price is made contingent on validation of historical results, this step can be particularly important.

Other typical confirmatory diligence steps might include a legal review of certain contracts or a review of operational items that will help with integration planning. A review of any items the seller has held back to this point, perhaps including key customer contracts and pricing arrangements, or employee-identifiable information, also occurs. In practice, though, the line between preliminary and confirmatory diligence is not clear. Simply stated, confirmatory diligence is whatever the potential acquirer needs to do that is still open in order to close the transaction.

KEY POINTS

1. Virtually all of the divestiture's preparatory activities are performed by a small group in a confidential setting. From the time of the announcement forward, the corporation's words and actions are scrutinized by an audience, whose reaction can significantly increase or decrease the value of the deal. (Section 6.1)

2. Final preannouncement preparation should include review of communications documents, marketing materials, audits, employee retention agreements, and coordination of timing. (Section 6.3)

3. A good way to facilitate the reinforcement of a consistent message after the announcement is to use a well-established media training tool, the message triangle. (Section 6.3)
4. The nondisclosure agreement provides critical legal protection for the seller. It precludes disclosure of confidential information, including the deal discussions, and prevents the potential acquirer from hiring or soliciting employees. (Section 6.4)
5. Sellers should not be surprised to be asked for exclusivity. However, this decision should be approached with caution, since agreeing to exclusivity with one bidder can effectively undermine the leverage that might be gained from the auction. (Section 6.4)
6. Tension can exist between bidders, which are trying to extract information during preliminary due diligence, and the broker, which imposes a time limitation on the process. A good broker can help achieve a balance: allowing bidders a sufficient level of access to the business while maintaining momentum and process discipline. (Section 6.5)
7. Debriefing sessions should be conducted after each management presentation and adjustments made to the presentation slides, script, and prepared answers. (Section 6.5)
8. Nonfinancial factors are very important aspects of the final offer. Fewer conditions and mark-ups signal that the party will be less difficult to negotiate the contract with. (Section 6.6)
9. While it may be viewed as simpler to select one bidder with which to move toward a close, negotiating leverage is surrendered once the competitive field is eliminated. For this reason, some sellers choose to keep two bidders in the process, right up until they sign the purchase agreement with one of them. (Section 6.6)

CHAPTER 7

STRUCTURING THE TRANSACTION

7.1 STRUCTURING THE DIVESTITURE TRANSACTION

The team's decisions related to the structure of the transaction follow a logical progression of evaluating and winnowing options throughout the course of the divestiture, as discussed in previous chapters and illustrated in Exhibit 7.1. In the assessment phase (discussed in section 2.4(a)), the corporation considers a number of *approaches* to addressing its strategic concerns about business units examined in its portfolio review, including retaining and investing, liquidating, or divesting. After the organization has fixed on a divestiture approach (discussed in section 3.1), preliminary consideration is given during the planning phase to alternative transaction *structures*, such as the outright sale of the shares or the assets of the business or, possibly, the creation of a spin-off or carve-out entity. As preparation for the transaction begins, the team and its financial advisor confirm or revise the recommended divestiture structure (discussed in section 4.4(b)), settling on the particular structure the corporation will present as its preference to potential buyers. During the selling process (discussed in section 6.5(c)), the corporation drafts the purchase agreement in accordance with its preferred transaction structure and distributes it for

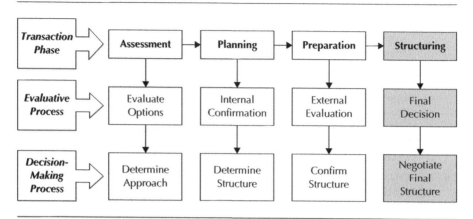

EXHIBIT 7.1 EVALUATION OF TRANSACTION APPROACH AND STRUCTURE

the review of potential buyers. After second-round bids are evaluated (discussed in section 6.6(b)), one or possibly two bidders are selected to perform confirmatory diligence and negotiate the definitive purchase agreements (executed by the single prevailing bidder), which will finalize the various details of the transaction structure.

Throughout this decision-making process, the team must evaluate a considerable number of technical details, along with their implications for both buyer and seller, so that the optimal structure can be chosen. From the overall approach chosen at the outset, to the wording of the agreements, it is the details of the structure that determine the tax liability, the allocation of risk between parties, and the financial reporting requirements. The cumulative impact of these details can be profound, greatly affecting the value of the deal, either positively or negatively.

We present and discuss the tax, legal, and accounting implications of the more common divestiture transaction structures in this chapter. We also discuss the importance of expanding the circle of internal and external experts and advisors, in order to properly evaluate the details of the transaction structure, while sustaining the transaction's forward momentum. Finally, we return to "live action" in the divestiture process, discussing the negotiation of the purchase agreement and compliance with regulatory requirements.

7.2 STRUCTURING PROCESS STEPS

The divestiture team's determination of a transaction structure, as described, begins early in the planning process and is confirmed or revised after financial advisors are retained. This determination involves a rigorous analysis of the implications of the various alternatives examined. During the selling phase, the corporation drafts the deal-related agreements, negotiates these agreements with the acquiring organization, and then submits the required regulatory filings. These activities take place within five steps.

Step 1. Bring in the required expertise. As the team enters the selling phase, it must expand its circle of internal and external experts and advisors and formalize their roles, in order to further analyze the transaction structure and, ultimately, to draft and negotiate the legal agreements. In section 7.3, we discuss this particular expansion of the divestiture team, which we refer to as the formation of the contract team. Our experience has shown us that success in structuring the transaction depends on careful planning for the availability of experts and on clear assignment of accountability to team members, so we address these issues in detail in this section.

Step 2. Analyze alternatives. In section 7.4, we present an array of different transaction structures and analyze the tax, legal, and accounting implications of these structures for the selling corporation. In the remaining sections of Chapter 7, and in keeping with the general orientation of the *Guide,* we return our emphasis to the most common divestiture approach, which is a sale-type transaction conducted through an auction process.

Step 3. Draft agreements. The next step is for the legal team to draft the various contracts and agreements for the sale. In section 7.5, we outline the key agreements for a sale-type divestiture transaction and discuss key considerations for team members drafting and reviewing them. In particular, we emphasize the value of utilizing a cross-functional group of executives to review, approve, and comment on items in the contract that relate to their areas of expertise.

Step 4. Negotiate agreements. We introduced the two-step auction process in Chapter 6, which described the typical pattern of bidding and price negotiations. Within this sale process, as discussed in section 6.5(c), the draft contract is usually distributed to potential buyers during the due diligence stage. The receipt of second-round bids and initial mark-ups to the draft contract allows the selection of the final participant(s), but it represents only the beginning of contract negotiations, which can continue until the agreements are signed and which rely much more heavily on the legal advisors. For these reasons, we deal separately with negotiation of the contracts in section 7.6. In this section, we present an overview of the contract negotiation process, and discuss key considerations for the contract team during this stage, which include empowering the negotiating lead and maintaining leverage.

Step 5. Comply with regulations. In section 7.7, we present several regulatory considerations. In the United States, antitrust legislation requires advance notification prior to the consummation of transactions that meet certain criteria. If the transaction is anticipated to meet these criteria, team members should be sensitized to the need for regulatory filings early in the process and the likelihood that all relevant documents may be subject to governmental scrutiny when the filings are made. Many other countries have their own antitrust requirements as well as other unique laws and regulations to be complied with, making it advisable to retain local counsel if the divested business has international operations of any magnitude.

Exhibit 7.2 illustrates these steps, each of which we discuss in the remaining sections of this chapter.

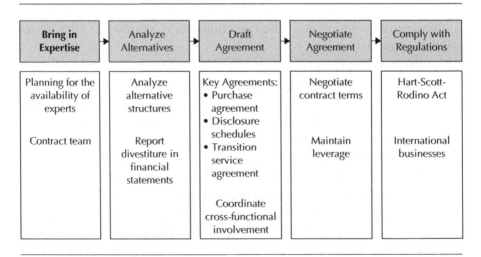

Bring in Expertise	Analyze Alternatives	Draft Agreement	Negotiate Agreement	Comply with Regulations
Planning for the availability of experts	Analyze alternative structures	Key Agreements: • Purchase agreement • Disclosure schedules • Transition service agreement	Negotiate contract terms	Hart-Scott-Rodino Act
Contract team	Report divestiture in financial statements	Coordinate cross-functional involvement	Maintain leverage	International businesses

EXHIBIT 7.2 STRUCTURING PHASE PROCESS STEPS AND CONSIDERATIONS

7.3 BRINGING IN THE REQUIRED EXPERTISE

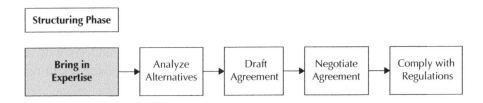

(a) PLANNING FOR THE AVAILABILITY OF EXPERTS   In section 1.4, we presented a staffing model for the divestiture, in which the core divestiture team is formed, then is expanded or contracted as required at key points in the transaction. The structuring of the divestiture provides a good example of this idea in practice. Normally, in the assessment phase, the core divestiture team evaluates alternative divestiture approaches. In the planning phase, the team must solicit input from corporate management and certain internal or external financial, tax, legal, and accounting advisors to preliminarily evaluate transaction structures. In the preparation phase, the divestiture team works closely with its financial advisor to select the structure it will take to market.

During the selling process, the team must turn its attention to drafting the purchase agreements and, ultimately, negotiating them with the acquirer. It is tasked with achieving what are seemingly contradictory objectives:

- **Sustain momentum.** In Chapter 6, we discussed the importance of sustaining positive momentum in the transaction. Momentum remains important in the transaction's latter stages; it is never good for progress on a deal to stagnate. Both parties to the divestiture transaction, especially when their spending on (and commitment to) the transaction becomes material, put even more pressure on their deal teams to get to closing quickly. Therefore, each has an expectation that the other side is making knowledgeable, empowered people available to keep the process moving. In this environment, either party would be irate if a key person were suddenly unavailable to the transaction for an extended period.
- **Negotiate a good deal for the selling corporation.** As we discuss in this chapter, there are numerous issues to be considered in the details of the contracts and agreements, which carry

profound financial and legal implications for the selling corporation. The divestiture team finds that it must balance its need to move quickly with fulfilling its fiduciary responsibility for mitigating risks and optimizing results for the corporation. Further, the team must manage intense, face-to-face negotiations with a potential acquirer that is trying to achieve the opposite result on nearly every deal point.

To achieve these objectives, the core divestiture team must once again widen the circle of people involved in the transaction. We refer to this particular expansion as the formation of the contract team.

Because of the nature of the issues that will be covered in the purchase agreements, the contract team will need to include key operating managers in addition to the technical experts. For large transactions, or in large organizations, the team may be able to dedicate the required internal staff to the contract team for the time they are needed and back-fill them with outside resources. More commonly, however, organizations struggle to make key internal people available and must borrow their time for divestiture issues. If this is the case, careful planning of their availability is a must, to avoid transaction bottlenecks.

Since the contract team's mission will include both an internally focused analytical aspect and a outward-facing negotiating aspect, its members' roles and responsibilities must be precisely defined.

(b) CONTRACT TEAM The contract team is responsible for the analysis and negotiation of the numerous elements of the transaction and is typically comprised of four types of roles: (1) negotiating lead, (2) legal team, (3) subject matter experts, and (4) executive management.

(i) Negotiating Lead. The negotiating lead is the single face of the selling corporation for the transaction, recognized as the person who communicates the definitive position on key issues throughout the negotiation of the contracts and agreements. This role can be filled by an executive from business development, finance, legal, or operating management. This person should have an appropriate level of experience in negotiating transactions, know the divested business in depth, and be vested with a visible level of authority to make decisions binding the seller. If the negotiating lead lacks mergers and acquisitions

experience but is otherwise suited for the role, the contract team should rely on its financial advisors to play a strong supporting role, as the advisors can help to fill any knowledge gaps.

(ii) Legal Team. Depending on the size of the transaction and scale of the organization involved, the legal team can be comprised entirely of in-house counsel or supplemented with external legal resources. Smaller organizations, faced with more limited resources, may choose to hire a law firm specializing in mergers and acquisitions to manage all aspects of the divestiture. The legal team's role in the structuring phase of the transaction includes:

- Drafting and revising agreements
- Assembling and reviewing supporting schedules
- Supporting negotiations
- Advising on issues in areas such as antitrust, intellectual property, employment, or securities law

The legal team should also coordinate the selling corporation's internal review and sign-off of the various sections of the agreement.

A single individual should direct the transaction from a legal perspective. This individual will support the negotiating lead and be the primary interface with the buyer's legal team. A good legal advisor orchestrates an efficient and effective negotiation by clearing many of the more routine contract points directly with the acquirer's legal team, allowing the negotiating lead to focus on the few important unresolved issues.

(iii) Subject Matter Experts. A number of areas involved in structuring the transaction stretch beyond the capacity of the negotiating lead and the legal team, regardless of their general level of knowledge about the divested business. As a result, the contract team needs to include subject matter experts responsible for covering areas such as:

- **Finance, accounting, and tax.** These areas are often coordinated by a senior financial executive, such as the selling corporation's chief financial officer, vice president of finance, or controller. Finance, accounting, and tax are involved in structuring the transaction and often advise and oversee the other subject matter experts to ensure the financial ramifications of each issue are understood. In this respect, the financial members of the contract team serve not only as technical advisors, but also link the various functional experts and executives looking at disparate elements of the transaction.

- **Human resources (HR).** The HR specialist is responsible for all issues relating to the employees of the divested business. HR determines how employees are impacted by the sale and oversees the operational transition of their compensation and benefit plans to those of the acquirer. HR also plays a major role in crafting the employee-related sections of the sale agreements.

- **Real estate, facilities, and technology.** Managers responsible for these infrastructure functions provide the operational knowledge to specify the real estate and technology assets (hardware and software) that are included in the sale and, importantly, are responsible for managing certain transition services that may be provided following the close of the transaction. Information technology (IT) is a particularly important function to include in the development of any agreements concerning postdivestiture transition services, since IT managers are normally deeply involved in the divestiture's disentanglement planning, as discussed in Chapter 5.

(iv) Executive Management.   The contract team requires the involvement of two groups of executives: the first to represent the interests of the selling corporation and the second to provide knowledge and information about the divested business.

- **Executive management of the selling corporation.** The executive management of the selling corporation normally prefers to rely on the divestiture team to manage the transaction while it tends to the retained businesses. However, executive management's involvement is needed for critical aspects of the transaction, such as ruling on transaction negotiating points that exceed the authority of the negotiating lead. Additionally, executive management has the final say on any agreements governing the behavior of the selling corporation, such as how the business is managed prior to the sale, which services are offered during the postsale transition, and whether any restrictions are placed on activity competitive with the divested business.

*   **Executive management of the divested business.** This group has firsthand knowledge of the operational details of the divested business, such as its assets, capabilities, products, services, and markets. As a result, executive management of the divested business is usually asked to coordinate information-gathering activities to ensure the completeness and accuracy of the contract and its supporting schedules.

Employees of the divested business are normally kept out of the contract negotiations, given their potentially conflicting personal and fiduciary interests during this time. That said, some members of its executive management group may be asked to make representations in the contract about certain aspects of the business. As the contract approaches finalization, these executives will review and approve certain sections of the agreements and corresponding disclosure schedules where they are making such representations.

7.4 ANALYZING ALTERNATIVE TRANSACTION STRUCTURES

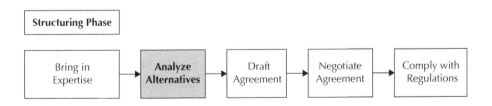

(a) TECHNICAL ISSUES AND IMPLICATIONS OF ALTERNATIVE TRANS-ACTION STRUCTURES In this section, several possible divestiture transaction structures are presented and discussed. Some forms involve the sale of the divested business to an acquiring organization. Other forms involve spinning off the divested business to shareholders or carving the business out in a public offering.

Each form of transaction can be subject to a widely differing level of taxation, impacting the net cash value to the selling corporation. There are also significant legal and accounting issues and consequences associated with the various structure options to be considered. With this much at stake, the team should utilize experienced and knowledgeable tax, legal, and accounting advisors to help it make informed decisions, as discussed earlier in this chapter.

Several technical tax and accounting terms warrant explanation in advance of the discussion of alternative structures.[1]

- **Basis: tax basis versus book basis.** The term "basis" refers to the net value of the divested business that is used to calculate the gain or loss generated by the divestiture. The "tax basis," generally the cost less accumulated depreciation, determines the tax gain or loss and, consequently, how much tax is due on the transaction. Its specific calculation is defined by the Internal Revenue Code. The "book basis," generally the amount of net assets or shareholders' equity, determines the accounting gain or loss that is reported in the selling corporation's financial statements. Its calculation is governed by U.S. generally accepted accounting principles (U.S. GAAP).

  Without getting into the particular requirements, it is important to keep in mind that, because the basis is calculated differently, the tax gain or loss will usually be a number different from the book gain or loss. While the book gain or loss is important, it is the tax gain or loss that determines the net *cash* proceeds of the transaction.

- **More on tax basis: tax basis in assets versus tax basis in stock.** As discussed in the sections that follow, in an asset sale, the taxable gain or loss is determined by the tax basis of the *net assets* of the divested business. This is often a value different from the tax basis in the *stock* of the business, which is normally

---

1   For further reading and more information on the tax aspects of divestitures, we highly recommend Myron S. Scholes, Mark A. Wolfson, Merle Erikson, Edward L. Maydew, and Terry Shevlin's, *Taxes and Business Strategy: A Planning Approach*, 2nd ed. (Upper Saddle River, NJ: Prentice Hall, 2002).

used in calculating the taxable gain or loss in a sale of stock. The tax advisors must calculate each of these values, which are determined by such factors as whether the divested business was organically developed or the result of a prior acquisition, and if acquired, how the original transaction was structured.

Because it is important to know the value of both the tax basis in the assets and the tax basis in the stock of the divested business, and because it takes some effort to arrive at these numbers, the contract team should ask its tax advisors to perform this analysis early in the planning phase of the divestiture.

A discussion of several alternative divestiture transaction structures and their implications for the selling corporation follows.

(i) Sale of Assets. In a divestiture structured as an asset sale, the selling corporation transfers specific assets and liabilities of one or more of its businesses to an acquirer, normally for cash. A sale of assets results in a taxable gain or loss for the selling corporation and an accounting gain or loss for financial reporting. The taxable gain or loss is determined by the amount of sales proceeds, net of selling costs, and less the selling corporation's tax basis in the net assets.

All other things being equal, the selling corporation should be able to command a higher valuation in a sale of assets versus stock, since the acquirer receives the benefit of a step-up in the basis of the assets that results in a tax deduction. In other words, the acquirer's tax basis in the business can be increased to the amount of the purchase price, and the excess of that price over the net assets acquired can be deducted from taxable income over a period of time. This has the effect of lowering the acquirer's after-tax cost below the cost of acquiring stock, where step-up is not normally available (except as described below in the discussion of the Section 338(h)(10) election), allowing it to pay more for the assets at the same after-tax cost.

From a business and legal perspective, an asset sale has some drawbacks. It may result in the retention of certain unwanted elements of the divested business, as acquirers often attempt to pick and choose the assets and liabilities that will transfer with the business. Negotiating which assets and liabilities transfer and which ones are retained can become a difficult and time-consuming part of the sale process. An asset sale can also introduce potential hurdles if there are any constraints on the transferability or assignability of any assets or contracts. Conversely, an asset sale may be the preferred structure if the corporation's objective is to sell off certain assets or elements of a business rather than an entire subsidiary legal entity.

(ii) Sale of Stock.   When a divestiture is structured as a sale of stock, the selling corporation transfers the stock of one or more of its businesses to an acquirer, often in exchange for cash. A sale of stock will create a taxable gain or loss and an accounting gain or loss. The taxable gain or loss is calculated based on the amount of sale proceeds, net of selling costs, and less the selling corporation's tax basis in the stock.

In a sale of stock, the acquirer does not benefit from a step-up, as the selling corporation's tax basis in the divested business would carry over to the buyer. This difference in tax treatment normally lowers the price the acquirer would be willing to pay for the stock, compared with the price of the assets. An exception to this is if both parties agree to make an election under Internal Revenue Code Section 338(h)(10), discussed next.

Conversely, the selling corporation tends to view a stock sale as cleaner, more straightforward transaction than an asset sale. When an acquirer purchases stock, it normally assumes ownership of the entire legal entity, with all of its assets and liabilities, contracts and agreements, and, generally speaking, liability for the entity's past actions. Concerns about the transferability or assignability of assets or contracts are usually mitigated by structuring the transaction as a stock sale.

(iii) Sale of Stock with a Section 338(h)(10) election.   If the selling corporation and acquirer jointly choose to make an election under Internal Revenue Code Section 338(h)(10), a stock sale can be treated for tax purposes as if assets were sold. This means that the selling corporation's taxable gain or loss would be calculated using the tax basis of the net assets, rather than the tax basis of the stock, and that the acquirer receives the benefit of step-up.

The relative ease of this structure may be more attractive to the selling corporation than a sale of assets, while remaining attractive to the acquirer with its benefit of step-up. While, on the surface, a stock sale with a Section 338(h)(10) election may thus seem to be the best of both worlds, it is often not the optimal tax structure for the selling corporation. As described next, that answer is determined only by examining the tax implications for both the selling corporation and the acquirer.

(iv) Tax Consequences of a Sale of Assets versus Stock. In order for the selling corporation to decide whether a sale of assets or of stock will deliver the highest after-tax value, the tax implications for both parties to the transaction need to be analyzed and understood. As described, the selling corporation normally can command a higher valuation when it sells assets (or stock under a Section 338(h)(10) election) due to the benefit of step-up that accrues to the acquirer.

However, this advantage can be eliminated by a higher tax liability, depending on the amount by which the selling corporation's tax basis in the stock exceeds its tax basis in the assets. This might be the case, for example, if the divested business came about through a stock acquisition, making it more likely that the selling corporation has a much higher tax basis in the stock. The optimal tax structure from the standpoint of the selling corporation, therefore, must take all of these factors into account. It is determined by comparing the benefit of receiving a higher sale price, based on tax benefits accruing to the acquirer, against a potentially higher tax liability on the sale, depending on the value of the tax basis.

As an example, consider a scenario where the acquirer is willing to pay $100 million for the stock of the divested business or $125 million for the assets of the business. The acquirer's higher offer for the assets is based on its determination of the present value of the step-up and its choice of how much of that value it is willing to share with the selling corporation. Assume that the selling corporation's tax basis in the stock is $75 million, its tax basis in the assets is $25 million, and that the blended federal and state corporate tax rate is 40%. As shown in the calculation in Exhibit 7.3, despite receiving $25 million less for the business, the selling corporation would actually be $5 million better off after tax if it structured the deal as a stock sale.

This type of calculation should be done early in the preparation phase for the divestiture, so that the selling corporation and its financial advisor can express a preference to potential acquirers.

	SALE OF STOCK	SALE OF ASSETS
Sale proceeds	$100	$125
Tax basis	75	25
Taxable gain	25	100
Tax (@ 40%)	10	40
After-tax proceeds	$90	$85

EXHIBIT 7.3   ILLUSTRATIVE CALCULATION OF TAXATION OF
AN ASSET VERSUS STOCK SALE ($ IN MILLIONS)

(v) Tax-Free Subsidiary Sale under Section 368.   Transactions involving a sale of assets or of stock, as described, normally result in a taxable gain or loss for the selling corporation. One approach that does not generate a taxable gain or loss would be a tax-free subsidiary sale under Internal Revenue Code Section 368. In this type of transaction, the selling corporation receives shares of the acquirer's stock rather than cash.

The favorable tax treatment, however, is mitigated by the fact that the selling corporation does not receive cash. The proceeds in this structure remain at risk as a result of the selling corporation's continuing ownership stake in the acquirer. Further, a continuation of involvement with the divested business could preclude the selling corporation from separately presenting the results of the divested business in its financial statements, as discussed in section 7.4(b). Any of these factors might conflict with the selling corporation's objectives for the divestiture. For these reasons, this type of structure is not seen often.

(vi) Spin-offs and Equity Carve-outs.   Two divestiture structures do not involve an outright sale of the business, nor do they ordinarily generate a tax or accounting gain or loss.

In a spin-off transaction, the selling corporation is divided into two distinct corporations, with shares of the divested business distributed to current shareholders on a pro rata basis. A spin-off does not normally produce cash proceeds for the selling corporation but can qualify as a tax-free transaction if it meets certain requirements. A spin-off is accounted for by a charge to retained earnings.

In an equity carve-out, sometimes referred to as a subsidiary initial public offering (IPO), a portion of the equity of a business unit is sold to the public, generating cash proceeds. This structure does not produce a gain or loss for tax or financial accounting purposes as long as the shares are held by the business unit itself, not by the parent corporation.

If the selling corporation believes that public equity markets are not appropriately valuing the separate components of its business, one of these approaches may generate more value for shareholders than from a sale of assets or stock. However, given that these transactions require far more effort from a legal, regulatory, operational, and financial standpoint, they are seen somewhat less frequently than sales. Understanding the trade-off between valuation upside and favorable tax treatment, on one hand, and increased complexity and costs, on the other, requires careful and informed analysis.

(vii) Asset Swaps.   In certain rare instances, two organizations may decide that their value is optimized by swapping business units. Generally speaking, an asset swap is analogous to conducting an asset sale and an asset acquisition at the same time. Therefore, the selling corporation usually would recognize a gain or loss for both tax and accounting purposes.

Rather than receive cash, the selling corporation may greatly prefer to trade a nonstrategic business for one it considers more closely aligned with its strategy. Admittedly, this situation requires an uncommon alignment of interest and willingness to cooperate between two organizations that might otherwise be competing with each other. Still, if such a match can be found, an asset swap may be attractive in the right circumstances.

(b) REPORTING DIVESTITURES IN THE FINANCIAL STATEMENTS
Although accounting considerations do not normally drive the corporation's divestiture structure choice, the question of how the transaction will be reported in the financial statements is a major one for many corporations. As described in section 7.4(a), one issue of importance is whether a given transaction structure results in the recognition of a financial accounting gain or loss. Another accounting consideration that receives a lot of executive management attention is where the financial position and operating results of the divested business, in addition to the gain or loss on sale, will appear within the financial statements.

Most senior executives, if asked, would probably prefer that the divested business is shown separately within the current and historical financial statements, to allow investors to more clearly see the condition and performance of the business operations that will continue after the sale. This might especially be the case if the divested business is underperforming, creating a drag on the consolidated results. As a result, the accounting representatives on the divestiture team will likely be asked, early in the process, whether the divested business can be presented separately.

U.S. GAAP do allow the separate presentation of a divested business, known as discontinued operations treatment, but only if specific criteria are met. If a transaction meets these criteria, the assets and liabilities, results of operations, and cash flows of the divested business are separately classified as discontinued operations within the financial statements and footnotes, and prior periods are restated for comparability. If, however, a transaction fails to meet these criteria, the divested business must remain included within the financial results of the continuing business through the date of sale.

Determining the appropriate financial statement treatment requires the participation and input of the organization's accounting experts throughout the structuring of the contract. In particular, they should closely review sections that spell out the precise form of the sale transaction and, as will be discussed later, those that define any post-transaction involvement between the buyer and the seller.

(c) **CRITERIA FOR DISCONTINUED OPERATIONS TREATMENT: FIVE KEY QUESTIONS**   Since discontinued operations treatment is important to many organizations, and the requirements for attaining this treatment are somewhat complex, this section goes through the accounting requirements in some detail. The criteria for determining whether a transaction qualifies for discontinued operations treatment can be distilled into five key questions, as illustrated in Exhibit 7.4.

1. **Is the disposal by a sale?** According to U.S. GAAP, only businesses to be divested in a sale transaction—for example, a sale of assets or stock—may be treated as discontinued operations. If the business is disposed of by a method other than by sale, the assets of the business are considered "held and used," meaning

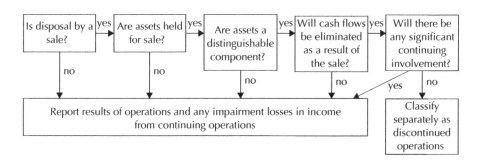

EXHIBIT 7.4   CRITERIA FOR TREATING DIVESTITURES AS DISCONTINUED OPERATIONS

its results must be included within income from continuing operations through the date of the sale. Assets are considered held and used if, for example, they are abandoned, exchanged for similar productive assets, or distributed to owners in a spin-off.

2. **Are the assets held for sale?** The assets of the divested business must be considered "held for sale" to qualify for discontinued operations treatment. All of these conditions need to be met for the business to be considered held for sale:

    ○   Management, having authority to approve the action, commits to a plan to sell.

    ○   The business is available for immediate sale in its present condition, subject only to usual and customary terms.

    ○   An active program to locate a buyer and other actions required to complete the plan to sell have been initiated.

    ○   The sale is probable and expected to be completed within one year.

    ○   The business is being actively marketed for sale at a price that is reasonable in relation to its fair value.

    ○   It is unlikely that the plan will be significantly changed or withdrawn.

Note that the goodwill of the divested business is sometimes recorded at a reporting unit level that also includes other ongoing operations. When a business is classified as held for sale, the amount of goodwill attributable to that business should be determined based on the relative fair values of the divested business and the portion of the reporting unit to be retained, and included along with the divested business's other assets and liabilities in determining the gain or loss on the disposal.

3. **Are the assets of the business a distinguishable component?** U.S. GAAP require the assets of the divested business, collectively referred to as the asset group, to be a "distinguishable component." An asset group is considered a distinguishable component if the operations and cash flow can be clearly distinguished, operationally and for financial reporting purposes, from the rest of the selling corporation.

4. **Will cash flows be eliminated?** The operations and cash flows of the component must be eliminated from the ongoing operations of the selling corporation as a result of the disposal transaction. If any cash flows do continue after the disposal, they cannot be considered "direct." Direct continuing cash flows (the existence of which precludes discontinued operations treatment) are defined as significant cash inflows or outflows that accrue to the selling corporation as a result of a migration of revenues or costs from the selling corporation's offering of similar products or services to customers of the divested business or from the continuation of activities through the selling corporation's active involvement with the divested business.

5. **Will there be any significant continuing involvement?** The selling corporation should not have any significant continuing involvement in operations of the divested business after the disposal transaction: that is, it does not retain an interest, or is party to a contract or arrangement, sufficient to enable it to exert significant influence over the divested business's operating and financial policies. Items that might be viewed as continuing involvement include:
   - Owning shares of stock in the divested business or the acquirer after the sale

- ○ Holding debt securities from the acquirer that include protections or covenants allowing influence over business operations or plans
- ○ Service-level agreements with extensive terms (e.g., greater than one year)

Items that would *not* constitute continuing involvement include:

- ○ Resolution of contingencies such as purchase price adjustments and indemnification issues
- ○ Resolution of contingencies related to operations of the divested business prior to disposal, such as environmental and product warranty obligations retained by the selling corporation
- ○ Settlement of employee benefit plan obligations directly related to the disposal transaction

(d) IMPAIRMENT LOSSES U.S. GAAP require the assets of the business to be stated on the balance sheet at the lower of their carrying amount or at fair value less costs to sell. Costs to sell are defined as the costs that result directly from and are essential to the sale transaction, and that would not have been incurred had the decision to sell not been made. Those costs include broker commissions, legal and title transfer fees, and closing costs that must be incurred before legal title can be transferred.

When a business is first classified into discontinued operations, a comparison is made between the aggregate fair vale and the carrying value of the assets. If fair value exceeds the carrying value, there is no impairment, and the balance sheet values are classified into discontinued operations at their current values. If, however, fair value is less than carrying value, then the corporation must formally revalue each of the tangible and intangible assets and liabilities of the divested business and record an impairment charge in the discontinued operations section of the profit and loss statement. This is obviously a lot more work for the accounting group. Additionally, impairment testing must be updated each quarter, so any changes in expectations of proceeds for the divestiture should be communicated and considered.

Finally, and significantly, if the criteria for discontinued operations treatment are not met, any impairment charges must be reflected within the financial results of the continuing business, which is another reason why corporations generally prefer for transactions to qualify for discontinued operations treatment.

7.5 DRAFTING THE AGREEMENTS

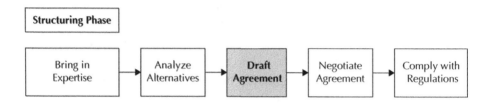

Once the selling corporation has determined which transaction structure best meets its objectives, it can begin drafting of the acquisition agreements. As discussed in section 6.5(c), the purchase agreement is initially drafted and distributed to bidders during preliminary due diligence, allowing the selling corporation to exploit the negotiating leverage provided by an auction to distribute a draft containing a preferred structure and favorable terms to the field of potential acquirers. The major contracts and agreements for a sale of assets or stock, the most common forms of divestiture, normally include:

- Purchase agreement
- Disclosure schedules to the purchase agreement
- Transition services agreement

(a) COMPONENTS OF THE PURCHASE AGREEMENT   The purchase agreement is the definitive legal document governing the divestiture. It sets forth the financial terms of the transaction, establishes the legal rights and obligations of the parties, lists required activities prior to and following the sale, provides a detailed description of the business being divested, determines remedies if that description is materially inaccurate, and allocates risk between the parties. The purchase agreement is organized into sections addressing specific issues. While individual contracts may be assembled differently to address issues relevant to specific transactions, most contracts cover in some form the points that are outlined in Exhibit 7.5 and described in the discussion that follows.

Purchase and Sale

Defines the business being sold, outlines the deal structure, and identifies parties to the agreement.

Closing

Sets the location and mechanism of the close: what is exchanged and when, the purchase price, and any price adjustments.

Representations and Warranties of the Seller

Seller represents its ability to enter into the transaction and describes in detail the state of business being sold.

Representations and Warranties of the Buyer

Buyer represents its ability to enter into the transaction: for example, availability of funds/financing.

Covenants

Governs conduct of both parties leading to and following the close. Usually includes a covenant not to compete with the divested business.

Employment Matters

Specific agreements and covenants regarding employment matters. Can be included within *Covenants* or in a separate section, depending on extent of issues to be addressed.

Conditions to Close

Conditions that must exist to obligate each party to close the transaction.

Termination

Conditions that must exist to allow for termination of the agreement.

Indemnification

Level of financial protection each party offers the other against losses arising from breaches of representations, warranties, covenants, or other performance obligations.

EXHIBIT 7.5 PURCHASE AGREEMENT—ILLUSTRATIVE OUTLINE (CONTINUED)

Tax Matters

Specific agreements and covenants regarding taxation matters. Can be included within *Covenants* or in a separate section, depending on extent of issues to be addressed.

General Provisions

Includes definitions and interpretations and addresses procedures regarding making claims.

EXHIBIT 7.5   PURCHASE AGREEMENT—ILLUSTRATIVE OUTLINE

(i) Purchase and Sale.   The purchase and sale section identifies the parties to the agreement and the general structure of the transaction (e.g., sale of assets, or shares of stock). This section also describes and defines the business being sold. Several issues require particular focus in this section.

- **Choosing the selling entity**. The specific legal entity selling the business determines where the gain or loss is recognized within the seller's tax reporting structure and the entity that will bear the liabilities resulting from the sale agreement. Legal and tax advisors should be consulted for guidance on this point. Based on their planning and analysis for the transaction, these advisors will normally want to designate particular entities to be the parties to the agreement.
- **Structuring the transaction as an asset or share sale.** The sale of assets or shares has significant tax implications for both the selling corporation and acquirer, as discussed in section 7.4.
- **Defining the business being sold.** The definition of the business should be written with care and precision. Its broadness or narrowness, depending on how the agreement is drafted, can potentially impact the noncompetition covenant, as further described in the "Covenants" section.

(ii) Closing.   The closing section of the agreement specifies the location and timing of the closing, the purchase price, and any purchase price adjustments. Several aspects are worth highlighting in this section.

- **Timing: sign and close simultaneously, or delay?** A key question is how long a time to provide between signing the agreement and closing the transaction. In many cases, both parties prefer to sign the agreement and close simultaneously. Often, however, it is necessary to delay the closing to allow financing to be secured or to obtain consents from shareholders, third parties, or governmental agencies. If there must be a delay between signing and closing, the selling corporation should try to keep it as short as possible. A short delay reduces the possibility of an unfavorable event, such as a material adverse change in the business, which might release the acquirer from its obligation to close.

- **Purchase price and adjustments.** This section specifies the purchase price, including the form and mechanism of consideration received, and any anticipated price adjustments. The type of consideration received (e.g., cash, shares of stock, assumption of debt, guaranteed consideration versus contingent) determines the ultimate value of the transaction and its accounting treatment, as discussed in section 7.4. The most common purchase price adjustments are for the amount of working capital at closing and for elements of the purchase price that are contingent on future events.

- **Working capital adjustment.** The purpose of a working capital adjustment is to balance the competing interests of the parties to the agreement. The selling corporation is interested in removing any excess working capital prior to the sale, while the acquirer expects the business unit to have a level of working capital sufficient to fund operations after the close. The working capital section should be as specific as possible to lower the likelihood of future misunderstandings. It should specify a reference amount, the level above or below which the purchase price will be increased or decreased, and include a predefined process for settling disputes (e.g., third-party arbitration). It should also define working capital precisely, with specific accounts listed (e.g., to include or exclude cash or intercompany accounts), and describe the accounting policies and practices that govern the calculation of the amounts.

- **Contingent consideration.** A technique to bridge valuation differences between the seller and buyer, or to share the risk for areas of uncertainty, is to make part of the purchase price contingent. Generally speaking, corporations value certainty and predictability in divestiture transactions and are disinclined to entertain price contingencies. Since contingent arrangements can increase the potential for postclosing disagreement and conflict with the acquirer, selling corporations might actually view these agreements as having as much downside risk as they have upside potential. Purchase price contingencies should therefore be viewed as a last resort in negotiations, and if agreed to, they should be defined in sufficient detail to minimize the potential for subsequent disagreement.

In spite of these drawbacks, contingent consideration is sometimes negotiated in divestiture transactions, most often taking one of three forms.

1. **Earn-out.** This form of contingent consideration is usually a formulaic approach whereby additional purchase price is paid to the selling corporation based on a factor applied to revenues or profits over a period of several years. Earn-outs typically include operating guidelines to govern how the business will be managed after the sale to allow the valuation to be maximized. For the reasons discussed earlier, selling corporations often prefer to avoid earnouts.

2. **Hold-back.** Payment of certain amounts sometimes is made contingent on the occurrence of a specific event, such as securing a key contract renewal or the successful launch of a new product. Timing in these cases tends to be shorter than for earn-outs, typically ranging from a few months to a year. Because of the short time frame and the binary nature of the contingency, these arrangements tend to be structured as a hold-back to a defined amount of the base price.

3. **Escrow agreement.** An escrow agreement is a vehicle for appointing a third party to hold part of the purchase price until specified uncertainties (e.g., the expiry of the survival period for representations and warranties) are resolved, at which time the amount is released to the selling corporation. While it is not uncommon for the acquirer to ask for an escrow agreement to ensure there is a funded account to go after in cure of a contractual breach, the selling corporation

is often reluctant to agree, arguing that its general credit should be sufficient to provide comfort that it can stand behind its obligations.

(iii) Representations and Warranties of the Seller. The primary function of the representations and warranties of the seller is to provide the buyer with a snapshot of the business at particular points in time, typically as of the date of the agreement and then again on the date of the closing, if they do not occur simultaneously. Representations and warranties of the selling corporation generally cover its ability to enter into the deal and disclose the state of the business being divested. Typical representations and important considerations for this section of the contract are described next.

- **Seller's ability to enter into the agreement.** The selling corporation makes a number of representations concerning its ability to legally close the transaction. These representations tend to be relatively uncontroversial in the negotiations. Typically, they cover several standard areas:
  - The seller is a valid organization authorized to enter into the deal.
  - The deal will not conflict with any contracts, laws, or regulations.
  - There is no litigation that would affect the seller's ability to close the transaction.
  - The seller has valid title to the assets (or shares) being sold.
- **State of the business being divested.** These representations are some of the most important aspects of the entire purchase agreement. The selling corporation makes detailed representations concerning the state of the business being divested and, importantly, discloses any exceptions to those representations in the schedules to the purchase agreement (see section 7.5(b)). The acquirer has the right to make a money damages claim for any items not accurately represented or disclosed in this section. Acquirers will, as a result, usually try to make this section very comprehensive, covering not only standard types of items

but also any items of concern that they come across in their due diligence. Examples of some commonly seen representations and warranties include these:

- o   The financial statements disclosed to the acquirer are properly stated.
- o   The contracts being transferred are valid, and the parties to them are not in breach.
- o   Business permits are in full force.
- o   Tax returns have been properly filed, and there are no outstanding claims.
- o   Employee benefit plans have been properly managed and regulations complied with.
- o   Environmental regulations have been complied with.
- o   Assets are sufficient to conduct the business.
- o   There are no undisclosed liabilities.
- • **Importance of full disclosure.** Given the range of the representations and warranties, and the potential liability associated with them, the selling corporation should have each section reviewed and approved by subject matter experts representing the applicable function and ensure that any exceptions to representations are fully disclosed in schedules to the contract. Section 7.5(d) addresses the cross-functional review in more detail.

(iv) Representations and Warranties of the Buyer.   This section lists the representations the acquirer makes about its ability to enter into the agreement. Unlike the selling corporation, the acquirer, especially if it is paying cash and has no financing contingencies, makes just a few representations and warranties in the purchase agreement. Some examples follow.

- •   The acquirer is a valid organization authorized to enter into the deal.
- •   The deal will not conflict with contracts, laws, and regulations.
- •   There is no litigation that would affect the acquirer's ability to close the transaction.
- •   The acquirer has sufficient funds or has secured financing.

When it signs the purchase agreement, the selling corporation makes a commitment to proceed exclusively with a particular acquirer. This commitment reduces the selling corporation's ability to reengage easily with alternative buyers in case the transaction does not reach close. The acquirer, in making its representations and warranties, says formally that it is able to close the transaction. The selling corporation should make sure that any concerns it has about the acquirer are addressed in this section. Most commonly, these concerns relate to the adequacy of the acquirer's funds and financing.

(v) Covenants.   Covenants govern the relationship between the selling corporation and acquirer over a period of time. Certain covenants apply from the signing of the agreement until the closing date and provide assurance that the proper actions are taken to facilitate the closing of the transaction and preserve the business pending the closing. Preclosing covenants normally include a list of actions allowed, or prohibited, without the buyer's consent. Other covenants survive the closing for a certain length of time, such as covenants requiring the cooperation of the parties with respect to the postclosing transition of the business or the sharing of facilities. Additional covenants can include such things as access to information, rights to use the seller's names and trademarks following the close, and agreements to keep the negotiations exclusive and confidential. If the acquirer is relying on third-party financing for the transaction, covenants may require it to perform certain activities between signing and closing to secure the financing.

Several specific types of covenants warrant particular focus, as discussed next.

- **Preclosing covenants create an awkward relationship between the selling corporation and the acquirer.** Covenants are largely intended to increase the acquirer's comfort that the selling corporation will not take major actions to change the business prior to closing and that it will be cooperative regarding the transition following the close.

  There is an inherent awkwardness in the period between signing and closing. During this time, the selling corporation still retains the benefits and the risks in owning the divested business but is made answerable through the covenants to the acquirer to act or not act in certain ways. If there will be an antitrust filing, the legal advisors must review this part of the contract closely to ensure that the acquirer is not perceived as assuming effective control of the business before the transaction has been approved by the appropriate governmental agencies.

These are additional reasons why the time between signing and closing should be minimized. From the perspective of either selling corporation or acquirer, few good things can happen between signing and closing.

- **Noncompetition covenant.** The covenant made by the selling corporation not to compete with the divested business is another very important section of the purchase agreement and is usually one of the most difficult to negotiate. The acquirer, from its perspective, needs assurance that the selling corporation will not enter into competition with the business it has just divested. The selling corporation, conversely, expects that its disposal of one business unit will not impinge on the ability of its remaining units to conduct business.

    Negotiation of this section requires the involvement of operating management with in-depth knowledge of the markets the unit operates in and with a good working knowledge about units not involved in the sale. This is the one section of the contract that may require extensive involvement of the selling corporation's senior management, as it needs to determine how much restriction it can tolerate to satisfy the acquirer's concerns.

    The covenant not to compete is composed of four elements, each of which can be fiercely negotiated, with the selling corporation looking to narrow each term and the acquirer seeking to broaden its definition.

    1. Definition of competitive activity and entities covered
    2. Geographic area
    3. Specified period of time
    4. Exceptions

    The selling corporation often looks to list certain areas, known as exceptions, or carve-outs, where the terms of the noncompetition covenant would not apply. For example, it may seek to exclude competitive activities of businesses it already owns, of businesses it acquires a small ownership stake in, or of businesses it acquires, where competitive activities are a small proportion of revenues. Each carve-out, then, can bring several additional definitions and percentage or dollar thresholds into the negotiations, another example of how detailed the contract discussions can get.

(vi) Employment Matters. This section addresses representations, warranties, and covenants of both parties specifically relating to employment matters. While these items can also be incorporated into the other contract sections, organizing them in a separate section facilitates review by the employment experts on both sides of the transaction.

In order to ensure that its former employees are treated fairly in the transition of ownership, the selling corporation may ask the acquirer to make commitments about how employees transferring with the deal will be treated; for example, to specify which employees will or will not transfer to the acquirer, or to sustain equivalent levels of salaries and benefits for a period of time following the closing. The selling corporation may also commit to certain actions to support the transition of employees to the acquirer's plans and to ensure a smooth transition of plan administration.

(vii) Conditions to Close. This section outlines the conditions that must be met in order for the parties to be legally obligated to consummate the transaction. If one party fails to satisfy a condition by the date of the closing, the other party has the right to terminate the agreement and walk away from the transaction. Typical conditions to close may include:

- Receiving governmental approvals such as antitrust clearances
- Obtaining key third-party consents
- Having no judgments or restraints
- Having no litigation
- No material adverse change occurring in the business
- Performance by either party of specific actions (such as obtaining financing)

The selling corporation wants to have as few conditions as possible to increase the certainty of closing. The acquirer will not want to be legally obligated to commit the funds to close until it is comfortable that the things it views as most important are in place, so the acquirer has an interest in making this a longer list.

(viii) Termination.   This section defines the conditions under which the agreement can be terminated. Parties might agree that the contract can be terminated prior to closing upon mutual agreement or if specific conditions are present. The section normally outlines the effect of termination; for example, specifying the sections of the purchase agreement that would survive termination of the agreement (e.g., confidentiality, publicity, jurisdiction, or governing law). The section should also list any penalties or specific performance obligations that would be required on termination.

There may be circumstances when the agreement should be terminated, but the selling corporation normally prefers to establish a very high threshold for an event of this significance. Having gone as far as signing the agreement, the last thing the selling corporation would want to do at this point is restart the sale process at the beginning. Thus, sellers normally allow very few conditions, and also make termination as distasteful as possible, by including disincentives such as breakup fees or other termination penalties.

(ix) Indemnification.   Indemnification requires the parties to pay damages in the event of a breach of their respective representations, warranties, and covenants. Indemnification provisions also serve to allocate specific postclosing risks associated with the transferred business. Even after all of the representations, warranties, and covenants are agreed, the parties often continue to hotly debate the indemnification section of the contract, since this section sets both the floor and the ceiling amounts for any damages claims that can be made under the contract. There are three typical elements of the indemnification section.

1. **Caps: placing a limit on the maximum exposure.** This section defines the aggregate level of each party's obligations and the allocation of legal and financial risk in the contract, through caps or limitations of the aggregate amount of claims that can be made. These aggregate obligations directly impact the ultimate value of the sale.

2. **Survival: establishing an end date for claims.** Survival represents a specified period of time during which claims can be made. Sometimes separate survival periods are established for tax and environmental representations (based on statutes of limitation), and some representations (e.g., incorporation, title, ownership) may survive indefinitely.

3. **Deductibles, baskets, and de minimis amounts: lowering the likelihood of nuisance claims.** Minimum dollar amounts can be established to ensure that only substantive claims for breaches of the agreement are made. A deductible is an amount that the acquirer is at risk for, since claims can only be made for amounts in excess of the deductible. A "basket" is a threshold amount that claims must surpass but is recoverable from the selling corporation if total claims exceed the threshold. Having a de minimis amount indicates that an individual claim cannot be made unless it exceeds a certain minimum dollar level, to mitigate the possibility of spending time and legal fees disputing minor items.

(x) Tax Matters. This section addresses representations, warranties, and covenants of the seller and buyer specifically relating to tax matters. It normally addresses the purchase price allocation; assigns responsibility for transfer taxes, tax filings, and tax liabilities; and outlines procedures for making tax claims. This section also may include a separate tax indemnification with its own survival and limits. While these items sometimes are incorporated into the other contract sections, organizing them in a separate section facilitates review by the tax experts on both sides of the transaction.

(xi) General Provisions. This section addresses some of the specifics of dispute resolution in addition to matters not covered elsewhere. It also includes definitions and interpretations of terms used in the purchase agreement.

Definitions and interpretations often can be overlooked but are critical to establishing how broadly or how narrowly statements made elsewhere in the contract are interpreted. The definitions and interpretations section is an important indicator of how seller-friendly or buyer-friendly the entire agreement is or, in other words, how the legal and financial risk is allocated between the parties to the agreement.

For example, if the "business" being sold is defined in this section, it has direct relevance to how restrictive the noncompetition covenant is to the selling corporation's postclose operations. Similarly, to the degree that representations and warranties are qualified to the extent of the "knowledge" of the seller, this section's definition of knowledge will broaden or narrow the risk assumed by the selling corporation. Other key definitions requiring careful reading include "materiality" and "material adverse effect," both of which are used to modify many of the representations, warranties, or covenants. This section needs to be read carefully and in conjunction with the applicable section of the purchase agreement where the terms are utilized.

(b) DISCLOSURE SCHEDULES TO THE PURCHASE AGREEMENT   The schedules to the agreement list all the disclosures the selling corporation has made and itemize any exceptions to the representations and warranties. Items included in the disclosure schedules are keyed to the appropriate contract section. Inclusion of an item on a schedule has the effect of *modifying* the relevant section of the agreement. For example, a representation may be made that there is no litigation *except* as disclosed in the schedules to the agreement. Another typical representation might say that the acquirer has been provided with a copy of every contract over a certain dollar amount and that the selling corporation is not in breach of any, except as disclosed in the schedules. Exhibit 7.6 illustrates some additional items often included in the disclosure schedules.

The disclosure schedules are prepared by the selling corporation and are reviewed by the acquirer, typically by individuals who were involved in the due diligence process. As such, they serve as a supplemental due diligence function on part of the acquirer.

The team should know that comprehensive disclosure is important–its purpose is to mitigate legal and financial risk. If an exception is not disclosed in the schedules, the acquirer has a basis for making a damages claim against the selling corporation for breach of representations and warranties. Consequently, the selling corporation should be diligent in ensuring that the schedules are thoroughly and comprehensively prepared. To facilitate this disclosure process, the selling corporation

---

- *Organization and good standing:* List of jurisdictions where qualified to conduct business
- *Company subsidiaries*
- *Included and excluded assets and liabilities:* Items transferring to the buyer in an asset sale
- *Real property:* Owned and leased
- *Permits*
- *Insurance:* List of policies, premiums, coverage limits, claims
- *Intellectual property:* Lists of copyrights, patents, and trademarks
- *Contracts:* List of all contracts above a defined dollar amount; agreements where consents are required in a change in control; agreements containing noncompetes or other restrictive covenants.
- *Financial statements:* Copies of financial statements the seller is making representations about; description of any departures from GAAP (especially for interim statements)
- *Litigation:* Threatened or pending claims
- *Compliance with laws or permits:* Exceptions
- *Environmental matters:* Any issues
- *Employment matters:* Employee lists, bonus and benefit plan descriptions
- *Related party transactions:* Contracts with affiliates; related party receivables and payables
- *Indebtedness:* Lists of all debt or loans; description of restrictive covenants
- *Taxes:* Outstanding audits; tax claims or liens

EXHIBIT 7.6 DISCLOSURE SCHEDULES TO THE PURCHASE AGREEMENT—ILLUSTRATIVE LIST

should make an individual responsible for managing and coordinating document-gathering activities throughout the sale, from the population of the data room, to completion of the schedules to the contract. This individual should ensure that knowledgeable people have reviewed the documents and flagged any potential issues. In addition, the legal advisors should review all the schedules and discuss any issues with management prior to sending them to the acquirer.

(c) TRANSITION SERVICES AGREEMENT Chapter 5 discussed the process of analyzing interdependencies and planning for disentanglement in detail. Most sale agreements provide for a commitment for the selling corporation to provide certain support and back office services to the acquirer for a limited period as the buyer transitions the unit to its ownership. This commitment is captured in the transition services agreement (TSA). TSA terms normally include the definition of included services, time period, pricing, and terms of billing and payment. The scope of the TSA is determined by two factors: the extent to which the divested business possesses a back office infrastructure that can support stand-alone operations and the nature and scale of any back-office infrastructure owned by the acquirer. The more dependent the divested business is on the selling corporation for back-office services and the less capability owned by the acquirer, the more likely it is that the TSA will have a broad scope and an extended transition term.

Management in charge of the selling corporation's affected functions, normally back-office functions such as customer service, accounting, human resources, facilities, and information technology, should be closely involved in the negotiation of the TSA. The IT function, in particular, should review the operational commitments to ensure that any technology implications have been properly considered. Additionally, accounting subject matter experts should review the TSA to determine if it represents significant continuing involvement for purposes of determining whether the transaction qualifies for financial reporting treatment as a discontinued operation.

(d) COORDINATING CROSS-FUNCTIONAL INVOLVEMENT IN CONTRACT DRAFTING AND REVIEW The purchase agreement can be an extraordinarily complex document, with significant legal and financial ramifications for the selling corporation. One must keep in mind that the legal team, while it does much of the work in drafting and negotiating the deal, does not normally sign the agreements that bind the selling corporation. That responsibility remains with executive management. As a result, the selling corporation should set up a process wherein specific management individuals are made accountable for reviewing and signing off on sections of the purchase agreement that relate to their areas of expertise. This will ensure that the appropriate technical and operational knowledge is brought into the contract review, so that the divestiture team thoroughly understands the implications of the various contract terms and conditions.

One individual, preferably from the legal team, should coordinate the actions of these reviewers, ensuring that individuals have provided required input, reviewed, and signed off on the appropriate sections of the agreement. Version control is especially important as contract mark-ups are passed back and forth between the seller and buyer during the negotiations. While some functions, such as finance and accounting, will want and need to review the entire agreement holistically, others, such as HR, will be needed to read and sign off on only particular sections. Exhibit 7.7 is an example of how one might assign responsibilities and manage the cross-functional review of particular contract sections.

7.6 NEGOTIATING THE AGREEMENTS

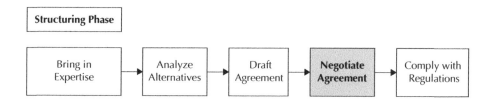

(a) NEGOTIATING THE CONTRACT TERMS IN AN AUCTION PROCESS   Chapter 6 described the typical auction process, where potential acquirers are selected to participate in two rounds of price bidding and due diligence. Throughout the course of the auction, the field of potential acquirers is reduced to very few (or just one) parties. Those parties are then invited to move into confirmatory diligence and to begin contract negotiations. Contract negotiations, the focus of this section, consist of three basic elements.

1. Drafting the agreement and distributing to potential acquirers during the bidding process
2. Reviewing mark-ups to the agreement made by the selected acquirer(s)
3. Conducting face-to-face discussions: lawyer to lawyer and principal to principal

	FINANCE/ ACCOUNTING	TAX	HUMAN RESOURCES	REAL ESTATE/IT	DIVESTED BUSINESS MANAGEMENT	SELLING CORPORATION MANAGEMENT
LEGAL						

Purchase and Sale
Establish parties to the agreement and transaction structure

- Purchase price
- What is being bought and sold (e.g., assets, stock)
- Included and excluded items

Closing
Determine location, timing and mechanism of the close

- Timing of signing versus closing
- What is exchanged (e.g., title, shares, funds)
- Treatment of debt and related security interests
- Purchase price adjustments (e.g., earn-outs)
- Working capital adjustment

Representations and Warranties of Seller
Review, sign off, and provide input for disclosure schedules

LEGAL	FINANCE/ ACCOUNTING	TAX	HUMAN RESOURCES	REAL ESTATE/IT	DIVESTED BUSINESS MANAGEMENT	SELLING CORPORATION MANAGEMENT
• Organization • Authority • Conflicts • Consents required • Title to assets	• Financial statements • Assets, liabilities • Sufficiency of assets	• Tax matters	• Employee matters • Benefit plans	• Real property • Environmental matters • Fixed assets	• Intellectual property • Contracts • Permits • Insurance • Compliance with laws	• Overall deal structure (Purchase and Sale) • Overall deal structure (Closing)

- Litigation
- Compliance with laws

- Undisclosed liabilities
- Brokers

- Intellectual property

- Absence of changes or events

Representations and Warranties of Buyer

Review, sign off

- Organization
- Authority
- Conflicts
- Consents required
- Litigation
- Availability of funds

Covenants

Review, sign off, and provide input for disclosure schedules and TSA

- Seller guarantees
- Solvency opinions
- Financing

- Financing
- Expenses
- Related party accounts
- Access to information
- Transition services

- Tax matters

- Transition services

- Transition services

- Transition services

- Transition services
- Non-compete
- Post-close cooperation
- Confidentiality
- Use of names and marks

EXHIBIT 7.7 Managing Cross-Functional Review of the Purchase Agreement—Illustrative Example (Continued)

LEGAL	FINANCE/ ACCOUNTING	TAX	HUMAN RESOURCES	REAL ESTATE/ IT	DIVESTED BUSINESS MANAGEMENT	SELLING CORPORATION MANAGEMENT
Employment Matters	Review, sign off, and provide input for disclosure schedules and TSA					
• Technical matters related to employment law			• Offers, terms • Benefit plans • Retirement plans • Administration • HR regulatory matters			
Conditions to Close						
Review, sign off • Approvals, consents • Judgments • Litigation • Performance obligations • Material adverse effect						• Approvals, consents • Judgments • Litigation • Performance obligations • Material adverse effect

Termination
Review, sign off
- Conditions
- Procedure Terminated
- Effect of termination

- Conditions
- Procedure terminated
- Effect of termination

Indemnification
Review, sign off
- Procedures
- Limitations
- Survival

- Procedures
- Limitations
- Survival

Tax Matters
Review, sign off, and provide input for disclosure schedules
- Technical matters related to tax law
- Tax covenants
- Purchase price allocation
- Transfer taxes
- Tax filings

EXHIBIT 7.7 Managing Cross-Functional Review of the Purchase Agreement—Illustrative Example (Continued)

LEGAL	FINANCE/ ACCOUNTING	TAX	HUMAN RESOURCES	REAL ESTATE/ IT	DIVESTED BUSINESS MANAGEMENT	SELLING CORPORATION MANAGEMENT
General Provisions Review, sign off • Definitions • Interpretations • Notices • Assignment • Entire agreement • Governing law • Jurisdiction • Service of process	• Definitions • Interpretations	• Definitions • Interpretations	• Definitions • Interpretations	• Definitions • Interpretations	• Definitions • Interpretations • "Knowledge individuals" [who are specifically named for representations subject to the knowledge of seller]	• Definitions • Interpretations

EXHIBIT 7.7 MANAGING CROSS-FUNCTIONAL REVIEW OF THE PURCHASE AGREEMENT—ILLUSTRATIVE EXAMPLE

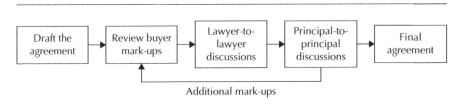

EXHIBIT 7.8 CONTRACT NEGOTIATIONS: PROCESS FLOW

These steps are iterated until both sides of the transaction are satisfied with the position taken and documented on all the issues, at which time the final agreement is reached, as shown in Exhibit 7.8.

(i) Drafting the Agreement. When the sale is conducted through a two-step auction process, as described in Chapter 6, the selling corporation normally prepares the first draft of the purchase agreement and distributes it to potential acquirers during their preliminary due diligence. The broker's second-round bid instructions request both definitive offers and proposed changes to the draft agreement. The selling corporation, by creating the first draft of the contract, is not only setting in place its preferred transaction structure but is also establishing the initial allocation of risk between parties through its selection of items and choice of language in sections such as representations and warranties. This is an important example of the leverage that is obtained by conducting a competitive auction. The selling corporation can prepare a seller-friendly draft and can keep it that way if there is a strong level of competition for the divested business.

(ii) Reviewing Mark-ups to the Agreement Made by the Buyer. The potential acquirers are asked to submit mark-ups to the draft contract to address what they consider to be major issues, such as concerns uncovered in their preliminary due diligence. By tying the mark-ups to second-round offers, the selling corporation uses the competitive pressure of the auction to help minimize the extent of changes to the agreement. That said, it is commonly understood that the acquirer's confirmatory diligence could raise additional contract issues (and generate further mark-ups), which is, in part, why the contract negotiations are an iterative process.

(iii) Lawyer-to-Lawyer Discussions. Legal advisors from each side of the transaction normally will speak after the buyer's marked-up draft has been returned. In the initial conversations, the legal advisors for the selling corporation seek to understand the buyer's comments and underlying concerns, and they may start to negotiate some points. They will then prioritize the major open issues to help focus the principal discussions. Depending on the level of empowerment of the legal team and the level of cooperation between the parties' legal advisors, a significant number of contract points actually can be negotiated and resolved between the legal advisors without requiring the involvement of principals.

A good legal team can play a much more valuable role than simply clarifying and resolving technical matters. The better and more experienced legal advisors have likely been involved in dozens, if not hundreds, of similar transactions and have a nuanced understanding of the human dynamics of negotiations that can help the deal immeasurably. They know, for example, when to call for a break in the conversations to allow parties to cool off if negotiations become too heated, how to orchestrate the trading of points to advance the negotiations, and precisely when and how to become confrontational on an issue if needed.

(iv) Principal-to-Principal Discussions. Face-to-face discussions between principals are most effective when legal advisors have organized and prioritized issues lists, allowing them to focus on resolving fewer items of greater significance. Items agreed on are sent back for redrafting, with the revised agreement then being circulated for review.

The negotiating lead serves as the principal for the selling corporation. In order to be most effective in this role, this person should be empowered with some predetermined level of negotiating authority to get the deal done. For example, the lead may be allowed to make price concessions up to a defined percentage of the preliminary bid, have authority to negotiate a contract survival period up to a certain number of years, or set limitations of liability up to some dollar amount. Setting a level of quantifiable limits makes the entire team more efficient by allowing the lead to act decisively in this critical part of the process. Knowing that every contract point cannot be anticipated in advance, a mechanism should also be established for obtaining corporate approval of items exceeding the negotiating lead's authority. This internal approval process should be kept as seamless as possible, to minimize any lags in responding to offers and counteroffers made in the negotiating process. To facilitate quick and informed review and approval, the negotiating lead should report regularly to senior management on the status of negotiations and key issues.

(v) Reaching the Final Agreement.   The preceding process iterates until all issues have been negotiated and resolved to the satisfaction of both parties, with a succession of marked-up contract drafts exchanged between the parties, followed by a series of calls and face-to-face meetings. The acquirer will not want to conclude the discussions until some time after it has completed confirmatory diligence, so that it can ensure all significant issues have been addressed in the contract.

In setting timing expectations for the sale process, corporations routinely underestimate the amount of time it takes to get a deal done. While it is not unheard of for motivated and cooperative parties to negotiate an agreement in a few days to a week, it is more reasonable to expect the negotiations to span several weeks, and in more complex or acrimonious cases, negotiations can last a month or more. A good rule of thumb is that one added iteration of the contract draft can extend the negotiations by up to a week. This fact underscores the need to minimize the number of iterations by resolving as many issues as possible during each negotiating session.

(b) MAINTAINING NEGOTIATING LEVERAGE   One of the worst mistakes a selling corporation can make in negotiations is agreeing too soon to enter into exclusive negotiations with one organization. Before taking this step, the selling corporation can manage a field of multiple potential acquirers to keep competitive pressure exerted on all parties. This gives the selling corporation a lot more leeway to dictate its preferences to the field, sustaining the price, and forcing potential acquirers to accept more seller-friendly terms to the contract than they would have otherwise. Once the competitive field is narrowed to a few players, the negotiating leverage between parties becomes more equal, with pressure on both the selling corporation and the acquirer to negotiate mutually acceptable contract terms.

If the field is reduced to one bidder, as it is during an exclusivity period, the negotiating leverage shifts further toward the acquirer. If there is no remaining competition, the acquirer has an advantage not only in negotiating the contract terms but could attempt to revisit the price discussions with unfavorable discoveries from its due diligence. The acquirer can simply walk away from the transaction if discussions break down, while the selling corporation could face the undesirable choice of agreeing to the acquirer's terms or restarting the sale process at the beginning.

For this reason, it is greatly preferable for the selling corporation to keep two or more parties active through contract negotiations and close with the party that can get to closing most quickly and under the most favorable conditions. Sustaining the level of negotiating leverage is often worth the added complexity of simultaneously negotiating with more than one organization. Potential acquirers, however, will usually ask for exclusivity as soon as they can get it, given their desire to get the negotiations onto a more equal footing.

Some selling corporations, especially for very large transactions, will take the idea of maintaining leverage one step further, fully preparing for two alternative transactions, such as an IPO and a sale transaction, and keeping one as a fallback for the other. That way, even if the auction is reduced to one organization, the option of IPO can always be held out as a way to keep pressure on the potential acquirer. Although this is by far the most complicated and expensive approach, for certain transactions, the differential in value could well justify the effort.

7.7 COMPLYING WITH REGULATIONS

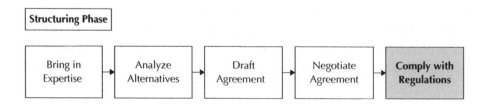

(a) FINAL HURDLE: REGULATORY APPROVAL Once the contracts are negotiated and signed, the divestiture team may have one more significant hurdle to contend with before the deal can close: regulatory review and approval. In the United States, the Hart-Scott-Rodino Antitrust Improvements Act of 1976 (HSR) requires premerger filings and a waiting period for transactions over a certain size. Since the federal government under HSR can either request additional information before approving a transaction, a time-consuming and expensive prospect, or choose to contest the transaction, careful planning and consultation with antitrust experts should be initiated early in the divestiture process.

For divested businesses outside the United States, the team needs to consider not only antitrust but any other laws or regulations unique to the country or region that may affect the transaction. For this reason, the divestiture team should engage counsel for each country or region of operations to guide the team through the local compliance process.

(b) HART-SCOTT-RODINO ACT The Hart-Scott-Rodino Antitrust Improvements Act of 1976 established a premerger program requiring those engaged in certain mergers and acquisitions to notify the Federal Trade Commission (FTC) and the Department of Justice (DOJ) of the impending transaction. The parties to such a transaction must submit a notification and report form with information about their businesses and wait a specified period of time, usually 30 days, before consummating the transaction. The objective of the act is to prevent transactions that the federal government would view as anticompetitive. A few points about the HSR requirements and their implications for the divestiture follow.

- **HSR affects a significant number of transactions.** An HSR filing is generally required for transactions with an aggregate value above $59.8 million,[2] an amount that is adjusted upward annually. Since the average divestiture value is approximately $175 million, as discussed in section 1.2 (c), many divestiture

---

2 The criteria for filing actually involve more than just the value of the transaction, and the amounts change annually, so sellers should retain antitrust counsel to perform a definitive assessment of whether a given transaction requires an HSR filing.

transactions fall above the filing threshold. The divestiture team should consider whether an HSR filing is a possibility early in its transaction planning and should retain expert antitrust counsel if a value anywhere near the filing threshold is anticipated.

- **FTC Notification and Report Form is the required filing document. Part 4C of the form is critical to the HSR review.** If a transaction does meet the criteria for HSR, then both the buyer and the seller must submit information about their respective business operations via the Notification and Report Form. This form requires disclosure of these items:
    - Identity of the parties involved and structure of the transaction
    - Financial data and certain documents filed with the Securities and Exchange Commission (SEC)
    - Certain planning and evaluation documents pertaining to the proposed transaction
    - Revenues by industry segment and geographic area, previous acquisitions or assets engaged in business in overlapping segments

    The requirement to provide certain planning and evaluation documents, sometimes referred to as the "4C request" after its section on the Notification and Report Form, is quite broad. It includes copies of studies, surveys, analyses, or reports prepared by or for officers or directors that evaluate or analyze the proposed transaction with respect to markets or market share, competition or competitors, potential for sales growth, or expansion into product or geographic markets. Typically responsive documents include offering prospectuses or memoranda, whether prepared by seller or buyer, and documents submitted to management including studies and presentations. Not just formal documents or presentations are included. Even informal communications, as seemingly innocuous as notes to the file or e-mails, can be viewed as responsive documents if they contain competitive or market analysis for the transaction and are prepared by or for the selling corporation's officers or directors.

- **The government can approve the transaction, contest it, or ask for more information.** Once the form is filed, the agencies begin their review, focusing on whether the divested business and the acquiring firm are competitors or are related in any way such that the transaction might adversely affect competition. They analyze the submitted materials but also may consult publicly available information as well as their prior experience with either the markets or the organizations involved in the filing.

After analyzing the information within the initial 30-day waiting period, the government can choose to approve the transaction, contest it in court by requesting injunctive relief, or ask for more information before making a decision.

- **Getting a "second request" is a very big deal.** If either agency determines that further inquiry is warranted, it can request additional information via a second request. The second request extends the waiting period, and the clock on the additional waiting period does not start until all parties are deemed to have complied with the request. The divestiture team should understand that, as a practical matter, getting a second request is a very big deal. Depending on how much information the government is asking for, the entire team could easily be faced with multiple months of internal and external effort and potentially millions of dollars of additional legal fees to comply.
- **Planning for the HSR filing.** While a second request can never be prevented, the team can certainly make the initial submission as complete and high quality as possible, to lower the likelihood of anything in the submission itself triggering the second request. If a transaction is projected to have a value anywhere near the $59.8 million threshold, guidance should be given to the entire divestiture team at the outset of the process to ensure there is a consistent understanding of the requirements of HSR and that 4C documents in particular are assembled and reviewed during the course of the divestiture so that time is not lost rushing through this critical process once the deal is signed.

In preparing all documents and communications related to the divestiture, the team needs to be precise and consistent in characterizing markets and in explaining the rationale for the deal. All documents should accurately characterize the market position of the business being sold based on a consistent set of market measures. Documents should be written factually, free of the hyperbole that sometimes makes its way into corporate documents and presentations concerning the effect of the strategic alternatives under evaluation, to avoid any ambiguities or misunderstandings once these documents are subject to governmental review.

(c) INTERNATIONAL BUSINESSES   If a divested business has operations outside of the United States, there are also the local laws and regulations that must be considered. In addition to having different forms of antitrust legislation, many countries in Europe and Asia have unique laws and regulations covering a variety of areas that could potentially affect the divestiture, such as privacy, employee benefits, intellectual property, foreign ownership, and taxation, to name a few. As one small example, European privacy legislation precludes the selling corporation from revealing certain employee-identifiable information. This impacts how the selling corporation can deal with the due diligence process, as a different approach must be devised to satisfy the standard diligence requests acquirers make in this area without running afoul of the privacy rules.

   If the divested business includes non-U.S. operations of any size, it is important to engage local legal and tax counsel at the inception the selling process, to ensure the divestiture team benefits from their expertise and so that they can plan ahead for complying with any local-country and/or regional requirements for the transaction.

KEY POINTS

1. Small details of the transaction structure have a big cumulative impact on the deal. They determine the after-tax valuation, the allocation of legal risk between parties, and the required accounting treatment. (Section 7.1)
2. Contract team members should be chosen once the selling process is under way, because of the increased demand for experts to analyze the deal and negotiate the contract

while sustaining the transaction's momentum. Availability of subject matter experts should be planned carefully to avoid process bottlenecks. (Section 7.3(a & b))

3. Choosing the most tax-efficient structure requires analysis of the tax implications for both the selling corporation (e.g., basis in the assets and stock) and the acquirer (e.g., step-up). (Section 7.4(a))

4. Corporations prefer to separate the reported results of the divested business from those of continuing operations, but the transaction must first meet specific accounting criteria. (Section 7.4(b))

5. Certain sections of the purchase agreement (e.g., representations, warranties, covenants) expose the selling corporation to legal and financial risk. The agreement and the disclosure schedules should be comprehensive and thoroughly reviewed and approved by a cross-functional group. (Section 7.5(a, b, & d))

6. Successful contract negotiations require an empowered negotiating lead and sustained leverage. The worst mistake the selling corporation can make is to surrender its negotiating leverage by reducing the field to a single potential acquirer too soon. (Section 7.6(a & b))

7. U.S. antitrust regulations generally require filings for transactions above $59.8 million. Team members should be sensitized to the probability that the government will scrutinize certain analyses prepared for the transaction. (Section 7.7(b))

CHAPTER 8

CLOSING

8.1 CLOSING, TRANSITIONING, AND LEARNING

In Chapter 6, we described the selling process, which leads to the selection of one or two bidders with whom to proceed into confirmatory due diligence. In Chapter 7, we discussed the detailed process of structuring the transaction, negotiating the purchase agreement, and making the regulatory filings that are often required.

Here we begin by addressing several items requiring the divestiture team's consideration in the period between signing the purchase agreement and closing the transaction, and then we look at the post-closing transition of the divested business to its new ownership.

We then shift our focus to the importance and value of the organization's learning from the divestiture experience. As we said in Chapter 1, many, if not most, corporations engaged in merger and acquisition (M&A) activity treat divestitures as isolated, tactical events rather than repetitive, strategic transactions that lend themselves to standardization and process improvement and value creation. As a result, we suspect that some organizations may not embrace the idea that the divestiture transaction is something worth trying *to become good at*. In our view, this would be an opportunity lost because a comparatively small investment of time can lead an organization to steadily improve its ability to optimize the results of its divestiture transactions, in the same way that many organizations take pride in increasing their effectiveness as acquirers.

Finally, we conclude the chapter with our summary thoughts and reflections on the divestiture process and on the value of the experience that the members of the team will take with them.

8.2 CLOSING PROCESS STEPS

In the closing phase, the divestiture team addresses a number of items requiring its focus in the period between signing and closing. After closing, the focus shifts to implementing the transition of the business to its new ownership. Once this transition is completed, the team should document its lessons learned for the benefit of teams tasked with the corporation's future divestitures. The elements of closing the transaction are described next.

- **Closing the transaction.** The closing happens either immediately upon signing the purchase agreement or, after a defined interval, once certain conditions have been met. If the signing and closing are separate, or bifurcated, there are several items requiring the attention of the divestiture team during this interval.
- **Transitioning to new ownership.** Following the closing, the selling corporation shifts its focus from contract negotiation to contract compliance, taking steps to ensure that operating management implements its various contractual commitments.

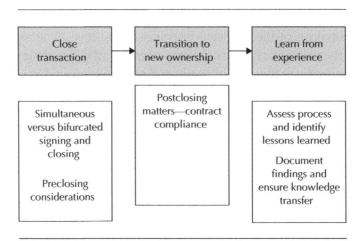

EXHIBIT 8.1   CLOSING PROCESS STEPS AND CONSIDERATIONS

- **Learning from the experience.** Once the transaction is closed and the business is transitioned to its new ownership, the seller should perform a retrospective analysis of the transaction and record all relevant information that can be accessed by those in the organization who are tasked with responsibility for divestitures in the future. This analysis would entail the identification of lessons learned—both positive and negative—and the documentation of those findings to ensure that the lessons are incorporated into the seller's institutional memory.

These steps are illustrated in Exhibit 8.1 and are discussed in the next sections of this chapter.

8.3 CLOSING THE TRANSACTION

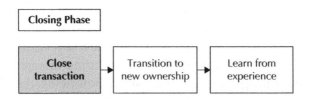

(a) CONSIDERATIONS LEADING UP TO THE CLOSE   In some transactions, the closing is effective immediately upon signing the purchase agreement. A simultaneous signing and closing can simplify smaller transactions, where there is no externally required waiting period. It benefits both the acquirer and the selling corporation by eliminating the risk of unforeseen events occurring during the period between signing and closing.

More often, however, it is necessary to separate, or bifurcate, the signing and the closing, establishing an intervening period in order to conduct certain activities. The next points outline and describe some of the activities normally occurring between signing and closing.

- **Buyer financing.** If the acquirer intends to use third-party debt to finance the transaction, it will normally need a period of time after the purchase agreement is executed to finalize the financing. Even though the acquirer should have obtained a bank commitment letter (and perhaps provided certain additional guaranties to the selling corporation) for the financing prior to signing the purchase agreement, it must then negotiate the definitive loan agreements and satisfy any conditions set by its bank. Additionally, depending on the magnitude of the transaction and the specific plan for financing the deal, the acquirer's bank may also choose to syndicate the acquisition debt to other participating institutions. These activities normally lead the acquirer to request that a period of several weeks exist between signing and closing.
- **Governmental approvals.** For transactions in the United States above $59.8 million,[1] the Hart-Scott-Rodino Antitrust Improvements Act (HSR) requires the acquirer and selling corporation to file a premerger notification form with the Federal Trade Commission and the Department of Justice. Once the HSR filing is made, the established waiting period for approval is 30 days. This period could be shortened by an "early termination" or significantly lengthened by a "second request" for more information, as discussed in section 7.7(b). Both the selling corporation and the acquirer should have antitrust specialist

---

1   This amount is subject to annual increases, and the details of the requirements are complicated. As a practical matter, if the transaction is anywhere in the range of this amount, antitrust counsel should be consulted for guidance.

counsel lined up and ready to assist during this period in the event of a second request.

- **Third-party consents.** In some cases, third parties other than the government are asked to provide their consent before the close of the transaction. For example, if the divestiture is structured as an asset sale, and if certain material customer contracts are not assignable to another corporation without the customers' prior consent, the acquirer may request that those consents be obtained before the closing. Given the potential for third parties to upend an otherwise successful divestiture transaction, selling corporations normally attempt to negotiate a relatively soft commitment to use best efforts to obtain the consents. Conversely, if nonassignable contracts are material to the value of the business, the acquirer may attempt to make its legal obligation to close the transaction conditional on obtaining certain consents. This aspect of the purchase agreement is sometimes hotly negotiated, especially in an asset sale.

- **Updating the purchase agreement disclosure schedules.** When the signing and closing are bifurcated, the selling corporation's representations and warranties in the purchase agreement provide a snapshot of the divested business as of the signing and then again as of the closing date. Further, in a sale of assets, some of the schedules identify the specific assets and liabilities that are transferring to the acquirer (e.g., customer contracts, fixed assets). As a result, the divestiture team should continuously update the related disclosure schedules so that they are current as of the date of the close. This process can be time-consuming, so the selling corporation should ensure it has made sufficient resources available to coordinate this effort.

- **Determining the amount of closing-day proceeds—estimated working capital adjustment.** If the purchase price is subject to a working capital adjustment, there may be a requirement that the selling corporation provide an estimate of the amount of working capital as of a few days before the close. If this is the case, the selling corporation needs to establish procedures for tracking activity within the relevant accounting subsystems so that it can reasonably estimate balance sheet balances as of the required date. Doing this requires careful thought and advance planning by the divestiture team, since the amount of the estimate directly impacts the cash proceeds that change hands at close.

- **Closing announcement.** The announcement of the closing of the divestiture transaction is ordinarily made via a press release. The selling corporation normally wants its management and investor relations groups to review and approve the language of both its and the acquirer's press release documents. Usually the selling corporation will not take any more action than issuing a press release after the closing, unless the divestiture did not meet publicly set expectations, in which case the communications plan is customized based on the particular circumstances.

- **Mechanics of the close.** Considering how intense the divestiture process can be, the actual close can seem anticlimactic in comparison. The closing itself, while technically taking place at the office of the attorney of either the selling corporation or the acquirer, is usually accomplished remotely between the two legal advisors, with the (electronic) exchange of signature pages of the agreements and with the confirmation of the wire transfer of the purchase price. The divestiture team has little to do at this point; it may simply receive an e-mail from the legal counsel informing it that the transaction has closed.

8.4 MANAGING THE POSTCLOSING TRANSITION

(a) POSTCLOSING MATTERS: CONTRACT COMPLIANCE Once the divestiture transaction has closed, the selling corporation's focus shifts from contract negotiations to contract compliance. The simplest yet the most important task to perform at this point is to prepare and distribute a contract compliance summary. The completed purchase agreement and supporting schedules for a typical divestiture can easily total hundreds of pages. Within those pages, the selling corporation has made a number of legal commitments to do, or not do, certain things. If those commitments remain buried within the pages of the purchase agreement, they could easily be overlooked, unnecessarily exposing the selling corporation to legal and financial liability. A contract compliance summary, normally prepared by legal counsel and distributed to operating management, distills the various commitments and the required actions necessary to facilitate their implementation. The items typically included in such a summary are described next.

- **Purchase price adjustments.** If part of the purchase price is subject to future adjustment, the finance and accounting group should be aware of the key dates and related responsibilities. In the case of a working capital adjustment, for example, the acquirer usually prepares a closing balance sheet and a calculation of the working capital adjustment within an agreed period of time following the closing. The selling corporation then has a fixed numbers of days to review the calculation and either agree to it or contest it. The process for agreeing on the calculation for contingent consideration, such as an earn-out, usually works in much the same way, except that it deals with longer time periods after the closing.
- **Transition services.** In Chapter 5, we discussed the disentanglement of the divested business in some detail, including the importance of making the same operating executives from the selling corporation accountable for the implementation of the disentanglement plan and the provision of transition services. The selling corporation should ensure that appropriate time and expense tracking mechanisms are put in place to facilitate timely and accurate billing for the transition services during this postclosing period.
- **Contractual covenants - noncompete and no-poach provisions.** The selling corporation makes a number of contractual

covenants in the purchase agreement. By far, the most important ones for operating management to be aware of are the noncompete and no-poach provisions. Depending on what terms were negotiated, the noncompete and no-poach provisions may place limitations on the scope of the business activity and hiring practices of multiple business units in multiple geographic regions for a number of years following the close. Senior management in every affected business division should be made aware of the specific terms of the provisions. Although some of these managers may have provided input in the negotiation phase of the transaction, they should now be made explicitly aware of the final terms and constraints. The terms of the noncompete provision should also be maintained centrally for access by corporate business development personnel, as the selling corporation's ability to make future acquisitions or investments may also be subject to limitations.

- **Administrative matters.** There are ordinarily a number of administrative matters requiring the attention of human resources, tax, and accounting, such as the items that follow.
    - **Employee matters.** In section 7.5(a), we discussed how the purchase agreement often includes a separate section focused on employment matters. This section would outline the postclosing administrative responsibility of the selling corporation to cooperate with the transition of employee compensation and benefit plans to those of the acquirer.
    - **Tax matters.** Similarly, the purchase agreement normally outlines clearly the parties' responsibilities for coordination of tax matters, such as allocating the purchase price and preparing interim-period tax returns.
    - **Trailing cash receipts and disbursements.** The selling corporation may continue to receive customer orders, remittances, or vendor invoices related to the divested business for some time following the close of the transaction. The accounting functions of the selling corporation and the acquirer should agree on a procedure and frequency for batching and forwarding any misdirected paperwork and payments.

8.5 CONDUCTING A POSTDEAL PROCESS ASSESSMENT

The temptation to disband the divestiture team immediately after the transaction closes is strong. After all, the process likely has spanned 6 to 12 months, and in all but a few organizations, team members have probably been asked to coordinate the divestiture in addition to performing their other responsibilities. Those who have persevered through this process would be understandably keen to return their undivided attention to their ongoing job responsibilities.

Additionally, as mentioned in the introduction to this chapter, we believe that there can be a tendency within corporations to look at divestitures as isolated events that, for them, will never happen again. Yet, for many, this will not be the case. As reported in section 1.2(c), divestitures represent a surprisingly large one-third of all M&A activity, totaling between 3,000 and 4,000 transactions per year. That means that the odds are actually quite high that many corporations will conduct multiple divestiture transactions over time, and unless they choose to view divestitures as a value-creation *process,* they risk having to relearn the same lessons over and over again on future transactions.

Conversely, with just a small additional investment of time and attention, corporations can reinforce the value-creation nature of the initiative and greatly enhance their ability to conduct effective and efficient divestiture transactions, just as many have applied process improvement methodology to become better acquirers. While the experience is still fresh in its mind, the divestiture team should be asked to do two things:

1. Assess the process and identify lessons learned.
2. Document findings to facilitate knowledge transfer.

(a) ASSESS THE PROCESS AND IDENTIFY LESSONS LEARNED We believe considerable organizational benefit can be derived from a relatively short debriefing of the divestiture team. The best way to accomplish this is to gather the core divestiture team in person for one day, with the objective of sharing lessons learned from the transaction and recommending process improvements for future transactions. The team leader should facilitate the session, going over each specific phase of the transaction with the team (e.g., planning, transactional preparation, disentanglement, selling and negotiating, and structuring), and gather the team's feedback and recommendations. These types of questions can help focus the team's feedback and ensure it is actionable:

- Did the corporation achieve the objectives it set for the divestiture transaction? In hindsight, were its expectations realistic? What should be done differently in the future to help set corporate expectations?
- Which aspects of the process went well, and why? What should be done in the future to ensure this happens again?
- Which aspects of the process did not go well, and what were the causes? What should be done in the future to improve the process?
- How did each of the external advisors perform? What were their strengths and weaknesses? Should the corporation consider using them in the future? If so, for what types of transactions would they be most useful?
- How effective were internal and external communications? What were the biggest unanticipated issues? Which audiences presented the biggest challenges? What might have improved the team's ability to communicate?
- How would the core divestiture team rate its own performance? What types of skills and experience contributed most strongly to the transaction's success? Were certain skills and capabilities missing that could have helped? How well did the team work together? How well did it manage cross-functionally within the organization? What advice would this group offer to future teams to optimize their performance?
- What were the biggest surprises in the divestiture process? How could a future team be better prepared for these items?

(b) DOCUMENT FINDINGS TO FACILITATE KNOWLEDGE TRANSFER
The team leader should then distill this feedback into a process feedback report that captures the team's observations and recommendations. One place to house this report is in the corporation's print and/or

electronic file for the divestiture transaction, along with the approval documents, communications plans, audit reports, marketing materials, diligence information, and final purchase agreements. As a practical matter, divestiture team leaders often begin their preparation by consulting the files on prior transactions, so the deal file is an obvious place in which to include the process feedback report.

The process feedback report should also be distributed to the corporation's business development and corporate finance groups. These groups, given their involvement in acquisition and divestiture transactions across the organization, usually play a major role in developing the corporation's M&A policies and procedures. They would greatly benefit from receiving process feedback as each transaction is completed, ensuring that policies and procedures can be shaped and improved over time based on the corporation's experience.

In more sophisticated organizations, the building of a process knowledge base may be accomplished even more systematically, for example, by developing a corporate intranet community for purposes of sharing teams' knowledge and experience and by developing directories of individuals who have accumulated specific areas of expertise.

Regardless of the form documentation takes, the objective should be the same: to provide a feedback mechanism for process improvement and knowledge transfer.

8.6 FINAL THOUGHTS

(a) 10 MOST IMPORTANT ELEMENTS OF SUCCESSFUL DIVESTITURES   During our collaboration on the *Guide*, we spent considerable time thinking about how to share our experience in a way that is informative, useful, and readily accessible by those who are actually working on a live transaction. We recognize that it is difficult enough to get through one's e-mail on many days, never mind read a treatise on divestitures. Consequently, we organized the discussion into specific topical elements, while presenting them within the context of a systematized process flow, so that readers can easily navigate to the points that are relevant to a particular phase of the transaction. We also listed the key points at the end of each chapter so that readers can scan this summary, see our observations and conclusions about the phase, and then turn back into the related detailed discussion as needed.

As an additional aid, we thought it would be useful to summarize the most important points of the book here. What are the 10 pieces of advice we wish someone had offered to us before we started work on our first divestiture transaction? The first 5 items, the enabling principles for an effective transaction, were introduced in Chapter 1. The second 5 items represent additional thoughts distilled from the remaining chapters.

1. **Empowered leadership.** The success or failure of most business initiatives stems from the quality of the people involved, and divestitures are no exception. A successful divestiture cannot happen without an effective team leader; the selling corporation should place a top performer in this role. While certain aspects of divestitures can be learned by doing, the leader must minimally have solid M&A experience and be an excellent communicator. The person chosen to be team leader should then be given sufficient autonomy to project authority. Internal and external audiences must know who is in charge of the transaction—it cannot be a faceless committee. The leader also needs to know he or she can call on resources across the organization as needed. With an average divestiture value of $175 million, there is a lot at stake, and the selling corporation would be foolish to shortchange the leadership of the transaction or the resources made available to that person.

2. **Team cohesiveness and ownership in the transaction.** In all but the largest corporations, the divestiture team probably will be smaller than most might wish for. As a result, it needs to compensate for its relatively small size by working cohesively. As we discussed throughout the *Guide,* even when the team is expanded, it is often done with borrowed or external resources, which can further complicate coordination. The core team members cannot afford to behave in a compartmentalized way, as can sometimes happen in large corporations. All must feel some personal stake in the success of the transaction and think holistically, calling attention to items beyond their particular responsibility and helping out the other team members when they can.

3. **Clearly defined roles, tasks, and deliverables.** In perusing the chapters of the *Guide*, one gets a sense of just how many things there are to do throughout the course of a divestiture transaction. In order to prevent team members from being overwhelmed and lose their direction and focus, exceptionally disciplined task management must be employed. That discipline can be exercised only by clearly defining and unambiguously communicating what has to be done, by whom, and when, *and* by holding the responsible parties accountable for delivering results.

4. **Frequent and regular communication.** Effective communication within the core team is critical to the management of a divestiture. Arguably, the key communication component should be regularly scheduled meetings run by the team leader. These meetings allow all team members to have a common understanding of the status and current priorities of the transaction, exert peer pressure to reinforce each person's accountability for delivering results, and more readily facilitate needed course corrections that may be necessitated by changing circumstances.

    Equally important is the communication with both external and internal stakeholder groups. A particularly fragile internal group that can easily be overlooked is the divested business's employees; their continued engagement and productivity is critical to sustaining the value of the transaction. We spent quite a bit of time discussing this in Chapter 6, because we believe that the team can become so absorbed with task management that it becomes too inwardly focused. There is a significant role to be played building and sustaining the confidence of internal and external stakeholder groups, and this responsibility cannot be left unattended without serious consequences for the selling corporation.

5. **Ample use of documentation.** While PowerPoint presentations have become a preferred communications media in today's business environment, quality analysis, informed decision making, and structured thought must underpin them. We are not advocating a bureaucratic approach. We believe, however, that people

in corporations are so busy that they must decide in advance how much time to allocate to each task, and they often use the requested deliverables to help determine the required level of effort. Anticipating this behavior, the team leader should communicate expectations for important deliverables so that the required depth and quality of the supporting analysis is clearly understood.

6. **Thorough preparation.** The team should overinvest in preparation. Once the divestiture receives corporate approval, the pressure to get the deal going can become intense. The divestiture team, feeling this pressure, might make the mistake of bringing the business to market too soon. If the team has not adequately prepared for the divestiture transaction and disentanglement, it will be forced into a reactive, catch-up mode throughout the course of the deal. Ironically, this is likely to result in prolonging the process.

    We hope that the points made in Chapters 4 and 5 resonate with readers—preparation should be thorough and the business should not brought to market until it is ready. One can easily see the difference in the management presentation, as one example, between a well-prepared, confident management team and one that has not anticipated bidders' questions. A well-prepared team and a seamlessly managed process will inspire and sustain a more enthusiastic group of bidders, which can add millions of dollars to the ultimate valuation of the business.

7. **The right advisors.** Good advisors pay for themselves. We spoke about the value of capable and experienced advisors in Chapters 4, 6, and 7. Far and away the most important ones are the financial advisor (broker or banker) and the legal advisor. It is important to find good, experienced advisors, and it is critical to make sure their capabilities fit with the selling corporation's needs. What works for one transaction may not work for another. For example, a small business unit operating in a niche market might be best suited for a boutique broker with extensive contacts in that particular market segment; a large business unit might be best suited for an investment banker

with experience in structuring and financing large transactions. The same principles apply to the choice of legal firm. A heavily regulated business, for example, might require very specific legal expertise and advice.

Consequently, the team should make sure it has clearly identified its particular needs for the transaction and must carefully vet the advisors accordingly. The team should thoroughly examine the candidate advisors' credentials and track record in the areas of most importance, remembering that everybody says they can do everything in their initial pitch.

8. **Understanding negotiating leverage.** When discussing negotiating leverage in Chapters 6 and 7, we made the point that one of the worst things the selling corporation can do is to surrender its negotiating leverage by agreeing too soon to enter into exclusive discussions with one buyer. In practice, it can be quite tempting to shut down a laborious auction and reduce the field to one enthusiastic bidder that offers a high valuation in an effort to preempt the remainder of the process. This move, however, is very risky. No matter how solid the buyer and how attractive its valuation, there are just too many things that can cause a bidder to walk away or reduce its offer at any time, since rarely is it legally bound to do anything until the purchase agreement is signed. And if this one bidder walks away, it is often extraordinarily difficult to resuscitate the auction process.

So, our advice is to try to avoid granting exclusivity. If granted, it should be done at a late stage in the selling process, when it is apparent that the buyer has invested significant time and money in the deal and has gotten far enough into the diligence that the probability of finding deal-breaking or valuation-changing issues is greatly reduced.

9. **Divestitures are rarely one-time organizational events.** Organizations that are faced with divestitures only occasionally may carry an internal bias, viewing the divestiture transaction as something that will never happen again. This belief could doom the organization to make the same mistakes over and over again.

As we said in Chapter 1, divestitures represent a large percentage of all M&A transactions, and the number does not appear to be declining. The implications are that many organizations will make multiple divestitures over time, and they are better served to look at the divestiture as a business process that can be improved, as we discussed in this chapter. With a comparatively minor investment of time, organizations can greatly improve the efficiency and effectiveness of their divestiture efforts, just as many have for acquisitions.

10. **Focus on value creation.** The divestiture team will be much more enthusiastic if it believes it is creating value for the corporation, as opposed to getting rid of a "nonstrategic" business. We discussed this element of organizational bias in Chapter 1: The divestiture can feel like an orphan transaction, especially in comparison to an acquisition. Team members may feel as if the corporation has turned its back on the business once it has been declared nonstrategic and not view their assignment to the divestiture team as a positive career step. From an attitude standpoint, there is a risk that the team gets caught up in an aura of failure, which can sap the high energy required to drive a successful process.

As we discussed in Chapter 2, there are many reasons corporations choose to divest perfectly good businesses. And the act of selling off one asset so that the proceeds can be reinvested more productively is a great value-creation opportunity for the organization and those who help make that happen. Increasingly, many organizations are using divestitures as a core portfolio management activity—recognizing that the market and competitive environment changes and that the corporation's business portfolio must also change to ensure its long-term success. It is critical that the team see its role in the divestiture as fundamentally about value creation for the corporation and not get caught up in negative thinking.

(b) HOW DIVESTITURE TEAM MEMBERS BENEFIT FROM THE EXPERIENCE We will conclude the *Guide* by addressing one final issue: Why should the divestiture team members invest a considerable amount of their energy and time into this process other than to be good corporate citizens? In Chapter 1, we noted that in contrast to acquisitions, which tend to attract a crowd of volunteers because they are seen as part of the organization's future, divestitures sometimes may be viewed as orphan transactions. This means that prospective team members may have to be convinced about "what is in it for them" so that they embrace, rather than grudgingly accept, the invitation to work on a divestiture transaction.

- **Experiential learning.** Increasingly, corporations are looking to foster employee career development through a combination of experiential building blocks and formal executive development programs. When evaluating their employees' readiness to assume greater responsibility, therefore, organizations often delve deeply into the particular assignments individuals have worked on. Participation on a divestiture transaction team brings a number of important skills to its members' resumes:
  - **Leadership development.** Whether it is serving as divestiture team leader, overseeing the work of outside advisors, or coordinating tasks and deliverables cross-functionally across the organization, all members of the divestiture team receive significant leadership development training. The important leadership skills of people management, leading by influence, and effectively communicating internally and externally are all exercised through the course of the transaction.
  - **Exposure to business operations.** The disentanglement process in particular allows team members to develop their understanding of the inner workings of the business much more deeply and to interact with key operational executives across the organization. In Chapter 5, we talked about how divestitures are much more complex than acquisitions in this respect. Divestitures are a major operations learning experience.
  - **Marketing, sales, and negotiating savvy.** Divestiture transactions can teach team members a great deal about how to present a business in its best light and how to negotiate a successful transaction for the corporation. We discussed

this in detail in Chapter 6. The team will be exposed to experienced financial and legal advisors who have done many deals, and has much to gain from working with and observing them in action.

o **Mergers and acquisitions technical knowledge.** As we discussed in Chapter 7, there is a significant depth to the divestiture's technical issues, spanning areas such as law, tax, and accounting. Even for those individuals who have worked on acquisition transactions before, negotiating and structuring a purchase agreement from the opposite vantage point creates a nuanced, deep knowledge of deals that can be used to great advantage on future acquisitions. One will literally have walked in the seller's shoes and emerges with much greater awareness of what each party to the transaction is trying to achieve.

- **Discrete project with quantifiable impact on shareholder value.** As a discrete project, the divestiture transaction progresses through a defined beginning, middle, and end. The success of the effort, a direct contribution to the corporation's value, is clear and quantifiable. As corporate initiatives go, divestitures can be surprisingly satisfying projects in which to participate.

- **Autonomy.** Many of the more accomplished executives we have seen tend to thrive in an environment where they are handed an objective, then are given plenty of autonomy to figure out how to accomplish it. Divestiture transactions, because they do not get lavished with corporate attention and resources, tend to be just such an environment, offering a clear objective and plenty of autonomy.

- **Networking opportunity.** Participating in a divestiture, especially one managed as an auction process, exposes the team to a wide array of organizations. This may include strategic acquirers (perhaps direct competitors), private equity players, their advisors, and other organizations actively involved in mergers and acquisitions. It is an incredibly interesting and energizing group in which to gain exposure.

We hope that you have found the *Guide* to be a helpful resource. The goal for any book of this sort is for the reader to receive a practical benefit—gaining insights and finding practice aids which make one's efforts more effective and efficient. We hope your time investment in the *Guide* has been beneficial, and we offer you our best wishes for a successful and rewarding transaction.

KEY POINTS

1. Signing the purchase agreement and closing the transaction simultaneously can simplify smaller divestitures. More often, however, it is necessary to bifurcate the signing and the closing in order to obtain financing, government approval, or third-party consents. (Section 8.3)
2. Once the divestiture transaction is completed, the selling corporation's focus shifts from contract negotiation to contract compliance. The simplest yet the most important task to perform at this point is to prepare and distribute a contract compliance summary. (Section 8.4)
3. We suspect that some organizations may not view the divestiture transaction as something they *want to become good at*. This would be an opportunity lost because a comparatively small investment of time can lead an organization to steadily improve its ability to optimize the results of its divestiture transactions. (Section 8.5)
4. Ten pieces of advice we wish we had received before our first divestiture transaction: (Section 8.6)
    (i)   Empowered leadership
    (ii) Team cohesiveness and ownership in the transaction
    (iii) Clearly defined roles, tasks, and deliverables
    (iv) Frequent and regular communication
    (v)   Ample use of documentation
    (vi) Thorough preparation
    (vii) The right advisors

    (viii)   Understanding negotiating leverage

    (ix)   Divestitures are rarely one-time organizational events

    (x)   Focus on value creation

5. Several reasons why team members should embrace the opportunity to work on a divestiture transaction: (Section 8.6)

- Professional development—it provides experiential learning.
- It is a discrete project with quantifiable impact on shareholder value.
- There is a lot of autonomy.
- It is an excellent networking opportunity.

INDEX

Note: a indicates Appendix; e indicates Exhibit.

Printed and bound by CPI Group (UK) Ltd, Croydon, CR0 4YY

23/04/2025

14660922-0001